Clemente!

Clemente!

Kal Wagenheim

Foreword by Wilfrid Sheed

OLMSTEAD
PRESS
An [e-reads] Book

Published in 2001 by Olmstead Press: Chicago, Illinois
e-reads: New York, New York

Originally published in 1973 by Praeger Publishers, Inc.: New York
New edition published in 1984 by Waterfront Press: Maplewood, New Jersey

Cover designed by Hope Forstenzer

Text designed and typeset by
Syllables, Hartwick, New York, USA

Printed and bound in the USA by
Sheridan Books, Ann Arbor, Michigan

ISBN: 1-58754-115-7

Library of Congress Card Number: 2001086662

Editorial Sales Rights and Permission Inquiries should be addressed to:
Olmstead Press, 22 Broad Street, Suite 34, Milford, CT 06460
Email: Editor@lpcgroup.com

Manufactured in the United States of America
1 3 5 7 9 10 8 6 4 2

Substantial discounts on bulk quantities of Olmstead Press books are available
to corporations, professional associations and other organizations. If you are
in the USA or Canada, contact LPC Group, Attn: Special Sales Department,
1-800-626-4330, fax 1-800-334-3892, or email: sales@lpcgroup.com

To *doña* Vera Cristina Zabala Vda. de
Clemente and *doña* Louisa Walker
Vda. de Clemente

Contents

Foreword

By Wilfrid Sheed

If there is such a thing as a *virtue* of pride, Roberto Clemente had it. Pride for him was not an indulgence but a moral obligation. Standing at the plate, or strolling with regal slowness to right field, he seemed to say, "You will pay attention." And as his throws came cracking into the third baseman's glove, with that strange extra venom he carried in his shoulder, they said, "Could a white man do better? Could even a black American do better?"

Clemente was a black Puerto Rican, but he was too sensitively tuned to say, "I'm doing this for Puerto Rico." Instead he would do it as the others did it—for himself. I, personally, am better than you. What do you make of that? Now, perhaps, you can accept my people. If Ego is the game, we'll beat you at that, too. Standing still as a statue in the October shadows, he looked, grotesquely, more like a patriot than anything usually seen on a ball field.

A trick of the light perhaps. Yet what famous athlete last died for a cause bigger than himself? Clemente could sometimes seem like a pest, a nagging narcissist, with only his burningly serious play to deny it. Yet when that plane crashed carrying relief supplies to Nicaragua we saw what he had meant all along. It was like the old Clemente crashing into the right field wall in a losing game: the act of a totally serious man.

By chance I met Clemente once, in the humble role of autograph-seeker. He was doing wind sprints down at the Pirate training camp in Bradenton, Florida. And although I claimed I was getting the autograph for my son (true, for a change), he looked at me with a *hidalgo's* contempt—at a grown man simpering over a blunt pencil; he turned his back abruptly and did another wind sprint, then slashed his name onto my scorecard and sauntered away. To hell with you, Clemente, I thought. But on the way out, I saw him funning with three old ladies from Allentown, Pennsylvania, and I have never seen sweeter courtesy.

Arrogance and gentleness. Where did it come from? Clemente was like a Martian to most North Americans, and has been written about as such. But not by Kal Wagenheim. By another chance, I met Kal in Puerto Rico in 1969, and on the strength of a passing recommendation by a mutual friend (if Dickens can use that phrase wrong, so can I) he dropped everything else and spent a week showing us round San Juan. The first day out, we got caught in one of those creative traffic snarls Puerto Ricans can apparently cook up even faster than Romans. Wagenheim was bumped and wearily got out to do battle. But the woman in the offending car turned out to be the mother of his cleaning lady, and before we knew it they were exchanging gossip and embracing hotly, like long-lost relatives—or like Clemente and his fans from Allentown.

In other words, Kal knows his Puerto Rico, not as a scholar but as a lover who chose to live and marry there, and even to identify with the independence movement. For a while he ran a fine literary-*cum*-political magazine in San Juan, and I imagine he would still give his right typing finger to see one local writer properly recognized on the mainland.

Fortunately, he also knows his baseball. As a boy first baseman, he got closer to the big leagues than most of us dreamers ever do, as far as an offer to play in the high minors in fact, until, at Fort Benning, he found himself staring curiously at a jet-stream fastball and decided (on the spot) that there must be better uses for his head than sticking it in the way of those things.

As it turns out, he also had a rendezvous with a subject, Roberto Clemente and Puerto Rico. This isn't just a baseball book, but a social history or meditation on an island, bitched by history and responding to it, like the Irish and other oppressed people, with public pride and private warmth: this culture, then, as personified in one man. And Wagenheim also knows what it means to be proud in the face of a big league fastball. Puerto Rico fights no wars of its own and must look elsewhere for its distinctive heroes. In the quaint

American game, with the ball and the stick and the diamond setting, it found itself an authentic one.

Acknowledgments

I wish to thank all the persons quoted in this book who kindly took the time to grant me an interview, and also—for their help in different aspects of the project—William J. Guilfoile, director of public relations for the Pittsburgh Pirates; Léon King, my editor at Praeger Publishers; and William Wagenheim, Harold Wagenheim, David Straus, Ronald Walker, Rai Garcia, Robert Jacobson, Neal Herschfeld, José Manuel Alvarez, and Ernest Potvin.

Roberto Clemente Walker

Born August 18, 1934, in Carolina, Puerto Rico.

Died December 31, 1972, in a plane crash, a few miles from his birthplace, while on a mission of mercy to aid the earthquake victims in Nicaragua.

Beloved son of Melchor Clemente and Luisa Walker de Clemente; husband of Vera Cristina Zabala de Clemente; father of Roberto, Jr., 8, Luis Roberto, 7, and Enrique Roberto, 4.

- First Latin American to enter Baseball's Hall of Fame, August 6, 1973.
- Eleventh man in the 103-year history of major league baseball to achieve 3,000 hits, a mark reached in his last year, 1972.
- Most Valuable Player, National League, 1966.
- Batting champion, National League, 1961, 1964, 1965, 1967.
- Winner of the Golden Glove for fielding excellence, twelve seasons, 1961–72.
- Batted above .300 for thirteen seasons, averaging .317 during his eighteen-year big league career.
- Played in twelve Major League All-Star Games, 1960–72.
- Won the Babe Ruth Award for his superb play in the 1971 World Series; tied world record by hitting safely in all fourteen games of the 1960 and 1971 Series.
- All-time leader of the Pittsburgh Pirates in games played, at bats, hits, singles, total bases, and runs batted in.
- Tied major league record by leading National League in assists for five seasons.
- Holds National League record with ten base hits in two consecutive games, August 22–23, 1970.
- Tied National League record by hitting three triples in one game, September 8, 1958.

Introduction

In a treatise about his own breed, Paul Gallico once said that sports writers are often cynics because they "learn eventually that, while there are no villains, there are no heroes either." But, he warned, "until you make the final discovery that there are only human beings, who are therefore all the more fascinating, you are liable to miss something."

Roberto Clemente Walker[1] of Puerto Rico—the first Latin American to enter baseball's Hall of Fame—was a fascinating human being. And if, as Gallico observes, there are no heroes, there are men who achieve deeds of heroic dimension. Roberto Clemente was one of these gifted few.

"Without question the hardest single thing to do in sport is to hit a baseball," says the great Boston slugger Ted Williams. "A .300 hitter, that rarest of breeds, goes through life with the certainty that he will fail at his job seven out of ten times." A baseball is a sphere with a diameter of $2\frac{7}{8}$ inches. The batter stands at home plate and grips a tapering wood cylinder that has a maximum diameter of $2\frac{3}{4}$ inches; he tries to defend a strike zone that is approximately seven baseballs wide and eleven high. The pitcher, from $60\frac{1}{2}$ feet away, throws the ball at a speed of about 90 miles per hour. As it spins toward the plate—hopping, sinking, or curving—the hitter has four-tenths of one second to decide whether he should let it pass by, jump away to avoid being maimed, or swing. To get "good wood" on it, he must connect squarely with a $\frac{3}{4}$-inch portion of the

[1] In the United States, "Walker" was incorrectly used as Roberto's middle name. It was actually his second surname. Hispanic people use the surnames of both parents, with "Clemente," the father's, being dominant, followed by "Walker," his mother's maiden name.

ball's round surface, and then hope that none of the nine defensive players catches it. Roberto Clemente had enormous success in this complex, difficult task. In September, 1972, when he smashed his 3,000th hit, he scaled a peak where only ten other men in the hundred-year history of baseball ever set foot. In his eighteen years as a major league player, he made a memorable impact upon a great sport. A lifetime average of .317, four league batting championships, a Most Valuable Player award, and twelve Golden Gloves for superior defensive play are just a few souvenirs that attest to his marvelous talent. During the 1971 World Series, his devastating *tour de force*, witnessed by millions on television, at last evoked the national recognition that he felt was long overdue. Roger Angell, in his superb book *The Summer Game*, says, "Now and again—very rarely—we see a man who seems to have met all the demands, challenged all the implacable averages, spurned the mere luck. He has defied baseball, even altered it, and for a time at least the game is truly his." During that 1971 World Series, and on many other occasions, the game was Roberto Clemente's.

But these great moments cost him dearly. Another famous Latino, Enrico Caruso, once said, "To be great, it is necessary to suffer." As you shall read in the following pages, Roberto Clemente endured severe physical pain and sacrificed a good portion of his life to perfect his skills.

There is much more to a great athlete than the one-dimensional view of his performance on the playing field. Roberto Clemente was a human being like all the rest of us, but when you peel away from each man the frailties that we share, there is a residue that defines each man's uniqueness.

The classical poets of ancient Greece would have rejoiced over Roberto Clemente. Unlike the Goliath-sized supermen of basketball and football, his physique was nearly perfect match for the "normal" ideal that one sees in time-weathered marble friezes and statues. He was strikingly handsome, with a superbly sculpted body: five feet, eleven inches tall, one hundred and eighty pounds, broadshouldered with powerful arms and hands, slender of waist, fleet of foot. His simple, traditional values might seem hopelessly naive to the cynic, but they would have inspired the ancient lyricists. He saw himself as a fine craftsman and viewed his craft, baseball, as deserving of painstaking labor. He believed passionately in the virtue and dignity of hard work. He believed, with equal fervor, that a man should revere his parents, his wife and children, his country, and God. But he was not a docile man. He believed just as fiercely in his personal worth and integrity. "From head to toes, Roberto Clemente is as good as the President of the United States," he proclaimed. "I believe that, and I think every man should believe that about himself."

It was this belief that caused Roberto Clemente to become deeply involved during a period of major social change, the 1950's and 1960's, when black and Spanish-speaking people quickened their pace in the struggle for equality. That long march is far from over, but Clemente's brilliance in his craft and his unyielding demands for respect off the field advanced the cause by great distances. His immense pride in his Puerto Rican heritage and in his blackness inspired many others to hold their own heads high.

Those who knew Roberto Clemente—as you will read in these pages—offer an appealing portrait of a remarkable man: a serious artist who wrote his own style of poetry in the air, with powerful strokes of a bat, leaping catches, and breathtaking throws; a man with an enormous well of sentiment, who could inspire tears and could himself be driven to tears by symbolic gestures of kindness and nobility; a man whose temper was quick and terrible like a tropical storm, but who bore no grudge; a man with an almost child-like zest for life, who spoke from the heart and damn the consequences; a man with a very special sense of humor that he shared with only a few friends. But above all, in talking with the people whose lives were touched by Roberto Clemente—in Puerto Rico, in the spring training camp at Bradenton, Florida, in Pittsburgh—one hears of the empathy, the deep concern for others, the concern that moved him one rainy New Year's Eve to fly off on a mission to help others, and to perish in the effort. In her book *Nobody Ever Died of Old Age*, Sharon R. Curtin tells of an elderly woman who "was near the end of her life and had never experienced magic, never challenged the smell of brimstone, never clawed at the limit of human capability." In his all-too-brief life—in those rich, eventful thirty-eight years—

Roberto Clemente experienced magic often, and others felt his magic. He knew many people, some for only a brief time, whom he touched very deeply. Through them, he touched me, too.

Kal Wagenheim
June, 1973

1

A salty breeze whipped in from the Atlantic and set the flags aflutter above San Juan's Sixto Escobar Stadium. It was a warm, sunny afternoon in 1953 as the Santurce Crabbers prepared for a Puerto Rico Winter League game.

Wearing the Santurce colors, shagging fly balls in center field, was Willie Mays, already a young star for the New York Giants. Over in left field, a dark-skinned youth whose uniform seemed a size too large made a running catch and let loose a throw to home plate that might have been fired from a cannon.

Sitting in a box near the Santurce dugout, fanning himself with a scorecard, was Branch Rickey, whose sharp eye for talent had built the St. Louis Cardinals and Brooklyn Dodgers into winning machines. He turned to his companion, local sportswriter Rafael Pont Flores, and said, "I'd like to talk to him."

Moments later, the nineteen-year-old leftfielder trotted up to the box, holding his cap in his hand.

"Young man," Rickey said, "do you like baseball?"

"More than eating, sir," the youth replied in halting English.

"Do you have a fiancée?"

"No, sir."

"A sweetheart, or a steady girl?"

"No, sir."

"Well," Rickey said, "find a nice girl and marry her. Get *that* out of the way and you can really settle down to the business of baseball because, young man, you are going to be a superstar."

The young man, of course, was Roberto Clemente.

He was born on an island whose people love sport with a passion. Long before Columbus sailed to the New World, the Taíno Indians of Puerto Rico played on ceremonial ball fields enclosed by rows of huge flat stones. Wearing heavy stone belts around their waists, they literally swung from the hips to "bat" a rubber ball through a stone ring set high in the air. For four centuries under the Spanish crown, cockfights and horse races were the twin national obsessions. Even today, racetrack betting parlors are found in every *barrio*. The cockfights still draw good crowds, and the police of Jersey City, New Jersey, were once amazed when they raided a basement and found a group of Puerto Ricans cheering on their favorite birds. The legal weekly lottery is not enough, because the illegal *bolita* (numbers) also thrives. Politics, too, is a popular sport. In fact, one of Puerto Rico's most widely-viewed weekly programs is a Sunday night debate between members of the three top political parties who hurl verbal brickbats at each other with such zest and eloquence that anything similar on American television pales by comparison. And then, of course, there is *beisbol*. Puerto Ricans play it twelve months of the year. They also root for their heroes in the U.S. big leagues, and after World Series-time flock to the local stadiums for Winter League games that continue almost until time for spring training.

Beisbol came to Puerto Rico on the winds of war. On July 25, 1898, when American troops raised Old Glory on Puerto Rico's south shore and claimed the island as a prize in the Spanish-American War, vast change was imminent. President William McKinley put an American general in charge. English became the official language on an island of more than 1 million Spanish-speaking people. Investors from the north gobbled up prime coastland and planted sugar cane. Carpetbaggers descended with such a hungry vengeance that one Puerto Rican leader bitterly told Congress, "We are the American Southerners of the twentieth century."

But the young men who had joined up to avenge the sinking of the *Maine* and to drive a doddering Spanish Empire from the Americas were not imperialists; they were clerks, farmers, and laborers. Their heroes back home were "Wee Willie" Keeler, who hit .379 for Baltimore that season; speedy Fred Clarke of Louisville, who stole sixty-six bases; and Boston's Eddie Collins, who led the league with fifteen home runs. Soon, in their spare hours, these young crusaders were playing pickup games of baseball.

The game was not entirely unknown in the Caribbean before the Spanish-American War; there are records of exhibition contests played in Cuba in the 1880's. But once America became solidly entrenched in Cuba and Puerto Rico, the game soared in popularity. Imperialism was sinful. Politics was controversial—some Puerto Ricans embraced the U.S. flag, others despised it, and most were confused. But *beisbol* was fun.

If America has its Abner Doubleday,[2] Puerto Rico has its Amos Iglesias, the offspring of Spanish and American parents, who was taken to the island as an infant. One afternoon around the turn of the century—the exact date and site are uncertain—in what is considered to be Puerto Rico's first official baseball game, young Amos pitched for the local Borinquen nine against a visiting team from Almendares, Cuba. Old-timers, men born under the flag of Mother Spain, still bet on their cockfights and horse races or whiled away the afternoons playing dominoes in sun-dappled plazas, but soon they were also watching their young, who were whacking and throwing round, horsehide-covered *pelotas* in schoolyards and fields in practically every *barrio* of the 100-by-35-mile island. Old men today still dimly recall the feats of those boys of summer—the fabulous Faberllé brothers, Fabito and Ciquí, Cosme Beitía, and José "Gacho" Torres.

By World War I, American and Puerto Rican "doughboys" had organized teams at the Las Casas Training Camp in the Villa Palmeras sector of San Juan. Barnstorming teams from Cuba and the United States docked at Puerto Rico for exhibition games. Cuba had already sent a few hometown heroes to the big leagues. In 1911, outfielder Armando Marsans and third baseman Rafael D. Almeida of the Cuban Stars joined the Cincinnati Reds (between 1871 and 1873, Esteban Enrique Bellan, of Cuban birth, played a few games with the Troy, New York, Mutuals of the old National Association, and in 1902 Louis M. Castro, a Colombian, appeared briefly for the Philadelphia Athletics). The first full-fledged Latino star was Adolfo

---

[2] According to legend, Doubleday organized the first game of baseball at Cooperstown, New York, in 1839. But the game clearly dates back to the old English game of rounders, and evolved gradually to its present form.

Luque, a righthander from Havana who won 194 games during his twenty-one-year career, including 27 victories for Cincinnati in 1923. But he and the others were light-skinned Latinos; they played together with their dark compatriots at home and were separated by the color bar in the United States. A crack pitcher such as José Méndez—Cubans called him *El Diamante Negro*, The Black Diamond—never had a chance, despite the fact that in 1908 and 1909, when the Philadelphia A's came to Havana, he won duels against their best pitchers, Jack Coombs and Eddie Plank, and later split a pair of games against Christy Mathewson of the New York Giants.

Blacks had not always been barred from American baseball. Before the turn of the century, more than thirty blacks were on the rosters of professional clubs. The first was Moses Fleetwood Walker, the son of an Ohio physician, who turned pro in 1883 with Toledo of the American Association. But there were signs of dissension. In Syracuse, for example, two white players refused to sit for a team photo with a black pitcher. Other incidents followed, and soon afterward league officials met and, reports a newspaper of the time, decided "to approve no more contracts with colored men." The noose tightened. In 1888, *The Sporting News* reported that only four or five black players remained in professional baseball. It said:

> The unfortunate son of Africa who makes his living as a member of a team of white professionals has a rocky road to travel. The rest of the players not only cut him in a social way, but most of them endeavor to "job" him out of the business. He gets the wrong instructions in coaching, and when a field play comes up in which he is interested, an effort is always made to have an error scored against him.

The atmosphere became so hostile that a group of American blacks who toured U.S. cities called their team the Cuban Giants and spoke a strange gibberish on the field, hoping that it would be mistaken for Spanish. By 1890, all blacks were gone from organized baseball. There were mild attempts to skirt the "gentlemen's agreement." In 1901, Baltimore Oriole manager John J. McGraw tried to pass off Charlie Grant, a fair-skinned black second baseman, as a "full-blooded Cherokee." But Charles Comiskey of the Chicago White Sox warned, "If Muggsy really keeps his Indian, I will get a Chinaman of my acquaintance and put him on third." (Grant played only a few games. He died in 1932 when struck by a car in front of the house in Cincinnati where he was the janitor.) McGraw was heard to comment several times that fireballing Cuban pitcher José Méndez was "worth a million dollars." But no one dared hire a black, and the color line would not be broken for another half-century.

Thus rebuffed, blacks formed their own teams and toured the country. They also went south to Puerto Rico, Cuba, and the Dominican Republic, where some of them—Satchel Paige, Buck Leonard, Josh Gibson, and later Monte Irvin and Roy Campanella— were acclaimed as heroes. Puerto Rico had not yet produced a major league player, but the island was wrapped up in its own ethos, and its local tournaments were followed with great enthusiasm. José Méndez, the great Cuban, settled in Puerto Rico for a while and became the mentor of such athletes as Chato Rivera, Liborio Caballero, Pepe Santana, and a young man named Monchile Concepción, who years later as a coach for Santurce in the Winter League, would pass on his baseball wisdom to a rookie by the name of Roberto Clemente.

Soon, every major town in Puerto Rico had its own strong team. Some of them (in English translation) were the Wolves of Arecibo, the Sorcerers of Guayama, the Eastern Grays of Humacao, the Lions of Ponce, and the Cardinals of Mayagüez. They battled among themselves and were also challenged by crack visiting teams. In time, the "Stop Eight League" was formed, with its home field close to Stop Eight of the old San Juan trolley line and, thus, drawing fans from miles around. They cheered for such local champions as Pancho Coímbre and Perucho Cepeda, who was reputed to be an even more ferocious batter than his son, Orlando, now a major league star. As attendance grew, the city of San Juan built a full-scale baseball park near the palm tree-lined Escambrón Beach and named it in honor of Sixto Escobar, the Puerto Rican boxer who had won the world's bantamweight title in the 1930's. The Winter League—which has since had dozens of major league baseball stars on its rosters— was founded in 1938 when Roberto Clemente was four years old.

"Your Blessing, *Mamá*"

Trees line both sides of the suburban street, and colorful shrubs adorn the front yard. It is a casual home of countrybred people. A dog and a cat lounge drowsily in the carport, which is enclosed by decorative iron grillwork. Young children play and chase each other about. The dog barks, a rooster crows from a nearby yard, an ice cream truck glides by out front, playing a loud, tinkling melody. It is the home Roberto Clemente bought for his elderly parents, don Melchor Clemente and doña Luisa Walker de Clemente, soon after he became a big league baseball player. Doña Luisa, aided by a young girl, has been busy in the kitchen. She dries her hands with a dish towel and sits in a rocking chair on the front porch. Don Melchor is in bed, resting, she explains; his heart has grown weaker since her son's death. Several weeks later, don Melchor's heart will stop forever, and the Clementes will go into mourning once more.

Roberto was the youngest of my seven children. He was very strong, with hands that were different from the others. When he was about five years old, if he got hold of a quarter, he would say, "I'm going to have my picture taken!" There were coin machines where you could take your picture. His older brothers would laugh and say, "This *muchacho* must think he's handsome!" He was born with that instinct, and it must have been his destiny, because people took pictures of him all his life.

I converted to the Baptist faith when I was quite young. I am now eighty-three years old, and my husband Melchor, who is still a Catholic, is ninety-two years old. Both Melchor and I are from the

Carolina area, and I think our parents were, too, although I believe that my father came from the town of Loíza. We raised Roberto as a Baptist—he went to church and liked singing the hymns—but he married in the Catholic church. When I was a very young girl, in the time of the Spaniards, baseball was unknown. But my sister and I used to play high-jump. I had lots of ability for that. I was very strong, and later on Roberto would compare his arm with mine and jokingly say that he got his good arm from me.

It was about three o'clock in the afternoon, on August 18, 1934, when Roberto was born, in a house made of wood and concrete on the old country highway in Carolina, right near the road marker that said "Kilometer 7, Hectometer 8." That's in Barrio San Antón, Carolina. We lived there for thirty-three years, but it was later taken down, and a doctor built his house there. All of my children were born at home, with the assistance of a midwife who lived nearby. From my first marriage—I was widowed—I had two children. The eldest, Luis Oquendo, died of an operation in Doctor's Hospital eighteen years ago, the exact same day as Roberto. We buried him on New Year's Day. Then there was Rosa María Oquendo, who died while giving birth to a child. Four or five years later, I married Melchor. Our first child was Osvaldo Clemente, then Justino Clemente, then Andrés Clemente. A daughter, Ana Iris, died at the age of five. Then came Roberto.

When he was very young, my eldest daughter, who was also just a child, started to call him "Momen." It means nothing in particular, just a child's word, but it stuck, and all his childhood friends called him "Momen."

Even as a young child, Roberto loved to play ball. He would lie down in bed and throw a rubber ball against the wall, back and forth, back and forth. As he grew, he would look for other children in the *barrio* to play with. Sometimes I'd dress him up nice and clean, and he'd come home full of dust and mud! I'd send him to the store on an errand, and he'd be gone for hours! I would say to him, "When you leave here, you have to tell us where you're going!" I raised my children at home, in a different epoch, not like nowadays. When I sent them on an errand to someone's house, I would tell them, "You say *buenos días*, give them what I sent with you, and don't you dare enter unless they invite you." In those days, a child was raised to be very humble, not like today. He would ask for *la bendición* of his parents. "Your blessing, *papá*. Your blessing, *mamá*." *Don* Melchor was a strict father, but he was very affectionate with his children. For more than twenty years Melchor worked with the Victoria mill in Carolina as foreman of the brigades of cane-cutters. He had a *paso fino* horse that he rode to the fields, and sometimes one of the employees would mount Roberto on the horse and ride him back and forth, from the house to the highway. He loved that. When Roberto was a little older, Melchor had some trucks which he used for hauling sand and gravel for the construction trade. All the boys would help their *papá*, loading the trucks with shovels. Outside of family work, Roberto's first real money was earned playing baseball.

Roberto was in high school when he signed up for baseball. He planned to attend the university in Mayagüez to study engineering, but he liked baseball. We didn't want him to sign, because he hadn't completed school, but they told him he could play and also study. Roberto was very well liked in school, the teachers were crazy about him. Once, the teacher said the schoolyard was dirty and full of weeds and would cost a lot to clean up. Roberto got up and said, "It won't cost anything! We've all got strong hands and arms, and everyone is going to pitch in, blacks and whites." That's what they did. They all got hoes and cleaned it up. He liked to organize things; he was a leader. Roberto was very thoughtful, very sentimental. Even when he was small, if some neighbor died, he went to their house to help out, and then he would come home and say, "Don't anyone go to work tomorrow, because so-and-so has died and we must attend the burial." When he grew older, he was always the first to offer his shoulder to help carry the coffin.

I am a very religious person. I am resigned to God's will, because what God has done, man cannot change. Today, only three of my children survive. But Roberto's death has left such a deep wound in my heart! Wherever I am, working, sitting, it's so painful. This doesn't mean I'm not resigned to God's will! Because I've always said, "God's will be done," but let Him give us some sign of Roberto! We never saw him get into the plane. He just disappeared. Not a single sign. When a dear one dies, and you bury him, you know that every year you can bring flowers to the grave and pray. My other children have died, but I know where their remains are. But a person like Roberto, so beloved by so many, my youngest son, so affectionate, so attentive—if his father became ill, he would come right away, take him here and there. I am a person who fears God, and respects His wishes. But give me a sign, Lord, something to show that Roberto fell there. Sometimes I think, 'Perhaps the sea is a tomb. It has earth and water. The sea is one of the largest tombs.' I feel better for a while, but then . . . I can't question God, because He made the heavens, the seas, the earth, and we humans are so tiny. It is not everyone's destiny to die old and weak in bed.

Roberto had a favorite Baptist hymn. Sometimes he played it on the organ in his home. He liked that hymn:

> *Sólo Dios hace el hombre feliz.*
> *Sólo Dios hace el hombre feliz.*
> *La vida es nada.*
> *Todo se acaba.*
> *Sólo Dios hace el hombre feliz.*

"Only God makes a man happy. Only God makes a man happy. Life is nothing. Life is fleeting. Only God makes a man happy." I believe that.

I hadn't seen Roberto for about eight days before he disappeared. He was so busy, working night and day, collecting things for the people in Nicaragua. One day I saw him on the television; he looked so gaunt and weary. I wondered, 'Why don't they let him rest, and have someone else go?' They tell me that his niece dreamed the plane would fall, and he laughed. *Don* Melchor dreamed the same thing. Then, about 3:30 in the afternoon of December 31, he called me from his home. "*Mamá*, I'm leaving now." "*Muchacho!* I thought you were in Nicaragua by now." "No, the pilot was delayed. I'm very sorry that I can't spend tonight with all of you. If I'm not back tomorrow, I'll be back the next day." That's exactly what Roberto told me: "If I'm not back tomorrow, I'll be back the next day." I'm still waiting for him.

2

In an album that his mother now treasures, Roberto Clemente once wrote, "I loved the game so much that even though our field was muddy and had lots of trees on it, I played many hours every day. The fences were about 150 feet from home plate. One day I hit about ten home runs in a game we started about 11 A.M. and finished about 6:30 P.M."

Roberto spent those idyllic days of childhood on the gently rolling land of Carolina, whose green fields shimmer eastward to the slopes of El Yunque Mountain, ever shrouded in clouds. That dark peak, according to the ancient Indians, was the home of the Supreme Creator, Yukiyú. On the slopes of El Yunque is the fabled rain forest where thousands of multicolored birds and blossoms grow in a cool, perpetual mist. But down below, in the fields of Carolina, the people are born, live, and die enveloped in tropical warmth.

Sugar was king when Roberto came into the world. Most of the lands and mills were owned by investors from the United States, but the brawn was supplied by Puerto Ricans, who worked for a few pennies a day, when there was work. In early winter, the *guajana*—the silvery flower of the sugar cane—glistens above the sweet stalks, some of them fifteen feet high, and the cane is juicy and ripe for harvest. Under the brutal sun, brigades of men like Melchor Clemente, Roberto's father, and his father before him, and their brothers, uncles, and neighbors, advanced with razor-sharp machetes, "doing battle" as they say, from the crack of dawn to late afternoon. It is back-breaking work, interrupted only by some coffee and bread or cheese at midmorning and midafternoon, and a hot lunch brought to the fields in multitiered kettles by their wives or children. There, sitting in a shady spot, they ate their green bananas, rice, beans, salt cod, and perhaps a scrap of meat until it was time to rise, machete in hand, and "do battle" once more. A few months later, when the narrow-gauge train chugged away toward the mill with the final load of cane, it was the time of the *bruja* (witch), *tiempo muerto* (dead time), and men sought credit at company stores to feed their families. In 1881, *don* Melchor Clemente was born into this stable, rural society, where customs were passed on from generation to generation. *Doña* Luisa Walker de Clemente, the widow with two children whom *don* Melchor married, is also from Carolina and was born in 1890. Like Melchor, she was born a Catholic, but she became a Baptist in her youth when her parents converted. Protestantism was long considered heresy in Puerto Rico, and it was not until the U.S. invasion of 1898 that this new gospel made real headway. Given their head, American missionaries came to the island and—"to avoid overlapping and wasting divine energy in competition," according to one church account—sliced it up into exclusive territories, for the Presbyterians, the Congregationalists, the Baptists, the Methodists, the United Brethren, the Disciples of Christ, and so forth. The town of Carolina, where the Clementes had lived for generations, fell squarely into "Division #3" on the missionaries' map, and *doña* Luisa's parents became Baptists.

Roberto, the youngest child in a large family, was an infant when Puerto Rico was still ensnared in the Great Depression. The island had always been poor, but now things were far worse. When he was six years old, average income per person in Puerto Rico was about thirty cents a day. The average life span was only forty-six years, as thousands of infants died of diarrhea, gastroenteritis, pneumonia, and influenza, and hundreds of thousands of adults were weakened by intestinal parasites. In Roberto's *barrio* of San Antón, it was not rare to see the neighbors solemnly bearing a tiny wooden casket—a dead infant—to the cemetery.

The Clementes were not poor by these standards. The short, wiry *don* Melchor "always worked," Roberto recalled. "We lived in a big wooden house," said Roberto, "with a large front porch, five bedrooms, living room, dining room, kitchen, and an indoor bathroom," a luxury in rural Puerto Rico at the time. But Roberto's father was not a common laborer. By the time Roberto was born, *don* Melchor was fifty-four years old and worked as a *capataz*, a foreman over the crews of cane-cutters at the Victoria Sugar Mill. He also brought in a few extra *pesos* by selling meat and other provisions to the workers. And in his spare time he rented out his beat-up truck for deliveries of sand and gravel to construction sites. A few months after Roberto's seventh birthday, the Japanese attacked Pearl Harbor, and the United States became involved in World War II. German submarines prowled the Caribbean, and even people with money had trouble finding food because of the wartime blockade on shipping.

Despite these hardships, Roberto remembered a happy childhood: "When I was a boy, I realized what lovely persons my father and mother were. I was treated real good. I learned the right way to live. I never heard any hate in my house. Not for anybody. I never heard my mother say a bad word to my father, or my father to my mother. During the war, when food all over Puerto Rico was limited, we never went hungry, They always found a way to feed us. We kids were first, and they were second."

Roberto was raised in a strict home, where sharp lines divided right and wrong, and a child gave unquestioning respect to his parents and his elders. *Doña* Luisa was a fervent churchgoer, and she often took Roberto to services, where he enjoyed singing hymns. Roberto worshiped his father. Once, when Roberto was a young child, *don* Melchor fell sick and was taken to the Presbyterian Hospital. Roberto was not old enough to be allowed in to visit him. He climbed a tall palm tree outside the window of his father's room so that he could see him.

When he was eight he joined his first neighborhood team and, according to his father, "played surprisingly well against boys his age and older." His first bat was fashioned from the branch of a guava tree, a glove was improvised from a coffee bean sack, and the ball was a tight knot of rags.

"Momen, as we childhood friends called him, had the combative fury of very few athletes," recalls Manuel Maldonado Denis, who grew up with Roberto, played pro ball on the island, and is now a professor of political science at the University of Puerto Rico. "I recall very well the day that his older brothers took him to play in the kid's league at the Barrio San Antón School. He couldn't have been older than ten and was probably younger. Some of us were much older. For example, there was his brother Matino, whose catches at first base were the sensation of the *barrio*;and Lorenzo, another brother, who gripped the bat cross-handed, and whose line drives shook the zinc roof of the school house;and Andrés, who threw underhand style. They were the Clemente brothers: Matino, Lorenzo, Andrés, and Momen. All you had to do was look at Momen to know that he had been born to play baseball."

In school, Roberto was "very shy and respectful" recalls his tenth-grade history teacher at the Julio C. Vizcarrondo High School in Carolina. When he came to her class at the age of fourteen, he chose the last seat in the room, and when she asked him a question, he answered with his face down, looking at the floor—a traditional sign of respect for one's elders. But despite his shyness, his former teacher retains one vivid image of young Roberto: "I will *always* remember his big hands, those big hands that would express what he would not say in words."

With schoolwork and chores at home, the day was never long enough for the sports-hungry Roberto. In high school, he starred in baseball and track and field, where he competed in the javelin throw, the high jump, and the 400-meter run. There was talk that he might even qualify for the Puerto Rican team that would compete in the 1956 Olympics. But baseball was his obsession. Every so often, his father gave him round-trip bus fare and sent him to San Juan to buy lottery tickets. If Monte Irvin was playing at Sixto Escobar Stadium, about a mile short of the place where he had to buy the lottery tickets, Roberto would get off the bus, peek in at the game for a while, and walk the rest of the way to town. "Once," a friend recalls, "a foul ball flew out of the park and Roberto kept it. He used to sleep with that ball, he told me! But his older brothers got to playing with it and it fell into a ditch where the hogs wallowed around in the mud. He cleaned it off and put it away, but his brothers always got hold of it."

"I would forget to eat because of baseball," he recalled years later, "and one time my mother started to burn my bat as a punishment. But I got it out of the fire and saved it." When he was not playing, he squeezed a hard rubber ball to strengthen his forearms.

And when the Winter League broadcast its games, he crouched close to the radio at home to hear how his idol, Monte Irvin, was faring.

"He's an Unpolished Gem"

Roberto Marín was lying in bed at his home in San Juan, listening to the Pirate game on the radio, when Roberto Clemente got his 3,000th hit. Moments later, he heard Clemente say from the clubhouse, "I dedicate that hit to the person I owe most to in professional baseball, Roberto Marín."

"You can imagine how I felt," says Marín, a youthful looking grandfather who lives in a suburb near San Juan International Airport. He has never been to Pittsburgh; in fact, he never saw Clemente play outside of Puerto Rico, except on television. Marín sells rice to wholesalers along the island's north coast. One day, more than two decades ago, while driving through Barrio San Antón of Carolina, he saw some boys batting empty tomato sauce cans with sticks. One fourteen-year-old "hit those cans pretty far." Soon afterward, he recruited that boy, Roberto Clemente, and gave him his first uniform—a T-shirt with the letters of the Sello Rojo Rice softball team. The team, composed of all-stars from the Carolina area, was organized to compete in a big softball tournament in San Juan. Sitting in a rocking chair in his dimmed living room, Marín recalls the beginning of his long friendship with Roberto Clemente.

I would drive him to and from the games. In those days, for a young kid to travel from Carolina to San Juan was almost like going to New York!

We used Roberto at shortstop because of his powerful arm, but then we moved him to the outfield. Slowly, his name became known for his long hits to right field, and for his sensational catches.

Everyone had their eyes on him. He was competing against top softball players, and as you know a good softball pitcher is about as hard to hit as a professional baseball pitcher.

Most everyone on that softball team liked to take a drink now and then. The end of the game was reason enough to have a party. But Roberto never, never drank. He would stay late with us, just eating and listening.

After the softball tournament, some teams in the double A amateur baseball league became interested in Roberto. He was like an unpolished gem. He had a strong arm, speed; he was a complete athlete. So he began to play with the Juncos team in the Double A amateur baseball league.

One day I said to him, "*Caramba*, Roberto, I think you're as good or better than many of the pros who play here in the Winter League. I'm going to talk with a friend of mine, Pedrín Zorrilla, who owns one of the clubs and is also a scout for the Brooklyn Dodgers." Every Tuesday my job took me to the town of Manatí. Pedrín Zorrilla had a country house on the beach there. Roberto and I drove out to see Pedrín. Roberto was very quiet, didn't say a word. Pedrín took a look at him and said, "*Caramba*, what a pair of hands!" The truth is, Roberto had huge hands. I always used to kid him that he was one of the few persons I knew who could wash his face and his head at the same time with just one hand! "He's an unpolished gem," I told Pedrín.

They didn't offer much to young players in those days and Roberto had no record to show. "I'd like to see him on the field," Pedrín said. So I wrote down Roberto's name on a piece of paper, gave it to him, and said he could see us whenever he liked.

The next weekend, Juncos was going to play an exhibition game in Manatí. Zorrilla was there. That day Roberto made two good catches in center, made a barbaric throw that caught a runner at home, and got a good hit. The manager of the Juncos team was Monchile Concepción, who has since died, may he rest in peace. Monchile was also a coach for the Santurce team in the Winter League, which was owned by Zorrilla, and Pedrín asks Monchile, "Who is that *negrito* out there?"

"That's Momen, a young fellow we're trying out. His last name is Clemente."

Pedrín looks in his pocket at the paper I gave him and says *"Adiós*, this is the same young fellow that Marín told me about. Tell him to come here." We arranged to see Pedrín the following Tuesday. Since Roberto was under age—about sixteen or seventeen years old—he couldn't sign a contract. Pedrín tells me, "Well, Marín, we can give him a $400 bonus, and maybe $40 or $45 a week, until he learns how to put his uniform on right." He was going to be on the same team with guys like Willard Brown, Buster Clarkson, and other black stars who played in Puerto Rico.

On the way back in my car, Roberto was all excited. He wanted to be a ballplayer. "What should I do? What should I do?" he kept asking me. "You've got to go see your father, we'll talk it over, and he'll decide," I said. When he got there, he told his *papá*, and his *papá* went to consult with a neighbor, who said, "When they offer $400, it means he's worth plenty more; so don't sign a thing."

His *papá* came to see me and said, "Marín, I want to go with you to see Pedrín Zorrilla, because I think they can give more money to my boy." We went in my car to Pedrín's house in Santurce. Pedrín told him very frankly, "If you want more money, I have no interest in him. I think he's good, but he's got no record to prove it."

We left, and the next day Roberto comes to my house again and says, "I want to sign." I went to *don* Melchor, his father, and said, "Look, Roberto says he wants to sign." They accepted the $400 and the $40-a-week salary, which wasn't bad in those days.

When I took Roberto to sign, we stopped at a restaurant and right away he asks for a big steak with plenty of potatoes. I tell him, *"Caramba, negrito*, you still haven't gotten your first hit, and already you're asking for steak!" Years later, in a phone conversation between me here and him in the United States—they were honoring him with a special day—he reminded me that the first big steak he'd eaten had been on me.

The Winter League lasted about four months, seventy-two games; they played about four times a week. There were so many black American stars that the natives had to be darn good to play. In those days, the blacks played for little money. Right after Roberto signed, they put him on the bench. I would drive him back and forth to the park, and after several weeks he still hadn't played. His team, Santurce, was the best in the league, and it was tough to break in.

One day, in the car, he says to me, "You've got to talk to the manager, because if he doesn't play me I'm quitting." We got to the park early. Roberto stayed outside, holding his little suitcase, completely silent. I went to Pedrín and told him, "*El negro* tells me he wants a chance." I never mentioned Roberto's threat about quitting. Pedrín says, "Remember, when I signed him I said I wanted him to first learn how to put a uniform on, that's all. It's just his first year."

"But the boy is desperate!" I said.

He told me to go talk to the manager. "Look," I said to the manager, "*el negro* is a bit upset, because we haven't given him a chance." "Well, Marín, I'll put him in when I think it's time. I'm the manager around here." I go back to Roberto and tell him, "He said he'll give you a chance as soon as he can."

Not much later, in Caguas, there were three men on base and it was Bob Thurman's turn to hit. He was a terrific batter, who played in the majors for a while, although he never got a chance in his prime because he was black. But he was pretty weak against lefty pitchers, and that's what Caguas had on the mound. So the time came. Clemente went in for Thurman and hit a long double to right field. That won the game, and Roberto got more chances from then on.

The best thing that ever happened to Roberto came the next season when he played next to Willie Mays, who was about five years older and was already a major league star. Roberto played left field and Mays was in center. They got along very well together, a young boy with a young star. Mays was a very good guy. When there was a grounder to the outfield, Mays would remind him, show him how one outfielder backs up another. I think it was the inspiration of playing next to a star like Mays, and doing a good job, that was most important. Anyway, that year Roberto became a first-class ballplayer. From then on, he went up and up.

Roberto had a tremendous amount of spirit. A few years later, when he was already established in the major leagues, I get a call from the prison in Río Piedras, inviting me to bring a softball team to play against the inmates. They knew I was a close friend of Roberto's, and since it was the off-season they asked if he could come to play with our team. I said to Roberto, "*Caramba*, they want a softball team to go to the prison to entertain the inmates. Can you come with us on Saturday?"

"Of course. Come pick me up."

At 8:30 in the morning on Saturday I go to his house, and he's wearing his Pittsburgh Pirate uniform! As if he were going to a big league game! We went to the prison and everyone was very happy. I was the pitcher for our team—I was slow, and the inmates had a pretty tough bunch. In the first inning they got about five runs off me, I couldn't get a man out! Roberto, who was playing shortstop, comes to the mound and says, "*Qué pasa?*" "They're hitting me," I tell him.

"Give me the ball. I don't even like to lose a game in jail," he says.

"But I'm the manager, you can't take me out."

"*Out*," he says firmly.

He had terrific speed, and he struck them out one after another. In the fifth inning we were catching up, but we were still a couple runs behind. He came to bat, with two men on base, and I was coaching at third base. He smacks one to right-center field and the ball really takes off. I'm waving the people home and he comes rounding second base. I signal for him to stop but he slides head first into third, and the third baseman goes flying. What a cloud of dust! He gets up, wiping himself off, and I say, "You're *loco*, an expensive big leaguer like you, sliding head first, and look at that poor prisoner over there, he still hasn't gotten up."

"I've always told you I play to win," he says. He was very proud when we won that game.

As the years went by, he used to come here to the house to visit me. One day—he was already quite famous—he asked me to baptize his second son, Roberto Luis, and to be his *compadre*. "What's this?" I ask him. "With all the big people around that you know?" "No," he says, "you're big people and I want you to be my *compadre*."

I didn't know what Roberto Clemente really was until he played the 1971 World Series. One time, there was a man on first, the winning run, and they hit one off the right field fence. Roberto grabbed it and without even stopping to brace himself he threw a perfect one-bounce strike to home that stopped the run from coming in. It was tremendous! I couldn't believe it! When he returned to the island, he came over to the house and says, "Now are you satisfied?" I gave him an *abrazo*, replying, "More than satisfied. I didn't believe my own eyes." "Now people know Roberto Clemente," he says.

During the off-season, Roberto couldn't keep still. He had lots of hobbies, making curtains, ceramic lamps. He had a farm, about nine acres, and he was always out there on his tractor. There was a nice house on the land, and when players came to the island they would stay there. He had another piece of land near the El Yunque rain forest, where he planned to build an artificial lake and fill it with trout. One day I called him to ask what he's up to. "Here I am, beneath the kitchen stove, fixing something." "*Muchacho!* You beneath the stove! Why don't you hire some man to fix it?" "No, I like doing this stuff." He always liked working with his hands.

Over the years, Roberto gradually changed in the sense that he was no longer so shy, he became much more talkative. He shed the complexes that so many colored players have in baseball; he always defended the cause of the Latinos. Once we took a trip to Saint Thomas in the Virgin Islands, him and his wife, my brother-in-law—who's a lawyer—and his wife, and my wife and me. We go to one of the car rental businesses at the airport in Saint Thomas. The man behind the counter tells me there are no cars available. But an American comes up and they hand him a set of car keys. Roberto went over. He simply asks why no cars are available and the man answers, "Well, a lot of Puerto Ricans come here, rent a car, leave it out in the mountains somewhere, and don't pay." Roberto says, "But not all Puerto Ricans are alike; you can't put us all in the same boat." He still hadn't identified himself, but when there was no other recourse, he whipped out his wallet, with God knows how many credit cards, and asks, "Will these do?" "Roberto Clemente!" the man said. Suddenly he couldn't do enough for us. But Roberto said "No, no, I don't want any favors; I want you to treat us all alike." By then, the governor of the island had been notified and sent a car over.

He had tremendous faith in a chiropractor named Arturo Garcia, and he learned a lot from that man. Soon he was helping people himself, without publicity. One day while we were preparing the food for a special homage we gave him in the town of Corozal, a fellow whom I had known for quite some time told me, "The greatest favor of my life I owe to Roberto Clemente." I didn't think

Roberto knew him, but Roberto gave him a big *abrazo* and asked him how he felt. That's when I learned that the man had been disabled and Roberto treated him for his injuries. The fellow was once a ship's cook and he said, "I'm going to prepare this meal myself."

The last time Roberto and I spoke, his plans were to play a couple of seasons more . . . but . . . it just didn't happen that way.

3

"*Uno más*," shouted Alex Campanis, the Brooklyn Dodger scout. For the second time, the dark, rawboned young man standing deep in center field at Sixto Escobar Stadium reared his right arm back and fired a bullet to home plate.

Roberto Clemente, then an eighteen-year-old amateur league player, was one of seventy-two young aspirants at a tryout conducted jointly by the Brooklyn Dodgers and the Santurce Crabbers in 1952. "How could I miss him? He was the greatest natural athlete I have ever seen as a free agent," Campanis remarked years later to columnist Dick Young of the *New York Daily News*. Watching them like a hawk, Campanis asked all the young men to throw from the outfield. Next, they ran sixty yards in full uniform. Roberto, his head bobbing up and down, his arms and legs flailing, ran the distance in 6.4 seconds. "I couldn't believe it," says Campanis. "*Uno más*." Again, Roberto ran it in 6.4 seconds. That was enough for Campanis, who thanked the other boys and sent them home. He asked to see Clemente hit, and the young man stayed in the batting cage for about twenty minutes.

"He starts hitting line drives all over the place," said Campanis. "I notice the way he's standing in the box and I figure there's no way he can reach the outside of the plate, so I tell the pitcher to pitch him outside, and the kid swings with both feet off the ground and hits drives to right and sharp ground balls up the middle."

Roberto was still in high school and neither the Dodgers nor the Santurce team signed him on the spot. But he continued to star in his second season for the Juncos team of the Double A Amateur League, and the hometown fans idolized him. Later that year—on October 9, 1952—Pedrín Zorilla signed Roberto to his first professional contract for a $400 bonus and a salary of $40 weekly. He would play with the Santurce Crabbers of the Winter League in their 1952–53 season. Since Roberto was a minor, the contract was actually signed by his father, *don* Melchor, and witnessed by a friend, José E. Marrero Otero. That first season, Roberto was used sparingly; he come to bat only 77 times and got 18 hits for .234 average, but he was just a green rookie playing against clubs with major leaguers on their rosters.

"I told him he'd be as good as Willie Mays some day. And he was," recalls James 'Buster' Clarkson, the great black American shortstop who starred in the Puerto Rican league for several years. Clemente and José Pagán, who were both breaking into professional ball at the time, called Clarkson "Papá."

"I could see he was going a long way," says Clarkson. "He had a few rough spots, but he never made the same mistake twice. He had baseball savvy and he listened. He listened to what he was told and he did it. Some of the old pros didn't take too kindly to a kid breaking into the lineup, but Clemente was too good to keep out." Years later, Clemente would tell a Pittsburgh writer that the best advice he ever received in baseball came from Clarkson: "I was just a kid. He insisted the other players allow me to take batting practice and he helped me. He put a bat behind my left foot and made sure I didn't drag my foot."

Roberto became a regular for Santurce the next year, in the 1953–54 winter season. During the sixty-game schedule, he came to bat 219 times and got 63 hits—17 of them for extra bases—finishing with a creditable .288 average. During that season he developed his "basket" catch, which until then was Willie Mays's trademark. He insisted he didn't copy from Mays. "I missed fly balls many times because I tried to catch too high," he explained, adding that Luis Olmo (the former Dodger outfielder) and Herman Franks (a Giant coach and later manager) urged him to catch the ball chesthigh instead of holding his arms outstretched. Later, he said, he dropped his hands even lower. "It worked good for me and made it easier to throw, too, after I make a catch." His fielding was spectacular that season, and major league scouts began to descend en masse.

"American baseball seemed so far away. With all the talent there, why should teams be interested in players on the island?" Roberto said years later, recalling how he felt in his youth.

Thus far, Puerto Rico had produced few major league players, and none of superstar caliber. Hiram Gabriel Bithorn had joined the Chicago Cubs in 1942 and pitched four seasons. Luis Rodríguez Olmo became a popular outfielder for the Brooklyn Dodgers in 1943, winding up his big-league career in 1951 with the Boston Braves. But they were light-skinned Latinos who had passed through the game's color bar. In the early 1950's, however, as Roberto grew to maturity, things began to change. A number of the American blacks whom Roberto had seen play in the Winter League were now on major league rosters. A dark-skinned Cuban by the name of Saturnino Orestes Arrieta Armas Miñoso—better known to American fans as "Minnie" Minoso—played his first full season with the Chicago White Sox in 1951, hit for a blistering .324 and stole 31 bases. In 1954, Roberto Avila of Mexico would lead the American League with a .341 average for the Cleveland Indians. Victor Pellot Power, a black compatriot of Roberto's, would sign a contract with the Philadelphia Athletics and become one of the fanciest fielding first basemen in the game. Another dark-skinned Puerto Rican, Rubén Gómez, had won 13 games for the New York Giants in 1953, and the next year, after compiling a 17–9 pitching record, would win a big game against the Cleveland Indians in the World Series. Suddenly, it all began to seem possible.

At least nine major league clubs approached Roberto with pen and money in hand during the winter of 1953. It is said that the New York Giants had first crack at him, but the Dodgers decided to outbid them, because the prospect of Clemente playing next to Willie Mays in the same outfield was too frightening. The Dodgers offered a $10,000 bonus, quite exceptional for a Latino player in those days (Felipe Alou of the Dominican Republic was signed for $200, and his hard-throwing countryman Juan Marichal received a bonus of $500). As the story goes, Milwaukee Braves scout Luis Olmo bid an astounding $28,000. But Roberto had already promised to accept the Dodgers' terms. Confused, he turned to his parents, and his mother sternly decided, "If you gave your word, you keep your word." So, on February 19, 1954, Roberto (still in high school and under age) co-signed a telegram with his father that was directed to the Dodgers, accepting the $10,000 bonus and a $5,000 salary to play with Brooklyn's International League farm team in Montreal.

Two days later, a United Press International dispatch out of Canada noted that "Roberto Clemente, a Negro bonus player from Puerto Rico," was expected to play center field that year "if Cuban Sandy Amoros, the league's leading hitter last season, catches on with the parent Dodgers."

"Buy yourself a good car, and don't depend on anybody," was the advice *don* Melchor Clemente gave to his nineteen-year-old son who waited in San Juan's airport with his bag packed, ready to fly north. His seventy-four-year-old father could have said more, but Roberto would have to learn for himself. He spoke only halting English, picked up from textbooks in school, but this could be overcome. The color of his skin would never change. Life was suddenly becoming quite complicated for the young man from Carolina. Now it was no longer just a question of hitting or catching a baseball. In fact, without knowing it he had already become a pawn in a power struggle between two major league teams, and his blackness was an important reason.

Jackie Robinson had ended half a century of "lily-white" competition in baseball just seven years before. Clubs still had informal quota systems; they feared, perhaps, that fans would turn away if too many black players appeared together on the field. This is why, despite scout Alex Campanis's urgings, Roberto was assigned to Montreal and not to the parent Brooklyn Dodger club. After the 1953 season the Dodgers brought Sandy Amoros up from Montreal, the fifth black on the roster, joining Jackie Robinson, Junior Gilliam, Roy Campanella, and Don Newcombe. On the days that Newcombe pitched, with four other blacks in the lineup, whites would be outnumbered on the playing field for the first time in the game's history. Those were the days that Roy Campanella might develop a sudden touch of fatigue, Jackie Robinson might have a stomachache, or rookie Sandy Amoros might be found sitting on the bench, wearing a Band-Aid around his "sore" finger.

So the Dodgers, to maintain their racial quota, kept Roberto in Montreal, where they risked losing him because of the complex "bonus" rule that prevailed at the time. Any player who received a bonus higher than $4,000 and was not on the major league club's 25-man roster was subject to being "drafted" by another club, the first choice going to the club that finished last in the league the previous year.

Roberto was totally unaware of these machinations, but the Dodgers were prepared to lose him, so long as he did not fall into the clutches of one of Brooklyn's strong rivals.

"That's right," Dodger vice president Buzzie Bavasi admitted later. "We didn't want the Giants to have Clemente and a fellow like Willie Mays in the same outfield. It was a cheap deal for us."

The "cheap deal" had the Dodgers outbidding the Giants for Clemente by offering him a $10,000 bonus, and later receiving $4,000 from the club that drafted him. "So, all right, it cost us $6,000, but the Giants didn't get him, which was the important thing," said Bavasi.

That solved the Dodgers' problem, but Roberto—heading northward for the first time in his life—would be immersed in a racial environment totally foreign to him. A black man is not a stranger to prejudice in Puerto Rico, where, on a scale of values, "white" is prized above "black." But the racial climate in Puerto Rico is far more complex—and benign—than in the United States.

Most of Puerto Rico's original Indians were killed or frightened off during the Spanish conquest, but a few fled to the hills, where they intermarried with later settlers. Next came a large influx of African slaves to work the big plantations along the coasts. Since the first Spaniards brought few women with them, the white, black, and red races were mixed in a genetic "stew" that bubbled quietly for centuries. Today, the whites and blacks constitute large minorities in Puerto Rico and blend gradually into the dominant middle, who are near-white, near-black, or sometimes strikingly Indian and fall into a catch-all group known as the *trigueño* (literally, "wheat-colored" but meaning tan, swarthy, darkish). The fuzzy lines between racial groups, plus the fact that many families have members of different colors, blunt the sharp edge of color-consciousness that prevails in the United States. Because of Puerto Rico's polychromatic society, there were never separate restaurants, or water fountains, or rear sections of buses for blacks.

It was the numbing heritage of slavery (abolished in 1873) that deprived blacks of the schooling and economic assets they needed to compete in Puerto Rican society, a society with such rigid class lines that even poor whites found it difficult to climb upward. But a black man headed Puerto Rico's Republican Party for years; another was the speaker in the island's House of Representatives. And, of course, Roberto grew up watching blacks, whites, and *trigueños* compete on an equal footing on the baseball diamond. Perhaps Vic Power, the Puerto Rican ballplayer, best summed it up when he spoke to Jackie Robinson a few years ago:

> In Puerto Rico I don't see no segregation. You can go any place you want, you can go to the restaurant, you can go to movies, you can go anywhere, but the funny thing about it is if you go to a lot of places like bank or hotel, the white Puerto Ricans they get the jobs. You don't see so many colored people working in nice jobs. I've been around these places, San Juan, Cuba, Santo Domingo, Mexico. They never segregate me, but you don't see no colored people working for the money you need to go to nice hotel or good restaurant. Puerto Rico is the kind of country you can go anywhere if you got the money, but if you can't get the money you are segregated anyhow.

In the spring of 1954, when young Roberto reported to Montreal, he played on the same field where Jackie Robinson entered organized baseball in April, 1946, and went on to win the International League batting title. Racial tensions were certainly less than the time in 1946 when Montreal's manager said, "Mister Rickey, you don't mean to say, do you, that Nigras are human beings?" America's laws had changed, but attitudes die hard. Altruism alone had not permitted Jackie Robinson to break baseball's color line. There was also mounting pressure from civil rights groups, and it made good economic sense. Federal and state laws were passed in the early 1940's to prohibit discrimination in hiring. On opening day of 1945, as picketers marched outside Yankee Stadium, the major league owners asked Branch Rickey of the Dodgers and Larry McPhail of the Yankees to form a committee to study the race question. Rickey later recalled a meeting in 1945 where 15 major league clubs were represented, and 14 adopted a resolution to oppose blacks in baseball. "It was a warning to me," he said, "an admonition strangely worded. It was read to me by one of the club presidents. He was violently opposed. He warned that the physical properties of the ballclubs, the parks, would go up in smoke."

Those same owners, and most of the same managers, coaches, and players, were active in baseball when Robinson joined the Brooklyn club for the 1947 season. It was rumored that the Philadelphia Phillies would refuse to take the field if he played, and that the Saint Louis Cardinals were planning a league-wide strike. But a blunt telegram from National League President Ford Frick to the Cardinals warned them: "I do not care if half the league strikes. Those who do it . . . will be suspended and I don't care if it wrecks the National League for five years. This is the United States of America and one citizen has as much right to play as another."

It was also good business to hire blacks. This was the era of the "bonus baby," and untested white high school stars were commanding six-figure amounts, but blacks—eager to get in—were available for a pittance. Between 1948 and 1958, not one of the 30 blacks who entered baseball received a bonus above $20,000, while nearly one-fifth of the 134 whites who signed contracts got bonuses higher than that.

By 1953, just before Clemente signed, there were 20 blacks on seven major league clubs, including such future stars as Willie Mays of the Giants, Henry Aaron of the Braves, and Ernie Banks of the Cubs. But in the South, where the clubs trained, it was as though nothing had happened at all. This was a time when Autherine Lucy was still struggling in the courts to become the first black student at the University of Alabama. The days of Supreme Court decisions, Martin Luther King Jr., Mississippi Freedom Rides, and civil rights marches in Washington were still to come. It was a time when Felipe Alou, the Dominican, was prohibited from playing on an otherwise all-white minor league team by the governor of Louisiana. Willie Mays, already a $100,000-per-year star in the 1950's, was barnstorming through the South after the season, together with Hank Aaron.

They were in Willie's hometown, Birmingham, Alabama, and Aaron recalls, "He went into a store to get some shoes. He pulled out a hundred dollar bill to pay for them. They wanted to know where he'd got a hundred dollar bill." In 1954 Ernie Banks, the great Chicago Cubs slugger, was in Alabama, where the club held spring training. He and the other blacks on the club were told they couldn't stay with the team in a downtown hotel in Mobile. As they waited for further directions, Banks ran into the bus station to buy a candy bar and was told: "Go to the rear where the niggers are!"

For many springs, Milwaukee Braves star Billy Bruton ate in the kitchens of roadside diners. When he tried to take his wife south for spring training and finally found a cottage that would rent to them, she was prohibited from sitting in the grandstand with the white players' wives. "All I could ask myself," he later said, "was, How long would I have to suffer such humiliations?"

On the ballfield, where black and white statistics judge a man's worth, the situation was more palatable. But black Cleveland star Larry Doby checked those statistics and found that he, Jackie Robinson, Roy Campanella, and Minnie Minoso were hit by pitched balls 75 percent more than Joe DiMaggio, Ted Williams, or Stan Musial.

In Canada, Clemente recalled later, "they don't have much segregation. But one day I am signing autographs and talking to white man and his wife outside park, and this other man say, 'You not supposed to talk to white woman.' I said, 'No, I talk to the one I want. I talk to my friends. You believe in that stuff if you want. I don't.' " When Montreal took its first road trip to Richmond, Virginia, Roberto learned what it was like to play with a group of men and be forced to sleep and eat apart from them.

Then there was the language problem. "I had studied English in high school, but I never really had to speak it until I joined the team in Montreal," he said. During one game, Roberto made an acrobatic catch, robbing an opponent of an extra-base hit. As they passed each other on the field, the disgruntled batter muttered, "You sonofabitch," and Roberto, thinking the man had paid him a compliment, replied, "Thank you."

"What are you thanking him for?" asked a teammate, who gave Roberto a full translation of the "compliment." The next inning, as they passed each other on the field it was returned in full.

Worse than the insults, worse perhaps than the racial segregation in the South, was the perplexing way that Max Macon, the Montreal manager, treated him. Roberto recalled that first season with a shudder: "If I struck out I stay in the lineup. If I played well I'm benched. One day I hit three triples and the next day I was benched. Another time they took me out for a pinch-hitter with the bases loaded in the first inning. Much of the time I was used only as a pinch-runner or for defense. I didn't know what was going on, and I was confused and almost mad enough to go home."

Whenever he asked Macon why he was being played so irregularly, the manager assured him that he was doing it for his own good. But Roberto was confused. Finally, Alex Campanis—the scout who had spotted Roberto at that first workout in Sixto Escobar Stadium—came to Montreal on a routine visit. Campanis spoke Spanish, and Roberto poured out his frustrations.

"I want to go home, Mr. Campanis. I know I can play better than these guys, but I am not being used. The other night, we get five runs in the first inning, he takes me out. Mr. Macon does not like me."

Campanis assured Roberto that Macon held no personal grudge against him and that they were only trying to protect his future as a Brooklyn Dodger.

"Do you trust me?" said Campanis.

"I trust you."

"Then believe me. Everything will be all right."

Roberto never dreamed at the time that the Dodgers had practically given up all hope of keeping him because of the "bonus draft" rule. However, on the slim chance that he might be overlooked by the other clubs, they tried to "hide" him by playing him irregularly, so that he wouldn't appear too attractive a choice.

But how can a club "hide" a promising young player like Roberto Clemente? Despite the fact that he appeared in only 87 games that season and had a modest average of .257, he looked too good to pass up.

First choice in the National League draft would go to the Pittsburgh Pirates, who were comfortably ensconced in last place that season. The Pirates, who were interested in Montreal pitcher Joe Black, a former Dodger star, dispatched their scout Clyde Sukeforth to Richmond, where Montreal was playing. During the pregame workout, he saw Clemente throw a few 300-foot bullets from the outfield. "I couldn't take my eyes off him," he said. Roberto was used as a pinch-hitter in the game, and Sukeforth liked his swing enough to inquire and learn that the young Puerto Rican was eligible for the draft. Sukeforth went to Pittsburgh and consulted with Branch Rickey, who had moved from the Dodgers to the Pirate organization and was engaged in a "five-year plan" to recruit young players for the perennial losers. A few days later, Sukeforth went to Montreal to see more of Roberto. That night, while having dinner with Max Macon, the manager, he said with a mischievous grin, "I notice you haven't been playing Clemente much lately."

Before Macon could reply, Sukeforth said, "You might as well use him. He's better than anyone we have in Pittsburgh right now. We're going to finish last, and we're going to draft him number one."

Then, rising from the table, Sukeforth waved and said, "Take care of our boy."

Despite Sukeforth's playful warning, the Dodgers tried to keep Clemente under wraps. Toward the end of the year he hit two triples and a double off lefthander Jack Collum in Rochester, and the next time he came to bat the manager replaced him with a pinch-hitter. He remained on the bench for the final 25 games of the season. Nevertheless, on November 22, 1954, at a meeting of major league clubs in New York City, the Pirates announced that Roberto Clemente was their first draft choice and eagerly paid the purchase price of $4,000. "If we didn't," said Pittsburgh's Latin America scout, Howie Haak, "any of fourteen other clubs would have."

Roberto, who heard the news while at home in Puerto Rico, later admitted, "I didn't even know where Pittsburgh was."

But together with the good news of Roberto's major league contract, tragedy hit the Clemente household that winter. Roberto's older brother Luis was in the hospital dying of a brain tumor. One night, while returning home from a hospital visit, Roberto's car was smashed by a drunk whose car was speeding at 60 miles per hour. He emerged from the wreckage without visible injury, but three of his spinal discs were jarred loose and would plague him during his career. That New Year's Eve, while the rest of the world celebrated, the Clementes sat at Luis's bedside as the life slipped from his body. They buried him the next day.

"Clemente Was Right at His Heels!"

In 1952, Pedrín Zorrilla signed eighteen-year-old Roberto Clemente to his first professional baseball contract, with the Santurce team of the Puerto Rico Winter League. Two years later, while acting as a scout for the Brooklyn Dodgers, he also signed him for U.S. baseball. A tall, heavy-set man with white hair, don Pedrín is one of the pioneers of professional baseball in Puerto Rico and also served in the insular House of Representatives from 1960 through 1968. His home, atop a hill in the Santurce section of San Juan, is a veritable museum of cups, trophies, scrapbooks, and other baseball memorabilia. Leaning back in a chair on his front porch, he recalls:

My love of the sport began when my father sent me to the United States—I was eleven years old—and I played sandlot baseball. The Puerto Rican Winter League was formed in 1938, and the next year some friends of mine—Rafael Muñiz, Luis Torres, and Miguel Pasarell—and I got a league franchise and founded the Santurce Cangrejeros, the Crabbers in English. There was a great deal of enthusiasm for baseball here in the 1930's, mainly because of the black teams that came to play: the Newark Eagles, the Black Yankees, the Cuban Stars. These were great athletes, unquestionably of major league caliber, but the racial barriers prevented them from playing. The strange thing was that white major leaguers such as Johnny Mize, Wally Moses, George McQuinn, and many others competed here against black Americans such as Josh Gibson, Satchel Paige, Monte Irvin, Larry Doby, Dan Bankhead, Willard Brown . . . something they couldn't do in their own country! That's something we Puerto Ricans could never understand, in a country with such good government, with so much democracy. The two greatest players I've ever seen, of *any* race, are the Cuban Martín Dihigo, who played all positions, and Josh Gibson, the catcher. Our Winter League was, and is, a tough league. I remember when the World's Champion New York Yankees came here in 1947, and our Ponce team beat them. Raymond Brown, who was well past his prime, was the winning pitcher.

By the 1950's, I had established good relations with the Brooklyn Dodgers—with Mr. O'Malley, with Mr. Bavasi, with Alex Campanis, one of their scouts—and the Dodgers and our Santurce club in 1952 organized a tryout camp for young players in Sixto Escobar Stadium. The park was filled with young men, and among them was Roberto Clemente. We saw that he had a strong arm, hit hard, but we never imagined what he would do later. He was still just a boy, and we lost track of him. Some months later, a good friend of mine, Roberto Marín, reminded me that I should see Roberto Clemente, who was playing with Juncos in the Double A Amateur League. I saw him in one game against Manatí, where he hit a double and made a beautiful slide into second base. Not long after that, on October 9, 1952, we signed Roberto to a contract on the Santurce Crabbers for a $400 bonus and $40 per week. Players at that time earned from $400 to $500 a month, depending upon their ability, and a few major leaguers got as high as $1,000 per month, plus housing expenses. In the old days, when the league just started, the average native player earned only $12 a week, and the black imports got from $15 to $25 a week!

The next year I signed him for Brooklyn, to play with their Montreal farm team. I still keep the telegram that we sent. It's addressed to Mr. Matt Burns, Brooklyn Baseball Club, 215 Montague Street, Brooklyn, New York, and it's dated February 19, 1954. It says: "I WILL SIGN A CONTRACT ON BEHALF OF MY SON ROBERTO CLEMENTE FOR THE SEASON 1954 FOR THE SALARY OF $5,000 FOR THE SEASON PLUS A BONUS OF $10,000 PAYABLE ON APPROVAL OF THE PRESIDENT OF THE NATIONAL ASSOCIATION. I WILL SIGN THE CONTRACT WITH THE MONTREAL BASEBALL CLUB OF THE INTERNATIONAL

LEAGUE. SIGNED, MELCHOR CLEMENTE, FATHER. ROBERTO CLEMENTE, SON."

Roberto went to Montreal for the 1954 season, but what I think helped him most is when he played that winter with Santurce, and Willie Mays joined the club. Willie was the batting champion of the National League that year with a .345 average, and it was really something to see Clemente and Mays in the outfield. Mays had to go all out, and Clemente was right at his heels! Even with Mays there, he was one of the team's stars. So he saw he could compete, even against the best.

"One of my favorite memories of Roberto is that year when Santurce, with Clemente and Mays, went to Caracas, Venezuela, to play in the Caribbean Series, to represent Puerto Rico against Cuba, Panama, and the host country. There were many major leaguers on the rosters. In the deciding game, Clemente was on first in the final inning, and Mays hits one to right, where the outfielder bobbled the ball for just a second. Clemente took off like a shot the moment that Mays connected, and he flew around third, although the coach tried to stop him. Gus Triandos was the catcher for the other team. The ball arrived at the same time as Clemente, spikes in the air, and we won the game. That exhibition of Clemente's great speed, and spirit, was one of the most emotional moments in my life. He made many fine plays in the United States, but to win a game for Puerto Rico, for our club, in the Caribbean Series, was a great moment. In fact, not long ago in Pittsburgh someone asked Clemente if he had ever played on a team with the slugging power of the 1971 Pirates. He said yes, the Santurce Crabbers, when they won the Caribbean Series!

Roberto defended the cause of the Latinos, especially the dark-skinned Latinos, and they owe him a lot. Clemente wasn't a star after he got his 3,000th hit, he was a star a couple of years after he rose to the big leagues. But the press denied him the credit that he deserved. I think this made him try to prove that a Puerto Rican was as good as anyone in America and could do what a Babe Ruth or a Ted Williams had done; that this wasn't a game exclusively for people from Pennsylvania, Alabama, and New Jersey; that in Puerto Rico, this tiny little country, there are great men, too—in every sense of the word.

4

Brooklyn Dodger lefthander Johnny Podres wound up to throw as Roberto Clemente stood deep in the batter's box, poised to swing at his first big league pitch.

It was April 17, 1955, and 20,499 fans had purchased tickets to Pittsburgh's Forbes Field for the Pirates' home inaugural of the season, a Sunday doubleheader. During the first three games of the season, played away from home, Roberto fidgeted on the bench next to manager Fred Haney, while a young Cuban named Román Mejías played right field. But now Haney had given Roberto his first crack at major league pitching and had placed him third in the lineup. It was the first inning, and Podres had retired the first two Pirate batters. In came the pitch.

Roberto smacked a hard grounder off Pee Wee Reese's outstretched glove, sped to first and beat the throw. He was batting a thousand. Moments later, Frank Thomas walloped a triple to center field and Roberto scored his first big-league run. In the second game of the doubleheader that afternoon, he would hit another single and a double. He was off to a fine start.

Those first few days, Roberto felt strange on the grassy terrain of Forbes Field. During the next fifteen years, until the Pirates moved across the Duquesne Bridge to the brand-new Three Rivers Stadium, he would come to know his right field "garden" as intimately as any place on earth. He would spend hour after hour studying the three angles of the outfield barrier that could send a batted ball caroming in impossible directions: The right field foul line touched the stands 300 feet from home plate, the wall then slanted to a point in straightaway right that was 375 feet distant from home, and then slanted out again to deep right-center, 416 feet away. And he would stand at home plate and look at the distant left field wall, the longest shot in the league, which began 365 feet away at the foul line and quickly faded to a point in left-center 457 feet off. Many a home run in San Francisco, Los Angeles, Chicago, Cincinnati, or Philadelphia would have fallen innocuously into the leftfielder's glove at Forbes Field.

The old stadium, which held 35,000 fans and was located at the corner of Bouquet and Sennott Streets, near Schenley Park, had been built in better days, some forty-six years before. Just a few blocks away, in the year 1758, a British general by the name of John Forbes, aided by young Colonel George Washington, had defeated the French at Fort Duquesne and renamed the place Fort Pitt, in honor of the English statesman who, years later, was literally driven mad by the rebellion of the American colonies. Fort Pitt was a prized location where the Allegheny and Monongahela rivers joined to form the Ohio. In the bowels of the earth nearby were some of the world's richest deposits of coal and iron. By the year 1900, Pittsburgh's Andrew Carnegie[1] had cornered one-fourth of all America's steel production, and his brilliant associate, the union-busting Henry Clay Frick, was piling up the fortune that would stock a gorgeous museum in Manhattan. While Roberto Clemente's parents and grandparents hacked away at sugar cane in the sun-scorched fields of Puerto Rico, "ethnic Americans"—from Latvia, Poland, Italy, Ireland, and the other impoverished lands of Europe—sweated in the inferno of Pittsburgh's mills and foundries.

Ballclubs, like nations and financial dynasties, have their golden eras and their declines. In 1955, when Clemente joined the Pirates, the city of Pittsburgh was in the advanced stages of urban decay. So were the Pirates. The team had finished at the bottom of the league in four of the previous five years and next to last the other year.

Pittsburgh fielded its first major league team in 1887. Three years later, Louis Bierbauer, a star player, jumped from the Phila-

---

[1] In 1898, while vacationing in Europe, Carnegie established at least a tenuous link with Puerto Rico when he cabled the White House urging that the U.S. military take the island as its prize in the Spanish-American War. A few years later, he established one of his 2,700 Carnegie Libraries in San Juan as a philanthropic gift.

delphia Athletics of the old American Association to the outlawed Players' League. When the Players' League folded, Bierbauer was expected to return to Philadelphia, but he signed with Pittsburgh. One Philadelphia paper called the Bierbauer affair "an act of piracy on the high seas." From then on, the Pittsburgh team was called the Pirates, or the Buccaneers, or, for the benefit of headline writers, the Bucs.

It had always been a tough town of blue-collar men who worked hard and played hard, and who loved an exciting baseball game. They found plenty to cheer about in the years 1901, 1902, and 1903, when the Pirates swept to three straight championships, led by player-manager Fred C. Clarke and the great Honus Wagner at shortstop. The Pirates, again led by Wagner, won another pennant in 1909, perhaps to celebrate the inaugural of their spanking new Forbes Field. During the 1920's, the team was also a strong contender and won league championships in 1925 and 1927. By then, there were stars such as Pie Traynor at third base and Kiki Cuyler in the outfield, and a speedster from Indiana by the name of Maximilian Carnarius (fans knew him as Max Carey), who led the league ten times in stolen bases. There were also the Waner brothers from Oklahoma—Paul and Lloyd—who became known as "Big Poison" and "Little Poison." Paul would become one of the handful of players to achieve 3,000 hits in his carrer. In 1927, the Pirates met the New York Yankees in the World Series. The Yankees had a "Murderers' Row" of hitters—Babe Ruth, Lou Gehrig, Bob Meusel, and Tony Lazzeri—who creamed the Pirates in four straight games. They would not recover to win another pennant until 1960.

In those dreary intervening decades, the Pirates fans had little to rejoice about. In 1935, Arky Vaughan, the Pirates' shortstop, led the league in hitting, and five years later an outfielder named Debs Garms—born in a town called Bangs, Texas—also brought the batting prize home to the banks of the Monongahela. Pittsburgh might have disappeared entirely into sports oblivion during the postwar years were it not for a muscular Californian by the name of Ralph Kiner, who led the league in home runs between 1946 and 1952.

So hopelessly inept were the Pirates of the early 1950's that humor was the only sane response. One national magazine called them "the boy buffoons of baseball." The man determined to rebuild the club was sixty-eight-year-old Branch Rickey, who had organized two great baseball empires in Saint Louis and in Brooklyn. Seeing himself—in *Life* magazine's words—as "an Alexander standing on the threshold of a New World," Rickey became general manager of the club in 1950 and tried a crash program of bringing in green young recruits. So ruthless was this sink-or-swim design that one reporter commented, "A pitcher who was knocked out of the box didn't know whether to take a shower or catch a train." Rickey enlisted such a motley crew, from so many sources, that at times the club resembled a vaudeville troupe. One journalist noted, "a mink trapper, a Mormon minister, a former maitre d'hotel of a swank Palm Springs nightclub, an X-ray technician, half an All-American basketball team, and one of America's only professional foot racers."

Needless to say, the Pirates in 1955, Clemente's rookie year, finished eighth, losing 94 of their 154 games. Roberto himself did not exactly set the league afire, but he was learning, together with the other young men, Dick Groat, Bob Friend, Vernon Law, who would win a world championship for Pittsburgh five years later.

As a twenty-one-year-old eager to excell, Roberto often became angry when he struck out and hurled his plastic batting helmet to the ground. During the first month of the season, Manager Fred Haney fined him $25 and warned: "I don't mind you tearing up your clothes if you want to, but if you want to destroy club property, you're going to have to pay for it." Years later, Clemente would laughingly recall, "Once, I break twenty-two helmets. Haney tells me it will cost me $10 apiece for each one. That's $220 and I do not make so much money. I stop breaking helmets."

After his strong first day for the Pirates, Clemente continued to sparkle. The next game, in New York City, the Giants swamped the Pirates, 12 to 3, but Roberto hit an inside-the-park home run. And when a Giant batter hit a line drive to right, Roberto caught it and fired immediately to first base for a double-play as he spotted the runner loafing back.

But National League pitchers soon spotted a flaw in his style; his head bobbed as he swung, and he took his eye off the ball. He received intensive coaching from Pirate batting coach George Sisler, a Hall of Fame member who twice in his career surpassed the .400 batting mark. Roberto improved slowly, but he couldn't resist bad pitches, and it became virtually impossible to give him a base on balls. That season, in 124 games, he walked only eighteen times. He had bad days, too, when he went hitless, made errors, or missed signs. He also missed a few games when he sprained an ankle in practice.

Shortly after joining Pittsburgh, Clemente received some friendly advice from Willie Mays, who had played with him in Puerto Rico. "Don't let the pitchers up here show you up. Get mean when you go to bat. And if they try to knock you down, act like it doesn't bother you. Get back up there and hit the ball. Show them." The pitchers did go after the rookie. As he later recalled, "When I was first in the league, opposing pitchers would knock me down. I told my pitchers they had to protect me [by throwing at the other team's batters], and if they couldn't I said I would pitch. The writers made fun of me with articles saying how Clemente wants to pitch."

"Some writers put words in your mouth, and that's what they did to Roberto when he was younger," says teammate Bill Mazeroski. "They tried to make him look like an ass by getting him to say controversial things and then they wrote how the 'Puerto Rican hot dog' was popping off again. He was just learning to handle the language, and writers who couldn't speak three words of Spanish tried to make him look silly."

Not all of the Pittsburgh players were friendly, Roberto recalls. "They would make 'smart' remarks about Negroes, right to my face." The club had only one other black player, a second baseman by the name of Curt Roberts, who also received his share of abuse. "I didn't like some of the things the white players said to Roberts, so I said some things they didn't like, either."

Life was even tougher away from the park. He said, "We are always meeting new people, seeing new faces; everything is strange; we have trouble ordering food in restaurants. You have no idea how segregation held some of us back." One day, a woman in Pittsburgh inquired whether during the off-season in Puerto Rico he wore a loin cloth. There were two other Latinos on the club—Román Mejías of Cuba and Felipe Montemayor of Mexico—but they were just as lost as he. Roberto had made one good friend, a Pittsburgh postal worker by the name of Phil Dorsey, but he often felt homesick. The fans, at least, were some source of human warmth. Years later he would say, "In my early days, I was glad to stand outside Forbes Field and sign autographs. I had no place to go anyhow and the fans made me feel wanted. I didn't mind at all. I was lonely. Somehow I think maybe some of those kids of many years ago are now regular Pirate fans and still my friends."

The fans had reason to seek him out; he was the hottest property on the Pittsburgh baseball scene in many years. In May 1955, the Pirates were defending a one-run lead against Milwaukee in the ninth. With two outs and the tying and winning runs aboard, George Crowe hit a drive to deep right that seemed sure to hit the screen for extra bases. But, wrote Roberto Creamer, who covered the game for *Sports Illustrated*, "Roberto Clemente, a brilliant young player, raced back and made a leaping one-handed catch for the final out." He began to show his muscle at bat, too. In one game at Forbes Field, he ripped a pitch by Warren Spahn over the distant left field scoreboard, and a few days later he hit a 430-foot triple against Johnny Antonelli.

Soon, fans and players throughout the National League knew that the Pirates' Number 21 was someone special. Roberto acquired his uniform number in a rather unusual way. According to a friend of his, just before the 1955 season got under way, he and his buddy Phil Dorsey attended a movie in downtown Pittsburgh. Just before the show, Roberto picked up a piece of paper from the theater floor and on it he wrote his full name: "ROBERTO CLEMENTE WALKER." Exactly twenty-one letters.

By early summer, Pittsburgh sportswriter Les Biederman would comment in *The Sporting News*, "There aren't many bright spots on the last-place Pirates, but one of the brightest is Roberto Clemente. . . . Although he has only a working knowledge of English and speaks with some difficulty, Clemente has no trouble at all playing the National Game. . . . The Pittsburgh fans have fallen in love with his spectacular fielding and his deadly right arm." Although Clemente hit the ball hard, the writer said, Roberto promised even more when the weather warmed up: "I no play so gut yet. Me like hot weather, veree hot. I no run fast cold weather. No get warm in cold. No get warm, no play gut. You see." Over the years, most sportswriters quoted Roberto phonetically, making his English sound worse than it was.

It had been a dismal season for the Pirates, but not bad at all for young Roberto. He had hit .255, including 23 doubles, 11 triples, 5 home runs, and 47 runs batted in. He could expect at least a modest raise above his salary of $6,000.

He survived his first year in the big time and already had displayed signs of the burning pride that would become his trademark. Before the season's end, in New York City, he was invited to appear in a postgame interview. The announcer recalled some of Clemente's finer moments on the field and then, trying to compliment him, said, "Roberto, you had a fine day and a fine series here. As a young fellow starting out, you remind me of another rookie outfielder who could run, throw and get those clutch hits. Young fellow of ours, name of Willie Mays."

There was an awkward silence in front of the live microphone, and then the rookie replied, with just a hint of irritation, "Nonetheless, I play like Roberto Clemente."

"Pittsburgh Phil"

"I'm forty-six years old, and I have a son nineteen. I'd be happy if my son would be like Roberto; the way he did things, the way he carried himself." Phil Dorsey wears his olive-green fatigue uniform with the master sergeant's stripes as he sits in the dining room of his comfortable home on Pittsburgh's Broad Street. His wife Carol watches the news on the color television in the living room. It is after suppertime, and he is due soon at a U.S. Army Reserve meeting. Dorsey, who works in a post office, is a heavy-set man of medium height, with broad shoulders, a thick mustache, and close-cropped hair. Their home is adorned by several photos of Roberto Clemente and gifts—a lamp, a ceramic punchbowl—that he had fashioned by hand.

I met Roberto in the spring of 1955, the first year he came with the Pirates. Even when he was off on a road trip or in Puerto Rico during the winter, hardly a week went by that he didn't call me. For eighteen years I've gone to the airport to pick up Roberto, or his family, or his friends, no matter what the hour. When I went to Puerto Rico he'd take the money from my wallet, so I couldn't spend a cent of my own, and tell people, "This is Phil, my brother from Pittsburgh."

Around opening day of the '55 season, I went down to Forbes Field with Bob Friend, a Pirate pitcher. I was his sergeant in the Army reserve. We were near the bullpen when Roberto comes out onto the field and Bob introduced us. I was about twenty-eight at the time and Roberto must've thought I was with the club because he asked how come they let me keep my mustache. "Oh, I'm not a ballplayer; I'm a sergeant in the reserves." He didn't have a car, and I ask him where he's going after the game. Back to his hotel downtown, he says. "Let's go someplace to eat," I said. So that evening we went out. Something about him never changed through the years; he was always a very particular dresser. His clothes fitted him like a model. So we became friends. I would go over to the hotel and wake him before game time, or invite him over to my house. I lived in the East Liberty section and some nights we'd walk home along Fifth Avenue. We'd go to a movie, or watch TV at my house. He liked the swashbuckling films: Errol Flynn, Tyrone Power, the Corsican Brothers. I would explain American slang words to him. We got along just great.

At first, when he didn't know a lot of people, we'd leave the ballpark and he'd sign autographs for two or three hours. Being black, he had some trouble. He was good-looking and single, and people, young ladies, would say, "Gee, Mister Clemente, could I have your autograph?" He'd be there signing and I'd hear girls say, "Gee, he's cute." As far as going out on dates, he was normal, but there was no one special he went out with. His mind was set on playing baseball. One time we were heading for the car in the parking lot near Forbes Field. We were both carrying clothes from the dry cleaners. Two white girls come up and say, "Oh, Roberto, can we have your autograph?" He stood there talking to them and by then there were more coming up. A cop comes over and says, "All right, what's goin' on here?" Roberto didn't say a word. The cop says, "I said break it up! Get away from those girls. Did you hear me, boy?" So we walk slowly to the car and the cop follows us, looks in the car and says, "Whose stuff is this you got in the car?" One of the girls says, "You better leave him alone. He's Roberto Clemente. He plays ball right over there." The cop says, "He don't look like no Roberto Clemente." He chased all the kids away. The next day, after the game, one of the girls stood outside at the gate and says, "Roberto, I don't know if you understand, but I'm sorry. People shouldn't act like that." Every so often, Roberto would get hate letters: "Go back to your jungle." I'd go through the mail with him and he'd say, "Hey, these people never been to Puerto Rico. It's got streets and roads and cars, and houses that are nicer than the ones that some of these people live in!"

But over the years he came to love this town. He used to tell me, "I wouldn't play for nobody else. People are wonderful here." Once, some people in the stands booed him and a fight broke out because the other fans got upset. Friends of mine would say, "Man, I don't care if the Pirates are losing 10 to 0; I come here to see if he's gonna throw the ball or get a hit." With a runner on base, people would yell, "Hit it to right! Clemente will throw him out!" Fans in the bleachers would offer him sandwiches during doubleheaders. On his birthday they'd bring him cakes. He got so much mail! We'd sit in the clubhouse and go through it. Some people didn't send stamped, self-addressed envelopes, and he'd take care of it out of his own pocket. That used to run into some real money.

In the early years, Roberto didn't pal around much with the players. He liked to read. When he went to New York or California, he'd pick up books in Spanish. He also read English. He liked good westerns or adventure stories, like *The Count of Monte Cristo*. He also had a good collection of records—Sinatra, Nat "King" Cole, and a lot of Spanish albums.

I told him he was paying too much staying in a hotel, which charged him for his room even when he was on the road because he kept his stuff there. Stanley Garland, a fellow who works at the post office with me, had just built a new home on Iowa Street. He's a real quiet guy, and his wife taught nursing at Allegheny General Hospital. So he took a room with them. He could get his rest there, because they were out all day and he liked to sleep a lot. I used to tack up big pieces of black oilcloth over the bedroom windows so the daylight wouldn't shine through. Roberto wouldn't eat much before a game. At eleven in the morning, before a night game, he might wake up and cook himself a couple of eggs and a piece of steak and then go back to sleep. I worked at the post office from 6 A.M. to a little after 2 P.M. I would wake him and he'd often be out to the park by 3 P.M. Most people didn't realize how much practice he put in, fielding and hitting. "You know, Phil," he'd say, "a lot of people don't understand that you have to push yourself to play day after day." Sometimes I'd shop for him or pick up his dry cleaning, so he could have his rest, and he'd pay me later. He liked fruit juices and canned fruits. He was a real meat eater. He loved steak, rare. One thing he didn't like were hot dogs. A company wanted to pay him five hundred dollars for some hot dog endorsement. He said, "I don't care if they give me a thousand; I don't eat them and I won't say that I do." I'd go to his place sometimes and cook. "Hey, you know, you pretty good cook!" I says, "Hey, I didn't have no sister, you know." If I put some gas in his car he'd ask, "How much?" "Aw, forget it." "*No*, what the hell you mean? You got a wife and family!" "Aw, Robby, don't worry about it." That's the way we were.

He could get dressed faster than anybody I've ever seen. I'd wake him up and say, "Listen, Robby, you gotta be at the park at such-and-such a time." He'd groan and say, "Gimme fifteen minutes more, Phil. You start the cookin'." He'd walk into the bathroom, his eyes still closed, and brush his teeth. "Phil, is the cookin' ready?" "Hey, it's just about ready. Hey, man, we gotta go, c'mon!" "Don't worry, Phil, I'll be ready, I'll be ready, this is me! This is me! This is *Roberto!* I'm ready!" "Well, c'mon, let's go, let's get outa here!" "Get the car started!" I'd get the car started and damn, he'd be ready. "Oh my, Robby, you're too much."

Roberto was like two different persons, because on the field he was all business. After the game we hardly ever talked about baseball, unless he brought it up. After night games in those days there were hardly any places you could get a good dinner. We'd go to the Crawford Grill in the Hill section. Sometimes we'd go to a movie or go to my house and watch TV or play cards, or shoot pool. My brother has a place out in Homewood, with five or six tables, and we spent lots of time there. If he didn't play ball, I think he could've made a living shooting pool.

Roberto was different when press guys were around, too. Some guys tried to make him say things that made him look bad; he wouldn't lie, so he preferred not to open up to them. One reporter would ask him how he hit a certain pitcher and then quote Roberto, "I heet thees peetcher—" Hell, he didn't talk that way. Another guy begins by asking, "Now, what about these fictitious injuries of yours?" Roberto looks at me and I explain, "He means you're telling a lie, that you don't have any injuries." That was the end of that interview. Hell, I remember that his back bothered him way back in 1956. When he got out of bed, he would lie on the floor and I'd have to crack his back even then—he taught me how. He had all sorts of injuries—spike wounds, sore arms, chips in his elbow.

So many people used to call Roberto about various things—stories, endorsements, banquets—that he finally got an unlisted number. So we finally had a card printed up with my number. It said "Pittsburgh Phil, representing Roberto Clemente." I would get a lot of his phone calls so he could get his proper rest. In the wintertime, he would call me from Puerto Rico at least once a week to ask about the family and see if he had any important messages. In 1966, the year he won the Most Valuable Player award, some big shots from New York invited him to speak. I wrote asking them when. They said they'd pay his transportation, but there might be a passport problem getting him in and out of Puerto Rico and how much would that cost. I called the people back and said, "Hey, what's this about passports? Puerto Rico is part of *this* country, and Roberto is a citizen." He tells me, "Hey, Phil, I don't want to go to that banquet. These people don't even know what they're talking about."

Some people would say well, he doesn't speak enough English and people won't understand him if he speaks at a banquet. "Whataya mean he don't speak good English?" I says. "Hey, Phil," he says, "don't get yourself worked up. Forget these people." But he spoke now and then, and once when they had a special day for him all the cash collected he donated to the Children's Hospital in Pittsburgh. Anything for kids, he would say. Sometimes he'd take my car, because people might recognize his, and he'd spend an afternoon with the kids at the hospital. He was always thinking of other people. When Olivo, the Dominican, came with the club a few years ago, he'd take him under his wing and say, "This is Phil. If you need something, see Phil." Same thing with Sanguillen. As the young people say, he was one beautiful person. In the car on the way to the ballpark, we'd go over who needed tickets. He had a few really good friends, like Henry and Elsa Coulong; she's from Puerto Rico, and we used to go over to her house on the North Side and eat rice and beans. So we'd go over the list and there were always people coming from Puerto Rico. A ballplayer only gets tickets for his wife and kids, plus two extra. Some big games, like a playoff, or during the World Series, there just weren't enough tickets to go around. So he'd buy tickets himself in order not to disappoint his friends. He did that plenty of times, but never told anyone. We'd get to the park, and he was a great kidder in the clubhouse. On the way in, he'd say, "Put my uniform in Giusti's locker." Then he'd get on Hooly, the equipment manager. "Hey, Hooly, how come now that I'm an old man I don't have clothes in my locker? I might as well go home, huh?" He'd see one of the single young guys lying on the floor before practice and say, "Why don't you go home at night, boy? You better get some sleep and leave them girls alone. They gonna *kill* you. C'mere, let me look into your eyes. Oh, oh, you got it bad." He'd get on Giusti something awful. One time Roberto had to make a banquet speech out in the boondocks and Giusti spoke the same night in Pittsburgh. So he gets up in the clubhouse, real loud, and says, "Giusti takes Pittsburgh, New York, Chicago, but they send Phil and me up in the snow, in the mountains, *so cold. . . .*"

"But Roberto," I says, "you *like* winter."

"Don't change the subject! Up in the snow, snow up to there, in the woods, and all the planes can't even land—"

Manny Sanguillen would call him "Mister Clementine." Sometimes Roberto would come into the clubhouse looking for me, and Sangy would say, "Oh, Mister Clementine, you look for Phil? He is with Mister Rennie Stennett, the good-hitting rookie. Mister Dorsey is over there, carrying Stennett's bats. Mister Clementine, the old man, is horseshit. Phil has new rookie he look out for now."

Then Sangy would come over to me and say, "Oh, Mister Dorsey, I sore right here. Could you rub me here?" Just to bug Roberto. Sometimes I'd rub Sangy, and ballplayers are superstitious. If they have a good game they want the same treatment the next day. Sangy, Clines, Stennett, I'd rub 'em and the next day they'd get some hits. Or I'd grab a bat, hand it to a guy and say, "Hey, there's two hits in that bat." Stargell'd say to me, "Hey, pick me a bat." I'd pick up Alley and crack his back for him. He'd get two hits and they'd all be around, "Phil! Phil! Give me a crack!"

When Roberto married Vera, I found them an apartment in the Homewood section. The next year I got them a place in Penley Park, new apartments, where Pagán, Alou, Sanguillen, and some of the other guys stayed. But after the kids were born it was too small, and we found a place called Chatham West in the Greentree section, which had three bedrooms and a little area where the kids could play. It was also convenient to the airport. He had people coming in from Puerto Rico all the time. I would rather pick them up than let him lose sleep. He'd be at the ballpark sometimes and he'd say "Hey, Maz [Bill Mazeroski], I didn't get no sleep last night. Them kids! That Robertito and that Luis. They open up my eyes and they look into them!" Then he'd go out and get three hits, and the guys would tease him.

Vera would come up for the first week of the baseball season, in April, with her youngest son. She'd go back a little later and get the other kids when school finished. By then we'd had a chance to prepare the apartment. We'd rent some furniture and buy some other pieces. Some women are just nice on being nice. But Vera is plain nice. She didn't put on any airs, she was just like him. The kids used to call me Uncle Phil. Sometimes I'd have all three of them over to the house, watching them so that Vera could go shopping.

When Roberto was going good, all kinds of people were after him to be his friend, or to get something from him. Once a guy wanted Roberto to star in a movie, but he wanted Roberto to put up the money! "Somebody should put up money for *you* to be in the movie," I told him. The guy takes us to a restaurant, and when the check comes suddenly he remembers he's got to make a phone call. There were all kinds of sharpies trying to make fast deals. In the last few years everyone was suddenly his friend. They'd insist on picking him up at the airport. "Where were these people sixteen, seventeen years ago," I'd wonder. Roberto used to tell me, "Phil, I know where *you* are. But some of these people, they must think I'm dumb. I can see they wanna get a little bit of the glory. But there ain't no glory left on the old man. When I go horseshit I don't see these people. I be going horseshit, I mean horse*shit*—I can't hit, I can't do nothin'—and I don't see these people. But Roberto Clemente goes three for three. Oh, Robby! You my man!" He told me, "Phil, the finest thing that anyone can have is a person they can really trust." About a year ago, a friend of Roberto's was killed in an accident in Puerto Rico, and he was very down in the dumps. He told Vera, "If anything ever happens, you get in touch with Phil." Even when he was single, I had his mother's phone number in Puerto Rico. He had already told me what to do. But he always thought that if something happened it would be during the season, while the club was flying from one town to another. For eighteen years, every spring, I'm usually busy around this time, getting the apartment ready for him and Vera and the kids. I'd be running here and there, doing something. The phone would ring all the time.

5

Pittsburgh had pennant fever in the summer of 1960. Executives in narrow-lapelled poplin suits and little old ladies in flowery cotton prints went about their errands downtown, brows wrinkled, transistor radios held to their ears. For the first time in a full generation, the Pirates might play in the World Series. Such a thing was unheard of, preposterous. In the first nine years of the decade, Pittsburgh finished last in the league five times and next-to-last three. Throughout those dreary summers, only the hardcore fan, driven by masochism, a perverse comic taste, or some animal kind of fidelity, had patronized Forbes Field. But now it was chic to follow the Pirates.

"Fans phone and ask what tickets we have left," said the Pirate ticket man. "We tell them, 'Right field.' They say, 'Where's right field?' We say, 'Behind Clemente,' and they say, 'Oh, that will be fine.'"

It had taken Roberto Clemente five grueling years to achieve such recognition.

He had "paid his dues" with thousands of hours of arduous labor, and now the talented, impetuous young man was acquiring the polish of a star. It had been a costly apprenticeship, marred by injuries largely due to a fragile spine that caused torturous backaches. He had also suffered flu attacks, a nervous stomach, spasms of diarrhea, infected tonsils, headaches, and bone chips in his throwing elbow. In his first five years as a Pirate, Roberto missed 143 games.

The back trouble—undoubtedly aggravated by the auto accident in the winter of 1955—had become quite serious in 1956. "My mother and father wanted me to quit in 1956 and go to school," he said. "My back hurt and I didn't play much in the winter [in Puerto Rico]. My people [the fans] at home didn't like that. They want me to play, but I said I am hurt. I talked to my mother and father and said, I'll try one more year. If I'm still hurt, then I quit." Despite the painful back, Roberto hit .311 in his sophomore year and helped the Pirates to climb one rung above the cellar. He showed such great promise that by season's end club president Branch Rickey predicted, "In three years, he'll really show you something."

After the 1955 debacle, seventy-four-year-old Rickey had kicked himself upstairs to the board chairmanship of the Pirates. He replaced himself as general manager with young Joe L. Brown, the son of movie comedian Joe E. Brown, who, perhaps fittingly, had earned fame for his mimicry of a sad sack pitcher being shelled by enemy batters. For his field manager, Brown reached down into the Pacific Coast League and chose Bobby Bragan, a restless, chain-smoking former catcher who had convulsed minor league fans with his zany umpire-baiting tactics. The squad was also strengthened by Bill Virdon, a fine centerfielder acquired from Saint Louis, where he had been the league's Rookie of the Year the previous season.

In the very first game of that 1956 season, the club reverted to its old tricks. A rookie catcher muffed a simple pop-up. The next day, first baseman Dale Long intercepted an outfield throw that would have caught the runner at third base; Clemente missed a sign for a squeeze bunt, and the runner on third was out by several yards. Bragan barked, "If that's the way you want it, it's going to cost you money. It's going to cost Long $25 and what's more it's going to cost Clemente $25." This harsh action worked like a shot of adrenaline. The club was soon fighting for first place in the league. Dale Long hit eight home runs in as many games. Clemente moved his batting average up to .348, fourth best in the league. But by mid-June, the club sagged. Long went to bat twenty-one times without a hit. Roberto swung at every pitch within range. The Pirates dropped to seventh place by year's end, twenty-seven games behind the champion Brooklyn Dodgers, but only a game behind the sixth-place New York Giants. Despite occasional injuries, Roberto had played in all but seven of 154 games and had hit .311. He had also exhilarated the fans with his fiery style of play. On July 25, the Chicago

Cubs were leading the Pirates 8 to 5 in the last of the ninth, but Pittsburgh had filled the bases with no one out. On the first offering from relief pitcher Jim Brosnan, Roberto smashed the ball to the deepest part of Forbes Field. Three Pirate runners crossed the plate to tie the score. Bragan, who was coaching at third, frantically waved his arms as a signal for Roberto to slow down. But Clemente almost ran him over and made a spectacular slide just ahead of the throw to win the game with a grand slam homer. After the game, Roberto told reporters, "I think we have nothing to lose as we got the score tied without my run and if I score the game is over and we don't have to play no more." Normally, a player who misses a sign is hit with a $25 penalty, but when the press asked Bragan, he smiled weakly and said, "Roberto is quite a player. He likes to hit and run."

And field, too. During the season he was credited with twenty assists and became a menace to batters who hit singles to right and took a wide turn around first base. Several times Roberto whipped the ball to Dale Long, who tagged them out before they realized what had happened. He was also making a habit of throwing perfect strikes from the right field fence to third base. But on routine throws, when no runner threatened to advance, fans became accustomed to seeing Roberto flip the ball underhand, in a high, looping arc, a habit he had acquired from his early days as a softball player. That season was the rookie year for Bill Mazeroski, who became such a fine fielder and clutch hitter that upon retiring he was selected as the Pirates' all-time best second baseman. "When I first saw Clemente play in 1956 he wasn't the hitter he would later become, but anyone who saw him throw knew he was something special. During those first few years he was always happy, full of vinegar, a guy who trailed laughter wherever he went. He struggled hard with his English. There were a lot of players on the club then who had never known anyone who spoke a foreign language, and we used to laugh at his broken English and he laughed with us. We also laughed at some of his ways." Mazeroski also recalls that Roberto was "sort of superstitious." During one game, Clemente hit three consecutive doubles, and his fourth time at bat, with two out, a man on second base, and the Pirates a run behind, he bunted. Manager Bobby Bragan was dumbfounded and, says Mazeroski, "In that fractured English,

Roberto said, 'Well, the law of averages was against me to hit another double.' "

Bragan recounted the anecdote in a way that made Roberto sound like a pack carrier in a Tarzan movie. "Bunting when we needed a run to tie was the dumbest play I've ever seen," the enraged manager said to Clemente. "You must be *loco* to pull a boner like that. There was only one thing for you to do. You had to be up there swinging for a home run." Bragan told the writers that Clemente replied, "Boss, me no feel like home run."

On the strength of his good 1956 season, Clemente got a new contract in the mail that winter calling for a healthy raise. To earn extra cash, he also played for Santurce and Caguas in the Puerto Rican league and demolished the pitchers with a .396 average in 225 times at bat. During that time, he dipped into his earnings and bought his parents a comfortable new suburban home for $12,500, a large sum in the 1950's when Puerto Rico's per capita income was about $700 per year. Of the house he said, "I do not think I am giving my parents something; I am trying to pay them back for giving me so much."

That April, manager Bragan told a writer, "Clemente's worth every penny of a half-million dollars to me. That's what the other clubs would have to give in cash or equivalent player material to get him." But Román Mejías opened the 1957 season for the Pirates in right field, as Roberto, his back hurting, sat on the bench. Some of the writers and a few of his teammates found it hard to believe that such a trim, muscular young man with no visible injury couldn't perform. There were murmurs of goldbrick, hypochondriac. Even when writers didn't openly accuse Roberto of feigning injury, they made light of his pain. In mid-April, a sportswriter went to visit him at Pittsburgh's Webster Hall Hotel, "in a room that was so hot Roberto must have thought he was back home in Puerto Rico."

"The impression here," he wrote, "is that Bragan thinks Clemente's backache is more mental than lumbar." He then commented, "Given a choice, I would rather look at Kim Novak's back than Roberto Clemente's . . . Maybe Joe Brown can swing a deal for Kim Novak."

The matter was more serious to Roberto. He recalled, "When my back hurt me in 1957 all the doctors said there was nothing wrong with me. They said my shirt was too tight. Another said I had to have my tonsils out, so he pulled them. But it still hurt. When I would ask my manager to take me out of a game in the second inning, the fans booed me. They said I didn't want to play and that's what the sportswriters began to write . . . Then a chiropractor in Saint Louis told me there was something wrong with my spine. He said my disc was out of place or something, and after he twisted it this way and that, it did not hurt so much any more. But it was too late. By that time I already had the reputation from the press as a player who does not like to play."

Manager Bragan grew more frantic as the Pirates' ship was becalmed in seventh place. Like a land-bound Queeg, he began to behave erratically. In late June, when a Cincinnati pitcher appeared to be throwing spitballs, he sent two of his players out on the field with buckets of water. That stunt earned him his fourth ejection of the season and a fine of $50. Another day, after a close decision, Bragan thumbed his nose at an umpire in full view of the fans. He was thrown out of the game, but moments later he wandered out on the field with a bottle of orange soda and offered a sip to each of the umpires. That cost him a $100 fine. A few weeks later, general manager Brown removed him "for the good of the team" and brought in Danny Murtaugh, a former Pirate infielder, to manage the club. Murtaugh had a reputation for calmness under pressure and would later earn the sobriquet "the rocking chair manager." From that day on, in early August, the Pirates won as many games as they lost, but they remained stuck in seventh place. It had been a sad year, too, for Clemente, who hit a feeble .253 and had played in only 111 games.

But the Pirates were optimistic about young Roberto. A team press release in the spring of 1958 said that although he had been "plagued all season long with back trouble . . . he should be in tip-top playing condition."

On opening day, before 43,339 fans in Milwaukee, Roberto got off to a dramatic start with two singles and a double as the Pirates won a fourteen-inning thriller. The fans yelled *"Arriba! Arriba!"* each time he came to bat, in response to Pirate broadcaster Bob Prince's chants from the radio booth.

"I think our friendship really started in 1958," Prince recalls, "the same time that Orlando Cepeda broke in as a rookie with the

Giants. We were playing the Giants and it was a real beanball contest. It looked like we were going to have a terrible fight. Cepeda's idol was a pitcher by the name of Rubén Gomez, and Gomez had been thrown at by our pitcher. In the melee that followed, Gomez picked up a bat and started to swing at our manager, Danny Murtaugh. In the meantime, Cepeda, who thought that his idol was in danger, picked up a big leaded bat and went after Murtaugh. If he hits him with this he can kill him. Willie Mays tackled Cepeda and spreadeagled him. Stopped him cold. There were about 35,000 people in the park. I happened to say on the air, 'This is a young Latin American player who's very excited and doesn't realize what he's doing. You must forgive him, because he didn't mean to do this.' Roberto heard what I'd said and the next day he brings Orlando to me and explains to him in Spanish what I'd said."

During the first month of 1958 Roberto was hitting nearly .400, but on April 30, against Los Angeles, he made a snap sidearm throw from the outfield, heard a cracking sound, and felt a sharp twinge. Later he said, "it feels like needles in there, so I don't throw until I have to." He sat out an occasional game and lost his batting eye, and his average slumped. In July, however, the entire team caught fire. Dick Stuart, a rookie who had hit 66 home runs in the Western League, was brought up and connected for two homers in his first two games. Third baseman Frank Thomas went on a fifteen-game batting streak. Roberto, batting only .275 in the first 113 games of the season, hit a sizzling .375 the rest of the way. On September 8, he tied a National League record by hitting three triples in a single game. By season's end, the Pirates were in second place, just behind Milwaukee. Bob Friend became Pittsburgh's first pitcher to win 20 games since 1951. Frank Thomas had hit 35 homers, and Bill Mazeroski contributed 19. Shortstop Dick Groat hit .300, and Clemente, despite his ailing back and arm, had played in 140 games and hit a respectable .289; he also led the National League with 22 assists from the outfield. The "new" Pirates drew 1.3 million fans to their home games, a full half-million better than the previous season.

Late in the 1958 season, when Roberto came to bat, Bob Prince would introduce him as "Private Clemente of the Marines." On October 4, 1958, he reported to boot camp at Parris Island, South

Carolina, as a six-month trainee, after which he would return to civilian life as a Marine reservist.

After Parris Island, Roberto was transferred to the Marines' advanced infantry training facility at Camp Lejeune, South Carolina, where he worked out occasionally with the base team. Six months of arduous drills, calisthenics, and hiking apparently did wonders for his back, because, although he missed spring training, he reported to the Pirates in fine shape. Recalling his Marine Corps duty, he said, "I worked like hell."

In 1959, a Pittsburgh pennant seemed within reach for the first time since 1927. But a grim opening day on April 9, with patches of snow still on the ground, was a bad omen. On April 25, in a game against Cincinnati, Roberto dazzled the fans with his exciting style of play. He was on first and Virdon was the runner at second when Smokey Burgess singled to right. Wally Post, the Reds rightfielder, saw that Virdon was well on his way to scoring and decided not to try for him. Instead, he lobbed the ball to second base. Clemente, who was just approaching third base, suddenly picked up speed and drew a roar from the stands. Legs churning, in a manner reminiscent of the daring Ty Cobb, he scored from first on a single. But the next month, after hitting two home runs in a doubleheader against Chicago, he was hit by a pitch in the right elbow. On May 25, still ailing, he was placed on the team's disabled list for forty days. The team was hobbled by other injuries: Burgess was beaned by a pitch and later split a finger while catching; Bill Mazeroski had a sore leg; Clemente's replacement in right field, Joe Christopher, suffered a deep gash in his left hand while diving for a fly ball. Roberto returned to the lineup on July 4 and missed only two games the rest of the year. The club rallied and salvaged a decent fourth-place finish, just nine games behind the league-leading Los Angeles Dodgers. In 105 games that year, Roberto fell just four percentage points shy of the "magic" .300 batting mark. Feeling strong, he played that winter for the Caguas club in Puerto Rico and in 215 times at bat had a solid .330 average.

In 1960, when Pittsburgh won its first pennant in thirty-three years, Roberto broke every personal record for the past five seasons, hitting .314, scoring 89 runs, collecting 179 hits, 16 home runs, and 94 runs batted in. He earned cheers, too, for his dashing defensive play, as he chased after line drives, his cap flying off, and made sensational catches. Again the sportswriters, in their vain search for superlatives, began to compare him with the Giants' great Willie Mays. "Willie is a very good ballplayer," said Roberto, "but why does everybody say I run like Willie, catch like Willie, throw like Willie, and hit line drives like Willie? I am not Willie. I am Roberto Clemente. That means I play only like Roberto Clemente. Many people tell me I want to play like Willie. From a little boy up, I always play like this. I always want to run fast, to throw long and hit far."

And hit far he did. On May 6, in a game at San Francisco's Candlestick Park, Roberto smashed a pitch by Sam Jones directly into a terrific wind. The shocked fans and players saw the home run ball land 450 feet away as Roberto calmly trotted around the bases. That month he hit safely in twelve straight games and was voted the league's outstanding player, and the Pirates, already tasting the pennant, were in first place.

As his fame spread, Roberto became a hero to his fellow Puerto Ricans. One fan recalls sitting in the right field bleachers in Wrigley Field. "We're surrounded by Puerto Ricans yelling, *'Arriba! Arriba!'* And every inning Clemente comes near the wall to talk with them in Spanish. The joy in the young boys' faces as their fathers laughed with Clemente."

In Pittsburgh, one writer would comment, "He plays the right field wall better than any man the Pirates have had there since Paul Waner . . . The Giants may think they have the most exciting player in the league in Willie Mays, but Pirate rooters rebut them with Roberto."

His teammates always were amused at Roberto's strong superstitions. Bill Mazeroski remembers that in 1960 "he thought a band was jinxing us. At most of the home games a dixieland combo used to play a song called 'Beat 'Em Bucs,' and before long the whole town was singing it. When we went to Chicago for the last two games of the season, the band went with us. The Cubs were in last place, but they beat us twice and when we got back home Roberto said, 'Keep that band out of here. Every time they play we get beat.' He doesn't tell everyone about his superstitions now because we needle him quite a bit. He'll wear a certain shirt, and if we win that day he won't change it until we lose. He had a *hell* of a time this year when we won eleven straight games!"

Back home in Puerto Rico, his mother was quite proud. A reporter sought her out that season, and as they chatted a big dog approached.

"That's Cappy, Roberto's dog. He is just five months old, and Roberto hasn't seen him since he was a tiny pup. He will be very happy to see how his dog is," she said. Mrs. Clemente was delighted with her son's success. "We wanted him to be an engineer, but God wished it differently. We had to accept that decision. I thank God for everything, because I know that my son is very happy playing baseball." She, too, had become infected by the game. When the reporter asked her, "Do you think Pittsburgh can win this year?" she replied like a veteran observer: "The season is young, but those Pirates are leading and they have a good chance."

Doña Luisa would have also been proud to know something that did not come out until years later. Roberto had quietly decided to share his banquet fees with Diómedes Antonia Olivo, a forty-year-old rookie pitcher from the Dominican Republic, whose days as an active player were numbered.

By June, the incredulous Pittsburgh fans were pouring into Forbes Field at an unprecedented rate. The park's public address announcer, Art McKennan, commented happily, "Last year, we had no more than fifty children lost in the ballpark all season. This year . . . parents are so wrapped up in the game they forget about their own kids. At this clip, lost kids will be up almost 100 percent by the end of the season." Pitcher Bob Friend remarked with delight, "The fans cheer when you strike a guy out. They explode when an easy fly ball is hit to the outfield. You'd never know they've had baseball here for sixty years."

On July 1, Roberto figured in a play that would feed the sportswriters' growing legend of his hypochondria, or was it a bit of tongue-in-cheek humor that sailed right over their heads? In an extra-inning game against Los Angeles, with runner Joe Christopher on second base, and two outs, Johnny Podres slipped two fast strikes past Clemente. On the next pitch, Roberto chopped a high bouncing ball over second base and beat the shortstop's throw, as Christopher slid home to give the Pirates a 2–1 lead. When Dick Stuart hit a pop single to left field, Clemente roared around third base, ignoring the coach's sign to stop and slid home with Pittsburgh's third run. This proved to be a crucial play, as Los Angeles scored a run in the bottom of the tenth but lost, 3–2. After the game, as reporters crowded around Roberto, he said, "My foot was sore. I ran all the way home so I could rest it on the bench."

During a crucial game in early August, Roberto made a catch at Forbes Field that fans and players remember to this day. Pitcher "Vinegar Bend" Mizell held a precarious 1–0 lead over the San Francisco Giants in the seventh inning. Up came Willie Mays, who ripped a line drive toward the right field wall. Roberto turned his back on the ball, took off in a terrific burst of speed, and at the last moment dove head first into the concrete barrier. There was a ghostly silence in the park as he rose groggily from his knees, blood gushing from his chin. Then the fans exploded with joy as he lifted his left arm weakly, showing the white ball in the brown leather glove. The game was saved, and an ambulance rushed Roberto to the hospital, where doctors took five stitches in his chin and prescribed a week's rest. Shortly after he returned, with the stitches not yet removed, Roberto knocked in all four runs of a 4–1 victory over Saint Louis, and in a doubleheader the next day had four hits in seven times at bat.

The Pirates clinched the 1960 pennant in Milwaukee on Sunday, September 25, when they beat the Braves and the second-place Saint Louis Cardinals were shut out by Chicago. Clemente was standing ready to bat against Warren Spahn when the news of the Cardinals' loss rippled through the stands and the team dugout. Clemente turned to Dick Stuart, who was kneeling in the on-deck batter's circle, and asked, "Did we win it?" Stuart nodded, just as the news was confirmed on the public address system. On Spahn's next pitch, Clemente shot a single to center field. When Hal Smith hit a double, Roberto again zipped past a coach's stop sign at third base and raised a huge dust cloud as he slid safely home on his belly. "Stop at third?" he said gleefully in the clubhouse. "I want to get to the bench quick, and talk about winning the pennant!" That night, when the Pirates returned home to Pittsburgh, a crowd estimated at 125,000 was on hand to greet them.

At season's end, the Pirates led the league by a comfortable seven-game margin and topped all teams in hitting and defensive play. In 1927, the last time the Pirates had competed in a World Series, they had been routed in four games by the New York Yankees. Now, in October 1960, the Yankees were again champions of their league, and the Pirates thirsted for revenge.

"ROBERTO CLEMENTE, bats right. High fastball hitter, fair on breaking stuff. Power on inside strikes, hits straightaway. Often takes first pitch. Pushes bunt occasionally. Dislikes knockdown by close pitch. Runs well, takes risk on bases. Excellent defensive rightfielder. Frequently bluffs fumble of ground balls to dare opposing runners to try for extra base. (Jam him good. Keep change and slider away, preferably down.)"

This terse "intelligence report," prepared by former big-league pitcher Jim Brosnan, was part of a review of the Pirate team published for the benefit of *Life* magazine's readers just before the 1960 World Series. Brosnan added, "Clemente features a Latin-American variety of showboating; 'Look at *número uno,*' he seems to be saying . . . He once ran right over his manager, who was coaching third base, to complete an inside-the-park grand-slam home run hit off my best hanging slider. It excited the fans, startled the manager, shocked me, and disgusted the club."

Praise, but always there was the small sour note: He was good, but he was a "showboat." That same week, *Sports Illustrated* also issued a scouting report on the Pirates, and again there were the small digs that so annoyed the sensitive Roberto. He was "beautifully built," said the magazine, "swings viciously at any pitch within reach," and "slides like an avalanche." But, the article noted, "opposing players call him a 'hot dog' and say he can be intimidated by fastballs buzzing around his head." He was "quiet, friendly, and intelligent," the report concluded, but "something of a hypochondriac."

Tremendous excitement mounted in anticipation of the Pirate-Yankee series. Part of it was due to Pittsburgh's long fast: The club hadn't won a pennant since 1927 and hadn't won a World Series since 1925. Some old-timers claimed that the 1927 Pirates had quit before the first pitch of that series, when they saw Ruth and Gehrig in batting practice. The current Yankees were nearly as awesome. In the past twelve years they had won ten league pennants and eight World Series, and the big bats of Joe DiMaggio, Charley Keller, Tommy Heinrich, Joe Gordon, and Bill Dickey of the 1940's had been replaced by a new generation of sluggers: Mickey Mantle, Roger Maris, Yogi Berra, Bill Skowron, and Elston Howard. The consensus was that the Yanks would murder the upstart Pirates.

But the Pirates didn't quit. In fact, before 36,676 cheering fans at Forbes Field on October 5, they beat the Yanks in the first game of the Series by 6 to 4, snapping a fifteen-game win streak that had swept the New York club to the league pennant. Things looked bad at first; before some fans were even seated Roger Maris got hold of a Vernon Law pitch and sent it sailing into the right field upper deck. But the Pirates fought back with three runs in their half of the inning. The fleet Bill Virdon started the rally when he walked and made a daring steal of second base. Dick Groat doubled to score Virdon, and Bob Skinner's single sent Groat home. After Skinner also stole second base against the harried Berra, Clemente drove pitcher Jack Ditmar out of the box with a run-scoring single that bounced like a jack rabbit into center field. The Yanks narrowed the score to 3–2 in the fourth inning when Berra hit a towering fly ball to right-center; Virdon and Clemente—deafened by the crowd's roar—both went for it and collided, but Virdon held the ball. Maris advanced to third on the fly ball, however, and scored on a hit. Pittsburgh pulled ahead 5–2 with two runs in the fourth and made it 6–2 in the sixth, thanks to Virdon's double against the right field screen. The Yanks rallied for two runs in their final chance on bat, powered by Elston Howard's pinch-hit homer, but that was all.

The next afternoon, the Yankees resembled the "Murderers' Row" of old, as they crushed the Pirates 16 to 3, tying the Series at one game apiece. The New Yorkers battered six Pirate pitchers for nineteen hits, including two colossal homers by Mickey Mantle. Pittsburgh got thirteen hits, including two singles by Clemente, but to little avail. Now the Series moved to New York for three games.

As the morning sun slanted into Yankee Stadium on October 7, Pirate coach Frank Oceak, swinging a slender fungoe bat, whacked fly balls against the left field wall, and Gino Cimoli tried to gauge the angles. "The balls really spin around that curve like a roulette ball. You can't charge them, or they'll get past you for a home run," he said.

The teams had a day off before the third game of the Series, but they were keeping loose. Over in the shady right field sector, Roberto Clementc tossed balls against the wall, spinning them one way, then another, throwing long bounces against the barrier, then short skips, studying the angles. "I don't want them to play no dirty tricks on me," he said. The Yankees were also preparing for battle, studying the reports on Pirate pitchers and hitters. When star lefthander "Whitey" Ford, due to pitch the third game, was asked which Pirates might give him the most trouble, he said, "Groat and Clemente; all those guys who hit to right field pretty good."

That evening, the sidewalk outside Yankee Stadium was filled with a long line of hardy fans. Dressed warmly to fight off the October chill, they sipped coffee from paper cups, ate sandwiches wrapped in wax paper, and prepared to bed down, hopeful of finding a bleacher seat when the ticket windows opened in the morning. The Pirates were bedded down comfortably in the Commodore Hotel, but few of them slept soundly. For Roberto Clemente and the other young players, this was *it*. They had toiled in the relative obscurity of western Pennsylvania for several years; now they would play in the House that Ruth Built, in the biggest, oldest contest of American sports, and the whole world would be tuned in on television or radio.

The afternoon of October 8, a total of 70,001 fans packed Yankee Stadium and saw New York again crush Pittsburgh, 10 to 0, as a beleaguered Danny Murtaugh had to bring in six pitchers once more. The victory was made even more humiliating when light-hitting Bobby Richardson, a 166-pound second baseman, lofted a grand slam homer into the stands. In the meantime, the thirty-one-year-old Whitey Ford, who had won his first Series victory more than a decade before, bewildered the Pirates with his breaking pitches and razor-sharp control; he allowed only four hits, one of them a single by Clemente.

That night, as the glum Pirates returned to the Commodore Hotel, fans on the sidewalk jeered and kidded them. Just before disappearing through the front entrance, Clemente turned and said, "You come back tomorrow."

And "tomorrow," thanks largely to a game-saving catch by Bill Virdon, the Pirates beat the Yanks in a 3–2 thriller before 67,812 fans. Vernon Law, the winner of the first game, gained his second victory, with relief assistance from diminutive Elroy Face, who threw a baffling forkball. Clemente struck out twice in the game but managed one hit, his fifth in four games.

The oddsmakers were shocked the next day as the Pirates won their second game in a row on alien territory. Before 60,753 fans, Pittsburgh beat the Yanks 5 to 2 and took the lead in the Series. The Pirates never lost the advantage after a three-run flurry in the second inning, sparked by Bill Mazeroski's double that hugged the left field line. In the fourth inning, Clemente helped to widen the gap. Facing his countryman and friend—a stocky lefthanded Yankee by the name of Luis "Tite" Arroyo—Roberto rapped a run-scoring single to left, his sixth hit and second run batted in of the series.

Both teams flew back to Pittsburgh for the sixth Series game and, if necessary, a seventh. The Yankees, now desperate, called upon their ace, Whitey Ford, who had only three days of rest. Many of the 38,580 fans at Forbes Field gleefully waved "Beat 'Em Bucs" souvenir pennants when the contest began. But they sat in stunned silence as the Yankees battered six Pirate pitchers for a dozen runs. Again Ford baffled the Pirates, pitching a shutout and allowing only seven hits—two of them by Roberto. Years later, Ford recalled: "He stayed so far away from the plate. I have a little sinking fastball that would go away from him. I thought I could throw it on the outside corner and he wouldn't be able to reach it, but he knew exactly what he was doing up there. He would just move in toward the plate as you were releasing the ball; he could reach over and hit it to right field with almost as much power as to left field."

This, however, was little consolation. In six games the Yanks had amassed a record total of 46 runs and 78 hits; the Pittsburgh fans shuddered when they considered the prospects for tomorrow.

The final game between Pittsburgh and New York has often been described as one of the most harrowing contests in the history of the World Series.

The first roar from the crowd came in the home half of the first inning, after Vernon Law retired the Yankee side in order. With a runner on base, Rocky Nelson, who had spent eighteen playing years in the minor leagues, wafted a fly to right that barely cleared the 32-foot screen and put the Pirates in front, 2–0. They drew blood again in the third, when Virdon singled two runners home. But the Yankees, undaunted, chipped away for a run in the fourth and burst into a 5-4 lead in the sixth, as they drove Law from the mound and also mangled Face's tricky forkball. The New York team added two more runs against Face in the eighth, and held a 7–4 lead.

The Pirates, their backs to the wall, rallied in the bottom of the eighth. The assault opened as pinch-hitter Gino Cimoli cracked a single to right. When Virdon hit a vicious ground ball to short, manager Murtaugh winced and the fans' hearts sank; it looked like a sure double play. But the ball took a freak hop and smashed into shortstop Tony Kubek's larynx, knocking him to the ground, unable to breathe. By the time Richardson ran over to recover the ball, Cimoli and Virdon were safe. Kubek was rushed to the hospital, and play was resumed. Dick Groat's hard single to left scored Cimoli and knocked pitched Bobby Shantz out of the game. In came righthander Jim Coates. Skinner's sacrifice bunt moved the runners to second and third. Rocky Nelson's fly ball was easily caught, making it two outs, and the rally seemed to be sputtering, with Pittsburgh still behind 7 to 5. Up came Roberto, hitless in three tries. Coates pitched and Roberto, swinging for distance, topped the ball, dribbling it weakly toward first base. "The biggest thing I remember about Roberto in that Series," says Whitey Ford, "is when he hit that ground ball. It looked like an ordinary out. But he ran so hard to first base, he beat Coates to the bag, and Skowron, the first baseman who fielded it, just had to eat the ball." Cimoli scored on the play, and Roberto, puffing at first base, had kept the rally alive. Coates worked the count to two balls, two strikes against the next batter, Hal Smith. Then he threw a belt-high fastball, and Smith made it disappear over the left field fence, near the 406-foot marker. The Pirates were ahead 9 to 7, and the fans were delirious. Groat danced across home plate, and the exuberant young Roberto, one observer recalls, "came leaping down the line like a kangaroo." Smith, his face split by a proud, ear-to-ear grin, was engulfed by his fellow Pirates, who hugged and backslapped him. Roberto grabbed the big catcher by the arms and lifted him joyously into the air.

After such a moment, no one had emotions left in reserve. But they would have to dig deeper, because the Yankees hadn't surrendered, and Murtaugh knew it. He called in Bob Friend from the bullpen to protect the two-run lead in the last inning. The mounting hilarity in the stands was quickly subdued when Bobby Richardson singled and Dale Long—an ex-Pirate now on the Yankee roster— also singled. The worried Murtaugh brought in Harvey Haddix, but Mickey Mantle ripped him for another single that scored Richardson. Moments later Gil McDougald, running for Mantle, scored on an infield grounder, and it was a brand-new ballgame.

No playwright could have concocted a more dramatic scene. Last of the ninth inning, final game of the World Series, the score tied at 9–9, and 36,683 fans, with millions of television viewers peeking over their shoulder, were beside themselves with tension.

Bill Mazeroski, whose hits had helped win two previous games in the Series, led off against Yankee pitcher Ralph Terry. The end was mercifully quick. Mazeroski let one of Terry's fastballs pass him by, but he smashed the next one solidly; it sailed far above the head of leftfielder Yogi Berra and disappeared near the 406-foot marker. For an instant, nine grieving Yankees stood on the field, while Mazeroski—the only Pirate in view—rounded first base. Then Mazeroski began to jump in the air, lifted by the crowd's lung-bursting cheers; he whipped off his plastic batting helmet and, like an Indian warrior gone berserk, whirled it around with his right arm as he ran and skipped homeward. There to greet him, to hug and pummel him, were Clemente, Groat, the entire team, and hundreds of fans who had stormed past the police cordon. As the joyous mob stumbled toward the dugout, one fan stayed quietly behind with a shovel and began to dig up home plate for a souvenir. Inside the Pirate clubhouse, twenty policemen fought against the crush of several hundred reporters, photographers, and fans who tried to shove their way inside. Champagne corks and beer cans flew through the air. One player emptied half a bottle of the sparkling wine over a teammate's head. Dick Stuart sloshed beer all over the reporters. Vernon Law—a Mormon and a teetotaler—stood there beaming, relishing the mad tableau. Pittsburgh's Mayor Joseph Barr pushed his way into the clubhouse and was doused with beer by Dick Stuart. At the game's climax, when Mazeroski connected, he had leapt to his feet, throwing his arms in the air and nearly knocking out his wife Alice. The usually imperturbable Murtaugh was in a rare state of ecstasy. His wife later said, "I never saw you so happy, Danny," and he replied, with a wide grin, "If you had been standing on one side of me, and Bill Mazeroski on the other side, and somebody said I had to kiss one or the other, it wouldn't have been you."

Roberto Clemente was happy, too. The Pirates were champions, and he had helped to make the difference. During the tension-charged Series, he had gotten more hits than any other member of the team, batted in three big runs, and fielded flawlessly, making nineteen putouts. Watching Clemente throw in those seven games, Tommy Henrich, the former great Yankee rightfielder, remarked on the radio, "What an arm that Clemente has! It's one of the most powerful I've ever seen!" But the reporters were crowded around Mazeroski and Smith, the men of the moment, and manager Murtaugh, and Groat, who had won the league's batting championship.

Clemente did not attend the uproarious postgame party at a downtown hotel. He dressed and walked out into the cool October afternoon. It was like Mardi Gras, as bands of revelers trooped about, singing, yelling, playing makeshift instruments—a town of losers trying to quench a thirst of thirty-five years. The mountains of paper and debris in the streets were incredible. Roberto, still a black-skinned, Spanish-speaking stranger in America, wandered across the street into Schenley Park. As he later recalled, with a mystical appreciation that was misunderstood by so many, he felt "the biggest thrill of my life."

"I come out of the clubhouse and saw all those thousands of fans in the streets. It was something you cannot describe. I did not feel like a player at the time. I felt like one of those persons, and I walked the streets among them."

"The Divine Madman"

Chain-smoking Salems and sipping beer, fortyish Rubén Gomez cuts a slim, youthful figure with his modest Afro haircut, tight dungarees, maroon polo shirt, and a watch with a thick leather wristband. El divino loco—the Divine Madman—the Latino fans called him when he pitched for the New York Giants and was one of the most colorful, hotheaded players in the big leagues. Today they still recall that big year, 1954, when he won seventeen games and threw a winning four-hitter against Cleveland in the crucial third game of the World Series. Rubén remains active in island baseball as a manager and part-time player, and still, when his name comes up, fans shake their head, smile, and say, "Ah! El divino loco!" He has an infectious smile and a tough, direct gaze when he listens—or talks.

I first met Roberto about 1953, when I was with the New York Giants and he was breaking in with the Puerto Rican League. I'm older than he—forty-five—but I've always kept in shape, and never in all my years did I have a sore arm. I still lift weights, do calisthenics, run at the beach, play volleyball, and when I play golf, I *run* to the ball each time I hit it. I love fresh air.

Roberto was a fine natural athlete, but he lacked training. The years went by and he became a magician with the bat, despite the fact that he had a "wrong" way of hitting. He would step far away from the plate—in the bucket, as they say—but he kept his arms and torso close to the plate, which is what made him so great. He was very dedicated to the game—I'm that way, too—any player who doesn't respect the public that pays to see him doesn't deserve to be in uniform. In that sense he was a 105-percent professional. I've seen many players, and if I had to choose an all-star outfield, it would be Willie Mays, Joe DiMaggio, and Clemente. I'd also somehow find a place in the lineup for Hank Aaron because of his bat, although he's not as great a fielder as the other three.

The only way to get Clemente out was by being a bit criminal, as we Latino pitchers say. You had to keep knocking him down with tight pitches. If you didn't, he'd murder you. I was lucky with him, because I threw lots of dusters, so he stayed real loose. I was famous for my dusters, especially when I pitched for the Giants with Sal Maglie, who was a master at it. But very few pitchers were nasty like me, and Roberto always got his quota of base hits.

Roberto and I were friends. He was a good husband, good father, a good *compañero*, and I'm deeply sorry that he is gone. My wife died five years ago. She was only thirty-three. His wife and mine were also close, and we saw each other often. He was crazy about my son. Gave him a kangaroo-skin golf bag, must've cost about $300 just for the bag.

I'm about the same color as Clemente and I passed through the same places in the United States. I used to get angry, I was a real hothead, but I learned to take things in stride; he was always a lot more sensitive. I suffered, too, in the South, although it got better each year, but I think the American blacks suffered more. If you had a Latin name it wasn't quite as bad. I started out in 1948 and in spring training we slept and ate apart from our white teammates and only saw each other in the ballpark. Many Latino players have complained about their managers. I don't know, I had no racial problems with my managers; I think that sometimes these are complexes. Sometimes a player doesn't get what he wants and right away he thinks race is the reason. I hear that all the time, and I think they're wrong. It was much worse before. Now there are pensions, good pay, we live like kings, and get paid a fortune for just sitting on the bench. The press glorifies us even though we're just human, like farmers or factory hands. On the clubs, the blacks, whites, and Latin are closer together now than nails to flesh. In fact, nowadays some blacks almost always hang around with whites, and whites with blacks—we Latinos are all over the place, on both sides.

In Florida I had to live in the black section—on the other side of the tracks. But it didn't make me less of a man or less of an athlete. And, as I said, it was a little different if you were a Latino. In Jacksonville, Florida, everybody knew me. I was with some black *americano* once and I said, "Let's go in that restaurant to eat." I went in, but the other guy didn't want to. The owner came over; said, How are you?; started to talk to me, and they served me. The other guy saw this through the restaurant window. He came in, and they wouldn't serve him. It just goes to show you how crazy the whole question of race is in America—if you speak Spanish you're somehow not as black. It's like the case of the African, all those people who come from those other countries. They put on their tunics and they're treated differently. I think that's why dark-skinned Puerto Ricans in New York, when they're on the subway, speak Spanish nice and loud, so people will know they're Latinos.

My first year in the United States, I was going to play with a minor league club in Fredericksburg, Maryland. I stopped at the Baltimore bus terminal for some coffee—I've always been a coffee drinker. I ordered, and the man behind the counter said there was no coffee. Maybe they just ran out, I thought to myself. So I sat there wondering, should I order iced tea, or should I go someplace else for coffee? Then an American guy, a white, sits next to me, orders coffee, and they serve him. I figured, maybe they didn't understand my accent, so I told the guy, "Look, I want the same kind of coffee." "I told you we don't have no coffee," he says. I was a pretty violent character in those days. I'm still a bit like that, but not like before—now it's my son who's like I used to be. Anyway, I grabbed the cup of coffee from the guy next to me and gulped it down fast. It was so hot, I burned my lip. I took a coin and threw it at the waiter. Hit him right in the eye! They called the police. I sat right there. When the police came I realized for the first time that I was in the South. So I refused to speak English. They spoke to me in English, cursing and everything, and I answered back in Spanish, curses and all. They finally gave up. The policeman said, "Let's leave him alone. He's not from around here, he doesn't even know what we're talking about." What a crazy country. If I'd been an American black, not even a Chinese doctor could've saved me.

Then I went to get into the bus. I saw it said "color line," but I sat down right in the front seat, plenty angry. One lady didn't want to get into the bus because I was sitting there. The driver spoke to me and I answered in Spanish. When the lady heard me answer in Spanish, she calmed down, got in and took a seat! I didn't want to speak English to the driver, so I wrote down the address on a piece of paper and handed it to him. He took the piece of paper, nodded, Okay, but started abusing me verbally. I destroyed him with foul words in Spanish! When we reached Fredericksburg, he motioned to me. I got up and, as I was leaving, leaned over and right in his ear I said in English: "You motherfucker, come out of this bus and I'll kill you!" When he heard that! He grabbed for a tire jack and tried to get off, but the passengers held him back. I was down on the road now, yelling, "Come on down, jack and all! I'll wrap it around your neck!" He drove away.

When I first joined the Giants, the press agitated me. They made me appear to be less than I was. They said I was too skinny to be a big-league pitcher, yet I would look around and see another guy on the club skinnier than me. I thought as a Latino that they were against my race. I was angry. After the game, I would get undressed fast and walk around naked, so they couldn't take my picture. I felt hurt, it was the old Latino anger, and I looked for excuses to avoid talking to the reporters. I could've had more press if I'd been more sociable. In that sense I think I was like Roberto, but the years taught me not to be that way.

6

It was a hot, windless afternoon in San Francisco on July 1, 1961. A record 44,115 fans filled Candlestick Park to see the thirtieth major league All-Star Game. The stands were dotted by red, yellow, and blue Chinese sunhats, worn to ward off the midsummer glare. The Sunday before, first-aid officials had cared for 104 cases of heat prostration in the same ballpark. Before the day was over, 95 more persons would fall victim to the stifling heat. That same day Roberto Clemente would establish himself as a star among stars.

All during the previous winter he had been bitter. When he arrived home in Puerto Rico he basked in the glow of the Pirates' upset victory over the Yankees in the World Series. In mid-October, he was delighted to read that Danny Murtaugh had been named Manager of the Year. In early November he felt glad for pitcher Vernon Law, whose two Series wins and twenty victories during the season had earned him the prestigious Cy Young Award. On November 18, he picked up a paper in San Juan and read that Pirate shortstop Dick Groat had been named the Most Valuable Player in the National League. Roberto felt disappointed; after all, while Groat had out-hit him, .325 to .314. He batted in 94 runs, nearly double Groat's production of 50. During the World Series, he had contributed nine hits and batted .310, while Groat, suffering a sore wrist, made two errors and hit only .214. His eyes scanned the list of players who had received votes for Most Valuable Player, and his pique grew to a rage. He was not second, or third, or fourth . . . he was *eighth* in the balloting. Soon, the sports press heard a roar of anger from the Caribbean.

"I was very bitter, I still am bitter," Roberto said years later. "I'm a team player . . . winning the pennant and the world championship were more important to me than my average, but I feel I should get the credit I deserve." That winter he swore to his parents in Puerto Rico that he would become the best hitter in baseball. When he reported for spring practice at Fort Myers, Florida. The writers, accustomed to his perennial complaints of physical ills, were surprised to hear him declare, "I'm healthy. I feel good, real good." Batting coach George Sisler took Roberto aside and predicted that he would win the batting title if he waited for good pitches. Roberto began to use a heavier bat, measuring 36 inches, to slow his swing and give him more control.

That April he got off to a sizzling start, and the fans in Pittsburgh responded. When Pirates radio announcer Bob Prince urged him on with *"Arriba*, Roberto!" the cry became infectious. *"Arriba! Arriba!"* the fans yelled from the grandstands and the bleachers, and Forbes Field in Pittsburgh sometimes sounded like a ballpark in Latin America. There was a new camaraderie in the clubhouse, and some players—who had once made snide secretive remarks about his injuries—began to kid Roberto and call him "Mister No Votes" for his failure to win acclaim.

Roberto was hitting .323 by the end of April. In fact, he was hitting so well that pitchers began to knock him down. This infuriated him—he took it as a personal attack—and knocked him off stride. Early in June, Lew Burdette dusted Clemente with so violent a headhunting pitch that he was ejected from the game. But Roberto began to dig right in at the batter's box, and he soon discovered that the best antidote for the duster was a line-drive baschit. When the All-Star Game vote was made public on June 30, Roberto was the overwhelming choice as the National League rightfielder. He became even fiercer at the plate. During a July 6 doubleheader in Chicago, the Pirates massacred the Cubs, 15–3, in the first game and Roberto had five hits, five runs batted in, and four runs scored. In the second game, apparently arm-weary, he got two more hits. By midseason, at the time of the All-Star Game intermission, Roberto led the league with a .357 average and had batted in 51 runs, more than his entire season total in some previous years. He had also acquired several tricks of the trade on defense. In a game against Cincinnati, with a runner on first, the batter looped a fly ball to short right field. Roberto had no chance to catch it, but he came tearing in, his arms outstretched, pretending that it was within reach. The runner on first held back warily. Roberto quickly fielded the bouncing ball and fired it to second base for a force play.

As Roberto and his All-Star teammates trotted out on the field to warm up at Candlestick Park, there was striking proof of the impact of black athletes upon America's favorite pastime, especially in the National League. Seven of the league's ten best hitters and its four top home run hitters were black. Blacks made up 17 percent of the 200 players on National League clubs, and 36 percent of the All-Star squad. As the game progressed, blacks such as Maury Wills, Henry Aaron, Willie Mays, Frank Robinson, and Clemente would be largely responsible for the team's victory.

During the pregame ceremony, all the players received vigorous cheers from the crowded stands, but none more than forty-year-old Stan Musial, the veteran Saint Louis Cardinal, who would appear in his twentieth All-Star game. Then old Casey Stengel reared back his left arm and threw out the symbolic first pitch. It appeared to be a holiday for old-timers. Forty-year-old Warren Spahn started for the Nationals and pitched a perfect three innings, setting down nine batters in a row. Whitey Ford of the American League was less successful. After an uneventful first inning, he faced Clemente in the second. Roberto swung and smashed a powerful line drive to the wire railing in right-center field, where Mickey Mantle and Roger Maris converged in a race to catch it (this would be their great year together, as Maris broke Babe Ruth's record with 61 home runs and Mantle hit 54). Maris jumped and made a backhand try for the ball, but it was beyond his reach. By the time Mantle returned the ball to the infield, Clemente was dusting himself off at third base with a triple. Roberto gave the Nationals a 1–0 lead when he dashed home on Bill White's sacrifice fly to Mantle in right-center.

Clemente helped stretch the lead to 2–0 in the fourth inning. Willie Mays reached second on an infield error, advanced to third on Orlando Cepeda's grounder, and stormed home—his cap flying off— when Roberto hit a sacrifice fly to right field.

The American League cut the advantage to 2–1 in the sixth on Harmon Killebrew's mile-high homer that barely cleared the wall in left, but the Nationals bounced back to 3–1 in the eighth when George Altman hit a pitch 375 feet into the bleachers. By now, a strong breeze stirred the warm summer air. The American Leaguers also seemed to stir. In a dizzy top of the ninth they tied the score, 3–3, on a melange of hits and errors. The wind grew so strong that Stu Miller, a diminutive relief pitcher, was literally blown from the mound as he prepared to throw, and the umpire called a balk.

In the home half of the ninth, the Nationals tried to break the tie but were frustrated by knuckleballer Hoyt Wilhelm, whose spinless pitches were made even more perplexing by the gusts of wind.

The game went into a tenth inning, and it appeared that the Americans would win a comeback victory when Nellie Fox scored all the way from first on a wild infield throw. Now the National All-Stars came up for their final chance, with their "big guns" due to bat. No one left the park.

Hank Aaron was sent up to bat for the pitcher and lined a single to center. He took second on a passed ball and tied the score at 4–4 when Willie Mays bounced a hard double just over third base. The wind grew gustier and one of Wilhelm's knucklers darted inward, nicking batter Frank Robinson and giving him a free pass to first base.

Now Clemente dug in, deep in the batter's box, as the crowd cheered him on, and the wind swirled dust and debris in the late afternoon air. The tightly fought contest, begun nearly three hours before under a relentless sun, was now approaching its climax in a biting wind storm. Wilhelm checked the runners at first and second, pitched, and Roberto cracked it to right field for a single. Mays, clapping jubilantly, raced across home plate with the winning run, and Roberto raced back from first to shake his hand.

Years later, Roberto would recall with some bitterness that in the locker room after the game the press crowded only around Mays. "They were talking to him and he kept telling them, 'I didn't do it. This man next to me did it. Talk to him.' But they didn't listen to Mays. I did my best, but the writers didn't care. I knew then how American writers stood."

But he would also recall, on another occasion, "When I got that big hit in the tenth inning, I felt better than good. What made me feel best of all is that manager Danny Murtaugh let me play the whole game. He paid me quite a compliment, and I didn't let him down, no?" From then on, Roberto proudly wore his 1961 All-Star ring, not the ring he had earned when the Pirates won the 1960 World Series. Symbols were important to him.

The 1961 season was filled with satisfying moments. Three days after the All-Star Game, at the same Candlestick Park, Roberto hit a grand-slam home run, and on July 29, he hit his 16th homer, equaling his previous high total for a season.

Well beyond midseason Roberto told a writer, "I'm dead tired. Last year, when we were winning, I wanted to go to the park every day. But now I'm dragging myself." But, as the season wore on, and as the red-hot Maris-Mantle home run duet captured the headlines, Roberto kept hitting and fielding like a champion. During one week, he made 20 hits in 36 times at bat for an incredible .556 average. In early August, against Cincinnati, he reached an important milestone with the 1,000th base hit of his career. As umpire Mel Steiner briefly stopped the game to give the ball to Roberto as a souvenir, a pitcher in the Reds bullpen remarked to his teammate, "That's Roberto's 1,000th hit." The other man drawled back, "Did he get 'em all off of us?"

Late in the season, as Roberto still led the league in batting, he approached a veteran writer during a plane trip and asked, "Who made the most money in Pittsburgh as a player?"

When he was told that Ralph Kiner had once earned $90,000 in a season, he exclaimed, "That much!"

He was not yet in that league, but the twenty-seven-year-old Roberto earned steady raises each season, and with the help of a lawyer back home, was investing his money. He was proud of the fact that he owned four small suburban homes, each of which he rented unfurnished for $90 a month, a good price at the time.

"A lot of Latin players turned to him for advice. I guess he considered me a Latin because I come from the Caribbean," said Alvin McBean, a pitcher from the Virgin Islands who became Roberto's roommate in 1961.

"He practically set the rules for my conduct," said McBean. "He believes people know you by the company you keep. He's set in his ways, doesn't like noise. On the road he gets up late for breakfast, takes maybe a thirty-minute walk, and then goes back to bed. He used to tell me, 'the more you rest, the prettier you become.'"

As for Roberto's physical condition, McBean said, "Robby likes to talk about how he feels. He wants you to talk to him, make him feel good. When he says he feels real terrible, I tell him he feels good, that he'll hit 4-for-4. But he is a great player. If he were on the Yankees, Mickey Mantle would be nowhere."

That season Roberto met a Puerto Rican couple, Alejandro and Aida Sárraga, who had lived in San Francisco for many years. He was a frequent guest at their home when the Pirates played in San Francisco. "He became like a member of the family," says Aida. "He called my father *el viejo*, the old man, in the way that many Puerto Ricans refer to their parents. Sometimes he'd massage his back when it was hurting. Before dinner, he'd go out on the terrace with the kids and pitch pennies against the wall. Later, we opened a restaurant downtown—the People's Fish and Chip—and Roberto came there often with the players, some of the Latins, and Willie Stargell, and Alvin McBean, whom I'll always remember because he liked to sprinkle sugar on his beans! Roberto often got us tickets to see him play. But the time I remember most is when he invited a group of us to see the film *West Side Story*. Where I worked, we had a baseball pool, and I had great luck winning. Roberto played that day, and that night I told him, 'I was praying for you to get a hit, but not a home run, because if you drove in a run, then I would have lost the pool.' The expression on his face! He became very upset— he soon got over it—but then I realized how much he loved the game, and how seriously he took it. It was his whole life."

The 1961 season ended on a drab note for the Pirates, who finished in sixth place, eighteen games behind Cincinnati. Roberto had to sit out the last five games after one of Don Drysdale's fastballs clipped him on the elbow; later that winter surgery would be required to remove bone chips. But it had been one hell of a year. With his .351 average, Roberto was the top batter in the National League and received his first Silver Bat Award. His 201 hits made up the highest Pirate total since the days of Paul Waner. His 100 runs scored and 23 homers were career highs.

He could have done better, he claimed, were it not for night games. "I like sunshine," he said. "It makes me feel good, and I see the ball better." The figures proved him right. During the Pirates' sixty-eight day games that year, he batted .411, compared with .302 under lights. Had he played for the Cubs, he might have been baseball's first .400 hitter since Ted Williams; at Chicago's Wrigley Field, where all games are played under sunshine, he batted .478.

At season's end, the great Stan Musial, then close to retirement, called Roberto "a fine all-around athlete and getting better all the time." He also shone on defense, getting 27 assists and leading the league's outfielders by taking part in five double plays. The *Sporting News* named him to its all-star team and awarded him a Golden Glove for fine defensive play.

The honor that touched Roberto's heart more than any other during 1961 was the boisterous welcome he received after his plane touched down in San Juan on October 10. He arrived together with Orlando Cepeda of the San Francisco Giants, another native son, who had led the National League in home runs and runs batted in. Roberto and Orlando were the first Puerto Ricans ever to win major titles in big league competition. More than 18,000 jubilant people lined the roadway, cheering the motorcade that took them to Sixto Escobar Stadium, where another 5,000 admirers waited to greet them. People now stopped to stare at Roberto; kids asked for his autograph. And back in Pittsburgh, Pirates general manager Joe Brown proudly called him "the best rightfielder in the business."

Now that Roberto was thrust in the limelight for the first time in his career, he began to speak up. He spoke of his gratitude, of his joy, but he also spoke of other things that had been on his mind for the seven often lonely, frustrating years that he had spent as a ballplayer in the United States. He had said some of these things before, but nobody had listened. Now, reporters from national magazines sought him out. In that winter of 1961, he told Howard Cohn of *Sport* magazine:

"Latin American Negro ballplayers are treated today much like all Negroes were treated in baseball in the early days of the broken color barrier. They are subjected to prejudices and stamped with

Photo: *Courtesy of Pedrín Zorilla*

Baseball clinic held by Brooklyn Dodgers and Santurce Baseball
Club, San Juan, 1952. Rookie Clemente is at lower right.

Roberto's first professional contract (Puerto Rico League) in
1952. His salary was $40.00 a week.

Scoring winning run in Winter League championship with Santurce Crabbers, 1953–54 season.

Santurce Crabbers in 1955. Left to right: Willie Mays, Roberto Clemente, James Clarkson, Robert Thurman, George Crowe.

Roberto and his friend
Phil Dorsey in front of
Dorsey's house in Pitts-
burgh just before
leaving for the 1960
World Series.

Photo: *Phil Dorsey*

Photo: *El Día*

With kids at a baseball
clinic in Puerto Rico.

Photo: *Courtesy of Pedrín Zorilla*

Signing 1969–70 contract with San Juan Baseball Club.

"Trainer" Arturo Garcia treating Roberto's shoulder in Puerto Rico in 1970.

Photo: *El Mundo*

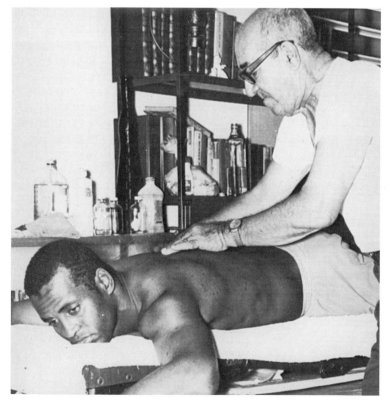

Roberto with his
youngest son.

Two shots of Roberto in action when he lined a pitch from Jon Matlack, New York Mets, for the double off the left-center field fence at Three Rivers Stadium that made him the eleventh player in the history of major league baseball to get 3,000 hits.

Photos: *El Día*

Roberto and Willie Mays of the New York Mets, who had crossed the field to congratulate him on his 3,000th hit.

Roberto's mother congratulating him a few moments after his historic feat. Listening to the phone conversation between her home and Three Rivers Stadium are two of Roberto's sons and his father, the late Don Melchor Clemente.

Photo: *El Día*

Photo: *El Mundo*

Photo: *El Día*

generalizations. Because they speak Spanish among themselves, they are set off as a minority within a minority, and they bear the brunt of the sport's remaining racial prejudices . . . Some players and managers lump together the Latin American Negroes with a set of generalized charges as old as racial-religious prejudice itself. 'They're all lazy, look for the easy way, the shortcut,' is one charge. 'They have no guts,' is another. There are more."

When he was asked if he received less publicity because he was a Puerto Rican, he replied with a pregnant "What do you think?"

"Hey, Tito. Can you take a picture for me?"

It was moments before game time in the 1963 Winter League and Roberto Clemente, in his San Juan Senators uniform, stood smiling near the dugout. Tito Stevens, then a reporter and now sports editor of the *San Juan Star*, had a camera with him.

"Sure," he said to Roberto, "but what do you want? One of you hitting, or fielding, or a posed shot?"

"No, not of me. Of that girl up in the stands," he said, pointing to a tall, beautiful young woman, Vera Christina Zabala.

They were both from Carolina, but they'd never met until a few weeks before. One evening, Roberto went to Oscar Landrau's pharmacy in town to buy medication for an ailing leg; he was chatting with his former teacher, Maria Isabela Cáceres, who worked there part-time. In came Vera, and he whispered, "*Doña* Maria, who is that pretty young girl?"

"She's one of my good students, and don't you *dare* go right up and talk to her!" *doña* Maria whispered back, shaking a finger at her former pupil.

Vera had attended the University of Puerto Rico for three years before becoming a secretary with the island's Government Development Bank. Of her two sisters, one had also become a secretary after going to college, and another was a teacher. Her only brother, Orlando, was an officer in the U.S. Army.

Roberto, momentarily forgetting that a "proper" Puerto Rican didn't just approach a "decent" girl (customs were different, of course, in the United States), called Vera at her office and invited her to lunch. "Everyone in the bank teased me," she recalls. Reared in the old-fashioned Hispanic tradition, she explained that she could not accept. Roberto tried a more subtle tack. He learned that the Velázquez sisters, whom he knew, were friends of Vera's. The girls organized a small *fiesta*, invited a proper crowd, and Roberto dropped in "by chance." Vera knew very little about baseball, but she was given a crash course. Their first date was at the ballpark in San Juan, where she sat in the stands with another couple as chaperones. As she later recalled, he was unable to show off on the field for his new girl because "it rained, and they had to postpone the game."

The following spring Roberto was in New York, and he told Buck Canel, a Spanish-language sports announcer, that he had finally found the girl he wanted. He fondly recalls that Roberto told him, "Buck, I'm going to get married. I know, I *know*, that she's never been out without a chaperone, and she's never kissed a man in her life. The first guy she's going to kiss is me."

And so, on November 14, 1964, about a year after they met, Roberto and Vera were married in the old Roman Catholic church that faces the plaza in Carolina. It was the marriage of the year: the handsome, famous athlete and the lovely young princess. Thousands of well-wishers crowded the church and overflowed onto the sunny plaza. Inside, Tito Stevens stood with Roberto in the sacristy moments before he would exchange vows with Vera and slip the wedding band on her finger.

"Are you nervous?" Stevens asked him.

"Who, me? Nervous? No, I feel great."

"Then why don't you spit out the gum you're chewing?"

A young prince and his princess require a castle, and they found one, complete with a "moat." Libertario Aviles, a prominent engineer, had built an imposing low-slung villa atop a hill in the San Agustín sector of Río Piedras. Roberto bought it from him for $65,000. A small bridge arched from the road across a depression in the ground and ended at the front door. It is one of the highest points for miles around, and from the rear balcony you can see forever: the ships in San Juan Bay, the palm-fringed Atlantic coastline, the planes landing like shiny silver toys at the airport, the purplish-gray haze atop the mountains to the east. Downstairs, next to the garage, is a small room that would soon brim over with trophies and plaques, but there would be space for a huge billiards table. Upstairs, a sunken sofa in the spacious living room faced a picture window and the splendid view from the balcony. Next was a formal dining room, and then an open-air garden with tropical foliage and a small lily pond. There were extra bedrooms for the future heirs. Roberto Junior—known by the diminutive "Robertito"—was born to Vera about a year after the wedding; a year later would come Luis Roberto, and three years hence, Enrique Roberto. "A whole outfield of Clementes!" their friends would say in jest.

"All his sons were born in Puerto Rico," says his former roommate Alvin McBean. "I asked him once why he spent so much money to send his wife down from the mainland for their births, and he told me, I was born in Puerto Rico. I want my children born there."

Roberto was three months beyond his thirtieth birthday when he married. Even before, there had been serious responsibilities to shoulder. His aged parents. Papo, the son of his dead stepbrother Luis. Rafaela, the daughter of his stepsister Rose María, who died in childbirth, was also being raised by Roberto's parents. There were many mouths to feed, and he never forgot. It had taken him some time to follow Branch Rickey's advice more than a decade before: *"Find a nice girl and marry her . . . then you can really get down to the business of baseball. Because, young man, you are going to be a superstar."* He hadn't done badly thus far—a ten-year veteran of the big leagues, twice a batting champion. But now—with his fame and his new happy domestic life—Roberto ascended to a higher plateau of personal serenity. Vera was a loving wife who bore him sons. Despite her youth, she had an almost maternal devotion to her husband. One of their friends would later comment, "Roberto never made an important decision without consulting Vera; only she really knew what went on inside this complex man."

During the three seasons prior to Roberto's marriage, the legend of his hypochondria became part of baseball's folklore. He claimed so many ills—and performed so well despite them—that his plaints evoked skepticism or laughter. After the 1961 season, he went to Johns Hopkins Hospital for the removal of painful bone chips that were "floating" in his elbow. The surgeon, Dr. George Bennett, had X-rayed the elbow and seen the chips a few weeks before. But when the doctor operated, there wasn't a chip to be found. Everyone was baffled. Not long after the operation, Roberto played a few games in Puerto Rico. When he reported to Fort Myers that spring, with a freshly signed $50,000 annual contract, he was ten pounds underweight and suffered from a nervous stomach. In the opening game of the 1962 season, however, he blasted a bases-loaded home run against Philadephia, and the writers, fans, and some of his teammates began to chuckle and remark, "*I* should be so sick!" At midseason, boasting a .336 average, he was chosen to play in the All-Star Game. On July 10 in Washington, D.C., before a crowd that included President John F. Kennedy and Vice President Lyndon B. Johnson, Roberto sparkled, punishing the American League's best pitchers with three hits. But as the summer wore on, his weight dropped to 162 pounds. Despite a late-season slump he helped the Pirates to finish a strong fourth in the league, played in 144 games, and batted .312; only eight men in the National League did better. That September, he said, "I will come back next year, and this time it will be good."

"This past season has been a nightmare to me," groaned Pirate general manager Joe L. Brown when 1963 was over. It was the second year that the National League would play under the new ten-team arrangement with an expanded 162-game schedule. The 1963 Pirates finished eighth, twenty-five games behind Los Angeles. Gambling on new talent, Brown had traded away three-quarters of the infield that won Pittsburgh's pennant in 1960. The new men hadn't panned out and those traded shone elsewhere. As the team lost, tension mounted. In May, against Los Angeles, Roberto— hitting a puny .278—tried a surprise bunt and was called out at first (photos later showed that his toe reached the base before the throw hit the fielder's glove) and exploded at the umpire. Two weeks later, after being called out at first on a double play, Roberto got into a heated dispute with umpire Bill Jackowski. As he continued to berate the umpire, first base coach Ron Northey stepped between them. Trying to brush past the coach, Roberto struck the umpire with his hand and was immediately ejected from the game. He received a written rebuke from National League President Warren Giles, who fined him $250 and suspended him for five days. Said Giles, "Your actions were the most serious reported to our office in several years."

This infuriated Roberto even more. "It was an accident. I hit him with my palm, not my fist, while I was trying to get away from the coach," he told reporters in the clubhouse. He complained that two years ago Leo Durocher had been suspended for only three days when he actually kicked umpire Jocko Conlan in the shins (Conlan, by the way, kicked him back). "What I did was mild compared to what Durocher did to Conlan. How can Giles say this when Durocher did what he did? I had good reason for losing my head. Durocher didn't." Still boiling, he wrote a letter of protest to Giles, but the punishment stood, and Giles replied, "Even though you may be very angry, you must try to control your temper in the presence of umpires." Dissatisfied, Clemente again turned to the press and said, "Every year I lose fifteen to twenty points on close plays at first base. I seldom argue unless I feel the umpire is wrong. I have a good record in the league office, but this is the worst year for umpiring I have ever seen. There are only two or three good umpires in the league."

Worse episodes lay ahead, this time with manager Danny Murtaugh, who was not in the best of moods as his former world champions floundered near the cellar. Much of the heat was generated by the newspapers, Roberto claimed. "The Pittsburgh press had me at odds with Danny Murtaugh. They never said it exactly that way, but they knew how to say it other ways. I caught the flu in San Francisco. Then we flew to Los Angeles and we had shrimp and steak on the plane. I got sick in my room at 3 A.M. I began to sweat, I had the shakes. I called the doctor at 6 A.M. His nurse told me to put wet towels on my stomach. Later that morning, they pumped out my stomach. I went to the ballpark and Murtaugh asked me how I felt."

Roberto answered, "Terrible." Murtaugh consulted with team captain Bill Mazeroski and decided that Clemente should play. He struck out twice that day against Don Drysdale, but also got a hit. The next day, before a doubleheader in Houston, Clemente lay on the trainer's rubbing table and complained of dizziness.

"I think you're the best in the league," Murtaugh told him. "You make good money. You have to put out."

"I can't play like this."

Then, as Roberto later recalled it, Murtaugh said, "You let me know when you are ready to play again. You're making too much money to sit on the bench. The next time you feel like playing you'll play and you'll play every day until I say you won't play."

"You talk like I don't want to play baseball," Clemente replied.

"I don't care what you think, and that's all I'm going to say," Murtaugh is said to have answered. The manager walked away in a huff. Roberto sat out the next three games, and soon there were hints in the Pittsburgh sports press that the manager was "tired" of his batting champ's attitude.

Another time, in Philadelphia, Roberto was playing with two stitches in his ankle. He hit a grounder to shortstop, fell as he left the batter's box and was thrown out at first before he got up. When he returned to the bench, he told Murtaugh that he couldn't play. "If you don't get in there, it'll cost you a hundred and fifty," Murtaugh said.

Clemente recalled later that he went into the clubhouse, where Murtaugh is said to have accused him of feigning an injury and demanded that he remove his uniform.

"No one takes my uniform off while I'm playing for Pittsburgh," Roberto answered. He later recalled that he and the manager "shouted at each other and came pretty close to fighting." When the squall subsided, the level of Roberto's fines had reached $650, but he stubbornly paid them and remained out of action that day.

Teammate Bob Friend later said, "Bobby always came to me and told me how Murtaugh was against him. I tried to tell him he was wrong but he just wouldn't believe me. Really, Danny was on Bobby's side all the way, but Clemente didn't understand."

One of the problems between Clemente and Murtaugh was communication, and the press often aggravated the relationship with its sideline comments. "Bobby is right about some of the writers being against him," Friend commented. "They hurt him more than anything, especially about the hypochondriac image."

But at the time Roberto felt that Murtaugh was responsible. Years later, he and Murtaugh would work together harmoniously, but when the manager quit after the 1964 season because of poor health, Roberto said, "I didn't say anything before because he was my manager and I respect him for that position. No matter what happened between us, I wouldn't put him down because he was my manager. But I didn't like what he did to me. He had no respect for me, and I had no respect for him. Nobody had better years under Murtaugh than me, but he acted like he didn't appreciate me. Instead of being friendly, he needled me."

When the 1963 season was over, however, Roberto had played 152 games and batted .320, only six points behind league champion Tommy Davis of Los Angeles. He won his third consecutive Golden Glove for defensive play. Yet there were some who still questioned his attitude toward the game. Of the sportswriters, Roberto would later say, "They think it is an act. When I said I had back trouble, they call me 'Mama's Boy,' or 'Goldbrick.' When my elbow was swollen big as a softball, they say it was in my head. If I am sick, I do not deny it. If my back is hurting and I am forced to punch at the ball, with no power, I tell the truth." That winter, he hit .345 for the San Juan club; the caliber of play in Puerto Rico is evidenced by the fact that his average was only fourth best in the league—behind stars like Orlando Cepeda of Santurce, Tony Oliva of Arecibo, and Walter Bond of Ponce.

During that winter season he made an unannounced visit to the home of a young Puerto Rican whose play in the island's amateur league had drawn the attention of many scouts. Willie Montañez, then only fifteen, recalls that there was a knock on the door and his brother Julio casually said, "Roberto Clemente's here."

"I nearly passed out," said Willie later. Clemente told him, "The Pittsburgh scouts have talked to me. They will be coming to see you soon. They like you, and will try to sign you. But you are a very good player, good enough to play in the United States, and I don't think they are going to offer you the money you are worth. You can get more if you want to wait, or maybe talk to other teams. Don't make the mistake of settling for less than you're worth." After chatting for a while, Roberto took a baseball from his pocket, autographed it, and left it with his open-mouthed young admirer. A few years later, after signing with Philadelphia, Montañez was one of the National League's best rookies, with thirty home runs and ninety-nine runs batted in. He still keeps the autographed ball in his trophy room.

In the early 1960's, Roberto drove a Chevrolet Corvair and then bought a Pontiac, but as the 1964 season began he sat behind the wheel of a new white and avocado green Cadillac, purchased from a Pittsburgh auto dealer for $5,400. "Harvey Haddix used to tell me, 'If you ever drive a Caddy you'll drive nothing else,'" Roberto told admirers, who flocked around the new machine. The car was just one symbol of Roberto's "arrival" that year; he celebrated his tenth anniversary in the big leagues, his thirtieth birthday, got married, and won his third batting crown with a .339 average that was the best in both leagues. It would be hard for him to top the 1964 season. He achieved a career high of 211 base hits, whacked 40 doubles (also a career record), and accumulated 301 total bases—more than such powerful batsmen as Hank Aaron and Joe Torre.

During that season, as he swung away toward his third batting title, he began to look and act like a champion. With his characteristic bluntness, he told a sports writer, "I believe I can hit with anybody in baseball. Maybe I can't hit with the power of a Mays or a Frank Robinson or a Hank Aaron, but I can hit. As long as I'm in Forbes Field I can't go for home runs; line drives, yes. I'm a better fielder than anybody you can name. I have great respect for Mays, but I can get a ball like Willie and I have a better arm. I can throw *blind* to a base." It sounded a bit cocky in print, but Roberto spoke the words softly, staring directly into his interviewer's eyes. Later, he would tell Myron Cope of *Sports Illustrated*, "For me, I am the best ballplayer in the world. I say, 'For *me*, for myself!'" And his old friend, the engineer Libertario Aviles, would try to explain to Cope that what sounded like the expression of a swell-headed prima donna might be misinterpreted. Aviles said, "You have to understand that the Latin is touchy. If you say to me, 'Who is the best engineer in town?' I will say, 'For me, I am the best.' It is a Spanish saying, an expression of self-respect. You are not to underestimate yourself, but that does not mean you are to underestimate anyone else's ability."

During that memorable 1964 season, more and more inquisitive reporters came around, trying to fathom the alchemy of Roberto's unorthodox hitting style. No other modern star could "step in the bucket" the way Clemente did, ducking away from the plate with his front left foot, and still connect with such force. He did so, he explained, because "in 1956 I was going good until I hurt my back. Since then I step to the side with my left foot faster so I don't have to twist my body so much." In order to compensate, he leaned his torso far forward and depended upon strong wrists and arms. Hitting was a science to Clemente. Like Ted Williams, he could lift a bat and tell that it was an ounce off the proper weight for him. In batting practice, he often stood motionless, his feet together, swinging lightly and rapping line drives in all directions to sharpen his eye. In a game, he rarely swung at the first pitch, preferring to study the pitcher's speed and delivery. Teammate Bill Mazeroski recalls that, after one of the few times Clemente went after a first pitch, and made an out, he came back to the dugout muttering, "Why did I do that? I never do that." As for Roberto's fabled throwing arm, Mazeroski says, "There was an iron gate in right-center at Forbes Field, and I've seen him throw a ball from near that gate to the plate on the fly, a distance of 460 feet."

That year, Sandy Koufax, the Hall of Fame pitcher, who had also started his career in 1955 and faced Roberto many times, called him "the strangest hitter in baseball. Figure him one way and he'll kill you another . . . He's very strong and is extremely quick with his hands. You look at him swinging sometimes on his front foot, sometimes on his rear, sometimes with both feet off the ground, and you're inclined to think, 'This guy can't hit.' " Koufax recalled that the longest ball he'd ever seen hit to the opposite field was "hit off me by Clemente at the Los Angeles Coliseum in 1961. It was a fastball on the outside corner, and he drove it out of the park; not just over the fence, but he knocked it way out . . . What makes Bob the kind of hitter I don't want to see at bat with runners on is that he's liable to hit anything. He could hit a *pitchout* for a home run."

Perhaps Clemente's greatest satisfaction was that he had finally gotten Bob Purkey's number. In the past six years, the right-handed Cincinnati pitcher had held Roberto to a meager ten hits and a .176 batting average, with his tantalizing melange of curves and "waste" pitches that were slightly off the plate. By 1964, a more mature Roberto waited for Purkey to get the ball over. That season, he walked 51 times (another career high) and in two games against Purkey walloped six hits. As the year wore on, Clemente had become such a menace that opposing clubs cooked up ways to rattle him. One August afternoon in Chicago, as Roberto dug in to hit, deep in the box as usual, the Cubs catcher complained to the umpire that his rear foot was outside the chalk line of that box. The umpire scratched out a new line in the dirt with his shoe and told Roberto to stay within bounds. Roberto, his eyes flashing with annoyance, growled, "Where you been? I've been batting this way for ten years." When he was thrown out on an infield grounder, Roberto yanked the helmet from his head and kicked it toward the Pirate dugout, prompting hoots from the crowd. A few days later, Philadelphia catcher Clay Dalrymple tried the same gambit, and again the umpire warned Roberto to stay within the box. On the next pitch, he smashed a single to right field, and opposing catchers began to search for new schemes.

As the season came to a close, Roberto said, "I will not play winter ball. I look forward to a rest. I play too much winter ball in the past. It makes me tired when I go to spring training. The last three winters, I just played half-seasons in Puerto Rico. Now, no more winter ball. In the spring of 1965, I'll report strong, you'll see." After his wedding that November, the hyperactive Roberto couldn't sit still. The next month, at the request of a judge who had organized a program to combat juvenile delinquency, he took part in several baseball clinics for low-income urban youngsters. He also accepted an offer to manage the San Juan club in the Winter League. The Puerto Rican fans were eager to see their home-town hero in action. Soon he was pinch-hitting and playing a few innings. The Pittsburgh front office, displeased, said, "Naturally we would prefer that Clemente rest. He can't improve any. He does not need to play. They put pressure on him to change his mind. The people in San Juan hounded him until he gave in to popular demand."

"They want me to play, yes, and I want to help San Juan win the pennant," Clemente replied. But also, now that he was a married man, "I did it to earn extra money." Despite his Golden Glove and batting championships, his salary was far below that of other stars.

The perils of domestic life, it seems, were even greater than those on the diamond. That December he was mowing the lawn of his palatial Rio Piedras home when the cutting blade struck a stone that flew up against his right thigh. Roberto stopped playing in the Winter League. But during the league All-Star game in San Juan he was prevailed upon to pinch-hit. "I could hardly walk, I couldn't risk running," he said. He drilled a hard shot to right field and hobbled to first base. But suddenly his leg crumbled beneath him and he felt "something like water draining inside my leg." It was blood. He was carried to a car and rushed to the hospital. The next day his leg was monstrously swollen and he couldn't walk. The doctor diagnosed it as an internal hemorrhage and three days later sliced the thigh open to drain the blood from the clotted bruise. Weeks later, Roberto trotted on the beach a few minutes each day, limbering up for the next season in Pittsburgh. The healing process was not aided by disconcerting news from the north. Ken Boyer, third baseman of the pennant-winning Cardinals and league leader in runs batted in, had been chosen Most Valuable Player. A good choice, but Roberto, the top batter in the league, was listed *ninth* in the balloting. In second place was Johnny Callison, a fine fielder whose average was 65 points lower than Roberto's. Later, the United Press International announced its major league All-Star team, and the outfield consisted of Willie Mays, Mickey Mantle, and Billy Williams. All fine players, but there was no room for the man who had just won this third batting championship and had his finest year.

"His Pain Didn't Let Him Sleep"

"I treated Roberto Clemente for eighteen years and never charged him a cent. I treated him at least a hundred times, sometimes for two or three hours in a row, until I fell from exhaustion."

Arturo Garcia, a semiretired chiropractor and sports trainer, runs a small trucking company from an office above a shoe store in Santurce. Semi-retired because athletes still come to his office and lie on the cot in the corner behind his desk, where he rubs them down with a potent orange ointment called "Atomic Balm," "cauterizes" their tendons with a black plastic cylinder that emits crackling purple sparks, and heats their aching muscles with a small infrared lamp. Now nearing seventy years of age, don Arturo wears thick horn-rimmed glasses; his eyes are hooded by puffy, drooping lids. He rises and walks with difficulty. But his forearms radiate power, and his hands are like two banana bunches. When he speaks, his voice is strong and sure.

Roberto suffered plenty of pain during his career. He was born with a weak spine and had many ailments. His pain didn't let him sleep. He would invent hobbies and stay awake until one, two, three in the morning. But according to the American newspapers he was just a hypochondriac. Once I went to Pittsburgh, and when the reporters there interviewed me I told them, "Anyone who says Roberto is a hypochondriac is a GOD-DAMNED LIAR! And if the doctor says he is, the doctor doesn't know a GOD-DAMNED THING!" I told them, because I speak my bit of English, but they never published a word.

During the past eighteen years, Clemente has brought his friends, relatives, and other players to see me many times. A few years ago, his father, *don* Melchor, had a severe attack of sciatica and pleaded to be taken to the hospital for an operation. Roberto said, "No, *papá*, not until *don* Arturo sees you." He took me to their house, and *don* Melchor was fine in two days. My treatment consists of physiotherapy, infrared lamps, electric shock, cyclotherapy—Once they wrote an article in the paper here about "The Magic Hands of Arturo García."

I've treated baseball players, boxers, sprinters, all kinds of athletes for more than forty years. Now I've retired and only treat friends of mine. I can't tell them no. I've got all my equipment right here behind the desk. I don't charge a cent. Every time someone enters bent over in pain, and I see him walk out healthy, it gives me great joy. The strange thing is, ever since I've stopped charging for my services, I've had more success! I don't go to church, but I'm a Christian and I have a small shrine at home, where I pray before going to bed and after arising. I believe in God. I'm on good terms with Him, because God has helped me a great deal. In six months I've had two thromboses, bronchial pneumonia, and my legs are a bit wobbly, but I walk. God has helped me.

Roberto used to marvel at how I could use my hands on him and remove his pain. I have strength in my hands. When I take hold of a patient, I close my eyes and I "see" with my hands.

I first met Roberto early in his career with Pittsburgh. He had stopped playing up there during the final two months of the season, because he has pains in his arms, his legs, and his waist. And he was unable to play with Caguas in the Winter League. In fact, he thought of quitting the game. Then the owner of the Caguas club—Rafael Ramos Cobián—came to see me with Juan Maldonado, head of public relations of the government's Parks and Recreation Administration. They showed me a series of X-rays of Roberto. I still hadn't met him. After studying the X-rays, I told them, "I'll have Roberto playing ball in ten days." I treated him for nine days, and the next day he was playing in the semifinal series at Sixto Escobar Stadium. He had three ruptured spinal discs that affected his entire body. I went to his home at Urbanización Comandante and kept treating him for sixty days. When Pirate general manager Joe Brown came with Roberto's contract for the next season, he asked if Roberto could play, and I said yes. After that Roberto came to see me at the end of each season. Even during the season, when something bothered him, he flew down and came to my house in Round Hill. He knew he was as welcome as if it were his own home. He would take off his clothes, get into the steam bath, then a hot-cold bath, and lie down on the massage table. Once they sent for me in Pittsburgh. I spent four days there with him, and I also treated other players— Steve Blass, José Antonio Pagán, many others. I have faith in my hands. I touch a muscle or tendon and I already know what the problem is. The doctor in Pittsburgh told me I was a *brujo*, a sorcerer. I didn't use any pills. I would touch them where it hurt and make them better. But I'm not a *brujo*, I can feel which is the bad tendon, I adjust it, and it's better. A couple of years ago, Roberto was in the Presbyterian Hospital of Pittsburgh with a bad vertebra and for three days they couldn't fix it. They even gave him twenty grams of Novocaine. Brown called and asked if I could fly up there. I had recently suffered a cardiac attack. So, I said if they could send Roberto down here I would have him back in two days. That's what happened and he had one of his best seasons.

When people called Roberto a hypochondriac, I told them, "I wish you could see the X-rays and know how to read them." When one tiny bone in the spine is out of place, this affects the sciatic nerve, which extends to other parts of the body. So a man's leg or finger can hurt, although the problem is in his back. But it can be adjusted and relieved. The other problem was Roberto's cervix. Did you ever notice how, when he went to bat, he moved his neck around? He had some vertebrae out of place and I put them back, but one of them remained chronic, kept slipping in and out. I taught him how to work it back in place with that technique. The doctor on the Pittsburgh team doesn't know *anything*. Nothing, nothing. All he knows is to give out little pills! Or injections, which are harmful. One day, during a doubleheader, a ball hit the Pittsburgh first baseman in the ankle. I examined him, there was nothing wrong, so I lightly taped the ankle. The doctor comes in and right away says, "To the hospital for X-rays." "He ain't got a damn *thing*," I told him. "Just use your *hands*, dammit, what are your hands *for*? You can *see* that nothing's broken!" Still, they sent him to the hospital and the X-rays were negative. "See?" I told the doctor. The trouble with doctors—my son is a doctor, and so are two of my nephews—is that they don't know a damn thing about this. "You've got to develop *touch, touch,*" I tell them. At school, we studied in a completely dark room with skeletons that had bones, skin, veins, tendons. I spent two and a half years in dark rooms. It wasn't reading books, it was *touch!*

For me, Roberto Clemente was the best outfielder that has ever existed. I've seen lots of great ones—Bob Meusel, Joe DiMaggio, Earle Combs, Ty Cobb, Tris Speaker. Those were outfielders! But as a complete player—who covers plenty of ground, throws hard and accurate; who uses his head on tough plays—nobody was like Roberto. In Montreal about four years ago I saw him catch a ball on top of the fence! He leapt, fell seated atop the fence and grabbed what would have been a sure home run. I've seen him throw men out from 380 feet away, a perfect strike. The Pittsburgh press gave him small-town publicity. If he had played in New York, with all the papers there, and all the Latin fans, they would have elevated him enormously! It wasn't the fault of the fans. The Pittsburgh fans adored him, they would even applaud when he struck out! As for the New York sportswriters, all they cared about were the Mets and the Yankees. If he hadn't had such a fine World Series in 1971—when they *had* to sit up and take notice—he would still have little publicity.

"Roberto gave the maximum when he played. And he wasn't hard to get along with, although he had his little squabbles with the managers. That's because—as can be expected—they favored their own, the white players. And since the team had plenty of colored players, that hurt Roberto. He especially defended the Latins. For Manny Sanguillen, the Pittsburgh catcher, Roberto was an idol. Clemente advised him, helped him. Roberto was an idol to almost all the Latins, because he fought for the cause of his *compañeros*. He used to tell me, "I don't care if they're Puerto Rican or not; they can be Dominican, Venezuelan, Cuban, Mexican, they're *latinos*, my people." Yes, he had his differences, but he also had great friendships in Pittsburgh. Mister Galbraith, the owner of the Pirates, cared a great deal for Roberto. When I was there, I ate in a different home every night, millionaires, people with class. I also ate at Roberto's house. His wife Vera is a marvelous cook, a *divine* cook! In fact, she is a divine woman in every sense of the word. She loved him a great deal—I used to kid Roberto, "This woman is too *good* for you!" But they loved each other a great deal. And Roberto had a natural love for children, it wasn't an act. Whenever he saw kids he would go up to them. He was humble, but he wasn't shy. He was the quiet type if you didn't speak to him, but if you did, and you were his friend, he would talk for hours.

And he remembered his friends. One time someone gave him a live lamb. He slaughtered it, cut it in half, stuffed it with ice, and came to my house. I see him lugging this *biiiig* box. "What's that?" "Laaaaamb!" he hollers. They would give him a sack of *morcilla*, blood sausage, which he loved, and right away he would bring me a big bunch.

The only time I reproached him is when I became seriously ill with my first thrombosis and he didn't come to see me in the hospital. I swore that I would never again give him another treatment, not for any amount. But the next time I was ill, he came with Vera, they embraced me, they were very affectionate. I reminded him that he hadn't come before, and he said, "You're right, *don* Arturo, pardon me, but with all my trips, I just couldn't." That erased the first time. So when he came to see me during the 1972 spring training, he was en route from Caracas to Florida, I couldn't say no to him. I worked on his sore arm for four and a half hours, until I found it, a very deep tendon, and I fixed it for him. He was strong enough for another four, five years, if he wanted to play.

Roberto was a good friend: sincere, humble. And I held him in high esteem. All the honors they kept giving him—one banquet after another—hurt him a bit. Too many honors make a man puff up ... like a peacock, and that's no good. But with all that, Roberto was never, as the Americans say, high-hat. To me, it's a source of pride to know that I helped him. When he got his 3,000th hit, I called him long distance in Pittsburgh and congratulated him. I felt proud, because I'd had a part in it. It's like an artist: When he finishes a fine canvas, he contemplates it. And since I did that with Roberto, I contemplate him a great deal.

7

eneral manager Joe L. Brown could speak frankly to Roberto; they had started out together with the Pirates nearly a decade before. Late in the 1964 season, he took Roberto aside for a private talk. The club finished eighth the year before and now floundered in sixth place. He was searching for a spark to set the Pirates afire and he thought the key was Roberto, who was heading toward his second National League batting title, and his fifth straight year as a .300 hitter. "Bob," he said, "you're one of the best players in the game today. But we want you to be more of a team leader."

"How can I be more of a team leader than I am?" said the surprised Roberto. "I talk to everyone when they have a good day or a bad day. I try to help everyone out there. What more can I do? I break my neck for the team and I do not even get so much as a *thank you* from the manager."

Roberto still felt bitter toward Danny Murtaugh, who had managed the Pirates since 1958. Later, he would comment, "I didn't feel I should speak out. I couldn't call a meeting of the players, for who would listen? When I tried to do that . . . Murtaugh would put me down. How could I be a leader for this man?"

In the spring of 1965, however, the situation changed. Murtaugh, in poor health, retired and was replaced by Harry "The Hat" Walker, a former outfielder for the Saint Louis Cardinals who had won a batting title in 1947 and as a minor league manager had led his clubs to three pennants. Walker was a zealous teacher of batting techniques, and some players resented his pedantry. In 1938, as a young rookie trying to foil a double play he had come into second base standing up and the throw hit him squarely in the Adam's apple, rendering him speechless for three months. "He's been making up for it ever since," commented one writer fondly.

Some players wondered whether the sensitive Roberto would hit it off with his loquacious new manager. But Roberto was having troubles of his own. He had barely recovered from a leg injury suffered that winter while using his lawn mower, when new disaster struck. A few weeks before the start of spring training, he had a raging fever and was racked by fits of vomiting and diarrhea. The doctors diagnosed his illness as a combination of malaria (contracted while on a barnstorming trip to Santo Domingo) and a systemic paratyphoid infection (apparently transmitted from hogs he was raising in Puerto Rico). When the illness subsided, he was twenty-five pounds underweight and barely able to stand. The Pirates opened their spring training camp on March 1, but Clemente checked in four weeks later. He had regained ten pounds but still felt listless.

"I don't think you're going to like him," a friend warned Roberto about the new manager.

"Why is that?"

"Well, he talks kinda funny. Always talking, talking about hitting. You could wake him up in the middle of the night and he'd talk baseball."

"What is so bad about that? I like to talk baseball, too."

The two men had a cordial beginning, and Walker coaxed his star along gently as he recuperated from his ailments. By early May, Roberto had a lowly .256 batting average and only one extra-base hit. When the team prepared for a road trip to Saint Louis, Walker decided to rest Roberto and keep him available as a pinch-hitter. Then, a series of misunderstandings arose. After the Saint Louis series, a friend told Roberto that Walker had criticized him during a radio interview with Cardinals announcer Harry Caray: "He said that Ted Williams and Stan Musial can play when they're hurt and he can't understand why you can't play, too." Roberto was stunned. Walker himself had suggested that he take a rest. Walker had been misquoted, but before Roberto knew this, he exploded in the dressing room, and told a writer that he wanted to be traded. This statement, in turn, was exaggerated by a reporter who overheard

Roberto's complaint, and soon the sports pages were alluding to a bitter conflict. A day later, in Chicago, Walker invited Clemente to breakfast in his room at the Knickerbocker Hotel and they had a friendly talk. The next day, with the Pirates back in Pittsburgh, Walker sent Roberto in to pinch-hit. Roberto drove in the tying run with a sacrifice fly in the ninth inning, and when Manny Mota singled home the winning run moments later, a joyful Clemente nearly carried his Dominican friend into the dugout.

Roberto erupted on a wild hitting streak, with base hits in thirty-three of thirty-four games, and his average soared to .340. So did the fortunes of the Pirates. The team had lost 24 of its first 33 games and was in last place when Roberto got hot. Not counting the first disastrous month, the team won 81 games against only 48 losses, better than the pennant-winning Los Angeles Dodgers, and finished in third place, only seven games out of first.

"When Clemente is out of the lineup, the Pirates just don't seem the same," a Pittsburgh writer commented. His leadership was becoming well established. Tales of his remarkable feats were now commonplace. Perhaps none was more unusual than the time he fielded a bunt; players would talk about that one for years to come. Second baseman Bill Mazeroski, who played in the game, recalls: "We had a trick play with two men on and nobody out. If the ball was bunted, Gene Alley, the shortstop, covered third base, and the third baseman broke in toward the plate. In a game against Houston, the batter bunted a ball in the air toward the hole the shortstop had vacated. Both runners held up briefly and Roberto raced in from *right field*, dove for the ball, and with his face in the dirt threw out the runner going to third base!" By mid-August Clemente was dog-tired, and his average sagged a bit. He also missed three games when he was hit in the elbow with a pitch. But at season's end, he had won his third National League batting title with a .329 average; he was only the fifth man in the league's history to do so and was now in the distinguished company of Honus Wagner, Paul Waner, Rogers Hornsby, and Stan Musial. Despite his ailments, he played in 152 games, hit 14 triples (second in the league) and made 194 base hits (fourth best in the league).

Many of Roberto's great moments on the playing field went unnoticed by the American press because they occurred in the Caribbean. Radio announcer Felo Ramirez, whose broadcasts of World Series and "The Game of the Week" were transmitted in Spanish throughout Latin America, insisted that "perhaps the greatest play I've *ever* seen Roberto make was in Nicaragua, in 1964 or 1965, after San Juan won the title in the Caribbean Series. They had Clemente, Cepeda, Pizarro, Conde, Pagán—it was like an all-star team! The San Juan team arranged a friendly series against the teams from Nicaragua and Panama. Know who won? Nicaragua! They had a bunch of old Cubans, almost retired, but they won! What a party they threw in Nicaragua. But during that series, Roberto made such a fantastic play that they nearly raised a monument in his honor out in right field. Ossie Echevarría, a Panamanian, one of the fastest men in baseball, was the runner on first base. A ball was hit to right-center, nearly by the wall. Normally, any runner would make it from first to third on such a hit, especially a guy like Echevarría. Clemente cut the ball off and threw it right into Wito Conde's glove at third—that ball looked like a jet! The runner was tagged out, and every fan in the ballpark just stood there, mouth open in amazement. They'd seen plenty of top players over the years, but never had they seen a throw like that! Three innings later, the same situation: Echevarría on first, another hit. Roberto cut it off and fired to third. Echevarría was between second and third base. When he slammed on the brakes, it looked so funny, like a character in a Walt Disney cartoon! He threw himself headlong back to second base. Incredible! It was impossible to run against Roberto's arm."

Even more than Roberto's natural talent, Ramirez admired his serious approach. "He was a perfectionist, like a great artist in any field. When he got to a new park, he inspected every inch of right field to see if the ground was hard or soft, how high the grass was. He was a fanatic about his waistline. Once he told me, 'I have a 32-inch waist always; when I'm a bit more, I'm no good.' In the off-season, I've seen him go to a field in Carolina with a sack full of beer bottle caps. He'd get some kids to throw him the tiny caps and he'd spend hours—hours!—batting. Then, for exercise, he'd bend down and pick them all up. He said that when he was done hitting those tiny caps, a real ball looked as big as a coconut!"

After the 1965 season, one of the wire services picked a major-league all-star team and chose Mickey Mantle ahead of Roberto for right field. Mantle, only two years away from retirement, had hit only .255, his lowest average in fifteen years for the Yankees. But the New York publicity machine continued to perpetuate his legend long after Mantle's prime. If Clemente complained of lack of recognition, however, writers muttered that he was a "sorehead." That October, before Roberto and Vera returned to Puerto Rico, they stopped off in New York to do some shopping, and Clemente learned another painful lesson about second-class citizenship. As he later recalled the episode:

"There is a furniture store in New York which is eleven stories high, and each floor has a different display. The quality and price of the furniture is best and highest on the ground floor, and the most modestly priced items are on the top floor. Both Vera and I were impressed with the furniture on the first floor. Beautiful. Very beautiful. She was eager to buy some, and I was delighted to please her. We asked a salesman, and he began to cough and fidget around, without telling us the price. 'Look sir,' he said, 'I think we have something better for you on the sixth floor. Come with me, please.' We went to the sixth floor, but the truth is, after seeing it, we still liked the furniture on the first floor. We let the salesman talk on and on, but we finally said we didn't like it and preferred the stuff downstairs. He finally told us, 'It seems to me that it might be a little too high for you; they're very expensive items.' By chance I had just cashed a check at the Chemical Bank for $5,000, four bills of $1,000 and the rest in small denominations. I pulled out that thick wad of bills and asked, 'Will it cost more than this?' He didn't know what to do for me. He asked my name, and after I told him he asked if I was *the* Roberto Clemente. When I said yes, he went wild and called the other employees over. Soon they were all around us. Then, smiling, the salesman asked me, 'Where shall we send the furniture, sir? You don't have to put anything down now. Just tell me where to send it.' I told him, 'Nowhere. We don't want it any longer.' The man kept insisting, he was very friendly now, but I told him, 'We don't want anything from this place, because you haven't treated me like a human being.' Before he knew who I was, just because I am black and Puerto Rican, he had already figured out what I could afford. I didn't want to do business with that kind of person.'"

Perhaps slights such as these and the lack of recognition for his true worth as an athlete spurred Roberto on to even greater accomplishment. Whatever the reason, the 1966 season proved to be his best ever. Recalling that year, manager Harry Walker would say, "No man ever gave more of himself or worked more unselfishly for the good of the team." Walker was having difficulty communicating with Mateo Alou, who had hit only .231 for the Giants the previous year. "Roberto," drawled Walker in his Mississippi accent, "I need your help. I'm trying to get Matty to hit the ball to left field, but I'm having trouble. He wants to pull everything to right. The pitchers work the outside corner on him and he becomes an easy mark. I *still* haven't convinced him that he'll hit better if he slices the ball to left and goes with the pitch. Will you tell him?" In fluent Spanish, Roberto translated Walker's advice to his Dominican teammate. Whenever Alou took batting practice, Clemente stood at third base, urging him, "Punch the ball at me, forget about pulling it to right; hit to left, to *left*." By season's end Alou raised his average by 111 points and won the National League championship. Walker also recalled, "During spring training, we were working with Gene Alley on his base-running and sliding. Clemente had a habit of taking a wide turn almost to the grass when rounding first base. We didn't ask him to join our little sessions, but one day he came over and asked if he could. Through his efforts in the spring, he became an even better runner. This is a great help to a manager. When a player as big as Clemente can look for help, then everybody can learn something. It does things to the other men on the ball club."

Despite his enthusiasm, the thirty-one-year-old Roberto got off to a tepid start, and by the time the season was one-fourth complete he had only a .285 average. But he came back refreshed after Walker gave him a three-day rest and during an eleven-game home stand in June batted .444, with twenty-eight hits, six of them home runs. Two of those homers landed deep in right-center at Forbes Field, between the Barney Dreyfuss monument and a light tower close to the 436-foot marker. Before the final night game of that home stand, he put Vera and ten-month-old Robertito on a plane for Puerto Rico. Soon she would bear him a second son, and Roberto insisted that his children open their eyes for the first time in *la patria*. After taking them to the airport, he told a writer, "My wife left Pittsburgh about a year ago for home to have our first child, but I didn't feel so sad then. This was a new experience for me. But this time something hit me. When the baby turned around and clapped his hands and my wife waved goodbye, I almost cried. I haven't felt like this since I first left home in 1954 and came to play ball for Montreal. When my mother said goodbye to me then, it was the same feeling I had when my wife and boy left now." But Roberto was functioning like a well-oiled machine. The night that Vera left, he consoled himself with a three-run homer in the eighth inning to beat the Cincinnati Reds. It was Roberto's year, and it was also the year of the "Black Maxes." The Pirates had become the zaniest team in baseball. After a group of players saw the film *The Blue Max*, a nostalgia-filled World War I aviation story, they were inspired to call themselves the "Black Maxes." Soon, catcher Jim Pagliaroni was strutting around the clubhouse with a World War I aviator's helmet and goggles. Pitcher Elroy Face wore a buccaneer's hat adorned with a skull and crossbones. Outfielder Willie Stargell was bewildering waiters in restaurants, ordering "gospel bird" (fried chicken) and "jungle plum" (watermelon). "Cliché awards" were given out for dubious achievements. Donn Clendenon, who had struck out 97 times by the month of August, was the team leader in "get-em-next-times," and pitcher Steve Blass, who had failed to finish 21 of his 22 starting assignments, led the club with "can't-do-it-every days." There were even loonier doings up in the Pirate broadcasting booth. Announcer Bob Prince (notorious for his loud sport jackets and for having once won a bet for jumping into a swimming pool from a third-floor window) conspired with Danny Whelan (then the team trainer) to invent the "Green Weenie"—a huge plastic hot dog that would put the "whammy" on opposing players. Soon, the Pirates were pointing green hot dogs from the dugout, and fans waved them joyously in the stands. During one game at Forbes Field, the Pirates were behind the Phillies 3 to 1 and the other announcer, Don Hoak, begged Prince to put the "weenie" to work. "Not yet," he was told. Finally, in the eighth inning, Prince waved the giant plastic sausage and the Pirates won the game with a four-run rally. Before signing off the air, Prince said to Hoak in mock-serious tones, "Remember, never waste the power of the Green Weenie." Even manager Walker was caught up in the summer's madness. The team was on a bus headed for the Chicago airport when it stopped for a moment near an old apartment house at 1946 West Addison Street. "There it is!" shouted Walker, pointing to the building, and nearly doing a cartwheel in the aisle. "That house right there! Number 1946! That's what I've wanted all year. The last time I was in the World Series was in 1946 and that number says I'll be there again in 1966!"

"We haven't got a sane guy on this ballclub," said catcher Pagliaroni proudly.

Clemente was not an active member of the Black Maxes, nor was he seen waving any Green Weenies, but he was bemused and buoyed by the club's jovial mood. That July, he was chosen to the National League's All-Star outfield, together with Willie Mays and Hank Aaron, and at Saint Louis's new Busch Memorial Stadium, playing in 105-degree weather, he helped beat the American League's best, 2 to 1, with a double and a single. During that long summer, he put together hitting streaks of fifteen and seventeen games. Four times he got four hits in a game. And he continued to shine on defense. Against Milwaukee he gunned down two baserunners in one game. Another time, with the bases loaded, he fielded an apparent line drive hit to right and fired it to the catcher for a force play against the surprised runner, who was jogging home from third base. On September 2 at Forbes Field, he reached another milestone, connecting against a fastball by Chicago Cubs ace Ferguson Jenkins for a dramatic fifth-inning homer into the upper deck in right field. It was his 2,000th career base hit.

Sportswriters sought him out, and he again used the occasion to speak out against the second-class status of Spanish-speaking players.

"The Latin American player doesn't get the recognition he deserves," he said in a wire service story that received nationwide play. "Neither does the Negro player, unless he does something really spectacular, like Willie Mays." It was common to hear political activists on the streets and campuses speak out on social issues, but it was a rare thing for a star athlete.

"We have self-satisfaction," he continued, "yes, but after the season is over, nobody cares about us. Zoilo Versalles was the most valuable player in the American League last year, but how many times has he been asked to make appearances at dinners or meetings during the winter? Juan Marichal is one of the greatest pitchers in the game, but does he get invited to banquets? I am an American citizen. I live not so far from Miami. But some people act like they think I live in the jungle someplace. To the people here, we are outsiders, foreigners."

Despite these bitter feelings, Clemente continued to perform, and back in his native Puerto Rico the question everyday was "*Qué hizo Clemente?*" What did Clemente do? As island sportswriter Rafael Pont Flores commented, "That question was asked more often in cities, towns, and hamlets in Puerto Rico than the daily queries about the results of the games."

One afternoon in September, as his friend, pitcher Al McBean, rubbed his neck in the dugout, he told a writer for the *New York Post*, "I am tired, tired, tired. Nobody but my wife knows how I feel. You know, I have such a hard time sleeping." To help him relax, the Pirates allowed Roberto to take a private room when the team was on the road. In previous years he had shared rooms with Gene Baker, a loud snorer, and Román Mejías and Al McBean, whose hanger-rattling when they tiptoed in was enough to awaken Roberto. By now his image as a hypochondriac had been so firmly engraved that the journalists, like most of his colleagues, made light of Clemente's troubles. One wrote, "Last year Clemente had touches of malaria and typhoid fever, a clinic of bruises and hurts, food poisoning, and insomnia. When all else fails, when his bones don't ache and his glands function perfectly, he always has that insomnia to fall back on. It is a comfort to him."

In the spring, manager Walker had told him, "Roberto, I wish this year you would go for power, hit 25 homers and get 115 runs batted in. We will need it for the pennant." The Pirates of 1966 fell a few games short, finishing in third place, but Clemente, the team player, had followed his manager's instructions. He hit 29 homers and drove in 119 runs for personal records in both categories. He also scored a career high of 105 runs, finished fifth in the league with a .317 batting average, and led outfielders in both leagues by throwing out seventeen base-runners. In late September, Walker said, "There's no question about it, Clemente has been the guts of this club. If he's not the league's most valuable player, I'm nuts." Several weeks later, the Baseball Writers of America confirmed

Walker's sanity, giving the MVP award to Roberto, ahead of Dodger pitcher Sandy Koufax, who had also enjoyed a fantastic year with 27 victories and 317 strikeouts. Roberto was the only candidate to appear on all twenty ballots cast by the two baseball writers in each city of the league, finishing with 218 votes to Koufax's 208.

Roberto was at the wheel of a bulldozer, landscaping a small farm that he had purchased in Puerto Rico, when reporters brought the news of his selection. "This is very relaxing," he said, patting the machine, "getting up at 5 A.M. and working like a laborer." Of the MVP award he said candidly, "It's the highest honor a player can hope for, but I was expecting it. Of course it could have gone to Sandy Koufax, but I had the best season of my career and I was confident that the sports writers would vote for me. I am thankful that they did."

Even more gratifying, he said, was the fact that he had also been named National League Player of the Year by *The Sporting News* in a vote by the ballplayers. "For one thing, I was selected by opponents. How would you say it? I was judged by my own peers, and one could hardly expect a greater satisfaction."

His fellow Puerto Ricans were ecstatic about the awards; it was the first time that a player from the baseball-happy island had been so honored. And Roberto understood the deep meaning of this. "When I was a kid I felt that baseball was great to America," he said. "Always, they said Babe Ruth was the best there was. They said you'd really have to be something to be like Babe Ruth. But Babe Ruth was an American player. What we needed was a Puerto Rican player they could say that about, someone to look up to and try to equal. Before I came here, you never had many outstanding players from the Caribbean. There were some good ones, like Miñoso, but no real outstanding player. I've had many good years. I've won the batting title three times and now I've won the MVP. This makes me happy because now the people feel that if I could do it, then they could do it. The kids have someone to look to and to follow. That's why I like to work with kids so much. I show them what baseball has done for me, and maybe they will work harder and try harder and be better men."

It had been a banner year for Latinos, who were now a major factor in big league baseball. Roberto was the first Spanish-speaking superstar, but others were also coming to the fore. His teammate Mateo Alou led the National League in hitting, and Mateo's brother Felipe of the Atlanta Braves, his chief rival, led in hits and runs scored. Other Latins among the top ten batters were Rico Carty of Philadelphia, also a Dominican, and Clemente's countryman Orlando Cepeda, who won the Most Valuable Player Award the next season. The league's leading pitcher was Juan Marichal, a Dominican, who won 25 games and lost only 6. Over in the American League Tony Oliva of Minnesota, a Cuban, had been the league's second best batter, and Bert Campaneris of Kansas City, another Cuban, led the league in stolen bases. By the next spring there would be seventy-five Latins on major league rosters, a jump of 50 per cent in a single year. But the road to the top for blacks and Latins was still by no means paved with roses. Base hits weren't all they had to concern themselves with. About that time black star Frank Robinson commented: "Conditions in Tampa [Florida] haven't changed to this day. It's downright cruel to send black rookies to places like that. A kid grows up dreaming of being a big leaguer. He's treated like a human being by the ball club, but when he steps out of the park he's lower than a mangy dog. His spirit is broken. It's a wonder he survives."

"This is the new Clemente," said Pirate first baseman Donn Clendenon as the 1967 season began. "He has great feelings for all the worries of the players. He keeps peace and harmony and he's our goodwill ambassador, the intermediary between us and Harry Walker and the front office."

"The first few years, Clemente was still fighting a battle within himself and for the Caribbean ballplayer," said Jim Pagliaroni, the Pirates' catcher since 1963. "He knew he had the desire and he knew he was great. But he was perplexed because some people didn't recognize this. Well, now they have, and you could see him change over the past couple of years. When he speaks in the clubhouse and on the field, everyone respects his word."

"It used to be that he rarely went out with us," said Roberto's friend, pitcher Al McBean. "He'd stay in his room, watch TV, order room service, and sleep. But now he goes out more often. He has changed, really changed."

Maturity and success had given the thirty-three-year-old Roberto more social confidence. Now he was an established superstar. That spring in Fort Myers, Harold "Pie" Traynor, the Hall of Fame third baseman who had starred for the Pirates in the 1920's, was asked, "How does Clemente rate with the best rightfielders in National League history?"

"He rates number one," said Traynor. Comparing him with Paul Waner, another Hall of Fame member who had played for Pittsburgh, Traynor said, "Waner was a great one, maybe a slightly better hitter for average than Clemente, good arm and good fielder, but I think Roberto has moved out in front of him in all departments."

And that year, in an autobiography, the great slugger Henry Aaron said of his rival, "Clemente . . . has no weakness. He's a lot stronger than he looks. He's got a batting style that's a little peculiar. He's got a little crouch in his stance, and when he swings at the ball his rear pops out and he looks like he's almost jumping at the ball. He always gets a lot of the fat part of the bat on the ball, though. . . . I admire Roberto Clemente as a ballplayer, and he's a friend of mine. I'm not going to get into any argument with him. Anybody who has led the National League in hitting as many times as he has can't be anything but great."

Despite Clemente's great 1967 season, the Pirates—who had finished a respectable third two years running—fell to sixth place. They led the league in batting, but the pitching staff collapsed, and Pittsburgh finished twenty games behind the pennant-winning Cardinals. Roberto, however, sustained his violent offensive. He won his fourth batting title with a .357 average, a personal record. This made him only the seventh player in history to win as many titles; the others were Ty Cobb (12 times), Honus Wagner, Rogers Hornsby, Stan Musial (seven times apiece), Ted Williams (six), and Harry Heilmann (four). He also led the league with 209 base hits and bested all outfielders with seventeen assists against enemy base-runners. That season, on May 15 in Cincinnati, Roberto enjoyed perhaps the finest single day of his career, but the Pirates lost 8 to 7 in ten innings. As one witness remarked, he was "a one-man gang," hitting three homers and a double and driving in all seven of the Pittsburgh runs. But he glumly told the writers, "I had a dream the other morning that I would hit three homers in a game and the dream came true. But this doesn't make me happy. It was my biggest game, but not my best game. My best game is when I drive in the winning run. I don't count this one, we lost."

Pirate coach Johnny Pesky, who played with Ted Williams on the Boston Red Sox, said he had never seen such a fearful display of power in one game. But again—after all these years—a writer popped the inevitable tiresome question: Did he model himself after Willie Mays? "I play like Roberto Clemente," he replied testily.

As he continued to punish the pitchers, some of them retaliated. After he hit a homer against Don Drysdale—the first of the season against the Los Angeles pitcher—he came to bat again and Drysdale whizzed a fastball past his ear. Roberto dug back in and sent the next pitch soaring into the stands for his second homer. But not all the pitchers missed. There seemed to be a vendetta against him and Maury Wills, another hot batsman who had been traded to the club that spring. A pitch by San Francisco's Ray Sadecki plowed into Wills's knee, putting him out of the game. "They let Sadecki take two shots at Wills," said manager Walker angrily. "He threw one right at his head on the first pitch and the umpires didn't do anything about it. Then, after he gets Maury in the knee, they give him a warning." Three days later, Saint Louis pitcher Larry Jaster struck Roberto on the elbow, and he, too, was out of commission. "They know we're hot and they started throwing at us," charged Walker.

Clemente continued his batting onslaught, but every so often he tired, and Walker gave him a couple of days' rest. His relatives in Puerto Rico, knowing that he was so injury prone, became concerned whenever his name did not appear in the box score in the San Juan newspapers. One morning, he received a phone call from his sister-in-law, who had just arrived in New York from the island. "How are you, Roberto?" she asked.

"Fine," said Roberto, a bit puzzled over the worried tone of her voice.

"Your name is not in the box scores, but if you say you're all right, then I'll let your parents know," she said.

That night, Clemente returned to the lineup and provoked headlines that let his parents know he felt fit. He hit two home runs against the Chicago Cubs and made a fantastic throw to stop a runner at home plate, helping the team to win a doubleheader. In one of those games, a Cubs rookie pitcher tried to get "cute," making Clemente lunge for bad pitches. One of those pitches, high and outside, was lined into the right-field seats.

By now he owned the most respected throwing arm in baseball, but every so often runners tried to challenge it. In a game against Saint Louis, his compatriot Orlando Cepeda—who should have known better—tried to reach home from second base on a single. Standing deep in the right field corner of Forbes Field, Roberto threw him out with a perfect, no-bounce strike to the catcher. An inning later, the speedy Curt Flood tried to score from first on a double, and he, too, was gunned down. Flabbergasted, Flood later said, "I didn't dream Clemente would try for me from that far out!"

But his phenomenal batting is what drew the most attention, and soon the writers sought him out as an oracle on hitting. He seemed to be the man most likely to reach the "magic" .400 batting mark; the last hitter to do so was Ted Williams, who registered .406 in 1941. "Nobody will ever hit .400," Clemente said. "We play too many games. We don't rest enough. Got to be strong to hit .400, but nobody can be strong enough with this schedule." Years ago, he said, the teams traveled by train and stayed for several weeks in one region of the country. Now they crisscrossed the continent in jets. Mentioning a recent trip from Pittsburgh to Los Angeles, he said, "After a night game, you go to to bed at 1 o'clock there, but it is really 4 o'clock in your head because we come from the East. That is what I mean about resting. Even when you think you're resting, you're really not." The .400 hitters, he added, had been in their heyday when baseball was played strictly in sunshine. "I don't see the ball well," he said. "In the daytime, it is all right, but at night it's bad. I have to crouch down and look like this to see the pitcher throw."

Despite all the adulation, he was unhappy because the team was losing. "The only time I get happy is winning a game, or better, winning a pennant." Referring to the first-place San Francisco team, he said, "I'd like to have the lead the Giants have. My father in Puerto Rico always say, 'The ox that walks in front of the others always gets to drink the clear water.' " But the waters were roiled and muddy for the Pirates. As they continued to lose, Roberto complained that some teammates were not giving their best. "There are a few players on this team who can be blamed for our poor showing. They know who they are." He refused to name them but insisted that the Pirates would not "be where we are today" were it not for some slackers. It is a tradition in baseball that when a club fares poorly the manager receives his walking papers. And in mid-July the Pirates fired Harry Walker and brought back Danny Murtaugh to finish out the year. Memories of the old Clemente-Murtaugh feud were revived by the writers, but Roberto quickly squelched them. "I play for any manager," he said. Murtaugh, chewing placidly on a jaw full of Beech-Nut Tobacco, responded that he didn't think he would have any trouble getting along with a .350 hitter.

That same month an incident occurred that wounded Roberto's pride and sustained his conviction that he and other Latin American players were not given the respect that they deserved. A segment of the film comedy *The Odd Couple* was to be shot at New York's Shea Stadium, just when the Pirates were in town, and the producers had asked members of both teams to take part. Roberto was offered $100 to appear, and he was under the impression that it was a documentary which would be shown to children. He did not know that the script called for him to hit into a triple play in a comedy. According to a story in the *New York Daily News*, Roberto learned the true nature of the film the night before shooting was to begin.

"I am in the hotel with Matty Alou and he ask me how much the movie people gonna pay me for being in big famous picture. I tell Alou they gonna pay me one hundred dollars. Then Alou, he laughs. He say I'm foolish. He say I should get one thousand dollars. I think it over for minute. I tell Alou that he is right." Growing angrier, Clemente said, "Alou says he knows all about the picture and it will make much money. I get mad. I would be in a movie for *nothin'*. But not for a hundred dollars. Would they ask Cary Grant to play baseball for one hundred dollars?" He grew even more furious when he learned that the script called for him to hit into a triple play. "They will show it in Latin America. They insult me. What will fans think? They will not understand."

The next day, out on the field, a director holding a megaphone and wearing a baseball cap walked up to Roberto, wrapped an arm around his shoulder and said, "Hiya, Roberto, how's my old buddy?"

Glaring at the man, Roberto said, "I am not old, and I ain't gonna be in your stinkin' movie. How you like that, old buddy?" The man's face turned red, and he scurried off the field, in search of the producer. Minutes later, Roberto stood in the batting cage. Still angry, he took his final swing and slammed the ball 440 feet over the left-center field wall. Turning and shouting to one of the film cameramen, he said, "Hey, take a picture of that home run and put it in your stinkin' picture. You can have it for nothin'."

His outburst was not just due to the film, but over a long career of being ignored or undervalued. As *Time* magazine said the year before, "All told, Clemente has three batting titles to his credit— but nobody has ever asked him to do a shaving-cream commercial." Again, it was not the money, but the man's pride.

Evidence showed that Roberto's angry attitude was not without foundation. In 1968, blacks and dark-skinned Latinos comprised more than 20 percent of all big-league baseball rosters, 26 percent of football rosters, and 44 percent of those in basketball. But, according to a study by the U.S. Equal Employment Opportunity Commission, they appeared in only 5 percent of the TV commercials that featured sports figures that year.

The Rand Corporation also issued a study with intriguing results. It noted that blacks and Latinos drew *higher* salaries than their white colleagues in major league baseball. But there was a reason. The career batting averages of players active during the 1967 season showed that blacks averaged .262, compared with .245 for whites—a 17-point difference. Black pitchers averaged 10.2 wins per season, compared with 7.5 wins for whites. The Rand study concluded *not* that whites are inferior but that, "on the average," a black must be better than a white player in order to make the big leagues. The low number of blacks and Latinos in jobs such as coaching, managing, and umpiring, said the study, "is difficult to explain on grounds other than racial bias." The study did not touch upon one very important aspect of baseball: the "image-makers" who write about the game. Although about one-fifth of the major leagues' 500 players are black or Latino, it is hard to find a single person from these ethnic groups in the press box. Not only are the vast majority of sportswriters white, but they are also middle-aged; their world view was shaped before Jackie Robinson entered baseball in 1947. By contrast, many players today were *born* after that date.

Dark-skinned Latino players feel that they are at the lowest rung of the ladder. Dominican pitching star Juan Marichal said in 1967, "Our skins may be lighter in some cases, but the breaks we get from baseball and on the outside are much less than even the American Negro gets." And in a private conversation Clemente once told a friend of his, "Here in America, I'm a 'double nigger,' for my skin and my Spanish heritage."

"C'mon Dago—"

Anthony Joseph "Tony" Bartirome sits atop the trainer's table at the Pirate clubhouse in Bradenton, Florida—the same table where for several springs he massaged away the aches and pains of the good friend he called Bobby. Tony, born in Pittsburgh in 1932, is of medium height and has typically Latin olive-colored skin and slick black hair. He played professional baseball for eleven years, including one summer in the majors as the Pirates' first baseman, and proudly holds a club record for having hit into the fewest double plays, none, in a full season. He has been the team trainer since 1963, and his uniform is a pair of slacks and a tee shirt.

Everybody knows what kind of ballplayer Bobby was, but I'll miss him most as a man. He was probably the best friend I ever had in this game.

On the buses and planes, in the clubhouse, he was a joy to be around, so happy all the time, always looking for something to laugh about. He had something going with each player. It's kind of unique in baseball when a person—especially a superstar like him—can get along so well with twenty-five different players. I've never heard anybody talk about Clemente being aloof. Any time a guy would be going bad—say, Oliver or Cash—next day you'd see Clemente sitting by his locker, talkin' to him. Nobody else around, just *reeeel* quiet talk. Players on other teams used to come to Clemente and ask, "What am I doin' wrong?" He'd *tell* 'em no matter what it cost our club—that guy could beat us a ballgame—but none of our players felt bad when he tried to help somebody. That's the way he was.

We had some real times on the road. We played poker on every plane trip. It was Blass, Giusti, Sanguillen, Davalillo . . . and Mateo Alou when he was here. They were all makin' real good money and as a trainer I'm just an average paid person. Lots of times—I love to play poker—I couldn't *afford* to play with those guys. Clemente would say, "C'mon, dago, c'mon over here and play."

"No, I can't afford it."

"Here! You play!"

He'd give me money to play with. I had nothing to lose. All I could do was win! He never let me sit out a game.

Money just didn't mean that much to him. In fact, he was very forgetful about it. One time, right here in this clubhouse at Pirate City, he was rushing out onto the field. He was always late. He would always put his glove atop his head, pull his pants up, and then quickly tie his belt, back when we used belts. One day he opened an envelope real fast, glanced at it and says, "Here, hold this check for me!" I just grabbed it, folded it up and put it into my pocket, together with my gauze pads and bandages. Heck, I forgot all about it. A week or so later he comes in and says, "Hey, you got my check?" "What check?" "That check I gave you the other day." "Oh, yeah!" I looked in my pocket, and sure enough. I'd completely forgotten, and he had, too. It was a check for $25,000, and I'd been carrying it around all that time! Another time, it was the night before we went on a seventeen-day road trip to the coast. We would all get meal money for road trips. Clemente, late again, is rushin' out onto the field. "Here," he says, and hands me an envelope. I put it in the same pocket I always do, with my gauze pads and stuff. Every day I take my uniform off after the game, hang it as is in the locker, and the next day when I put on a fresh uniform I just switch the stuff in the pockets. It must've been ten days later, after ten different uniform changes, that I notice the envelope and wonder what the hell is this? Clemente's name is on it. Oh, hell. That night, when he came to the park, I walk up to him and ask, "Did you get your meal money before we went on the trip?" "Yeah, I got my meal money." He walked away. It was about $240. "No you didn't, *I've* got it." "Naaah." "Here! It's got your name on it. It's your meal money." "Oh, yeah, yeah. Forgot all about it."

It used to really piss me off when the writers called Clemente
a hypochondriac. I tried over the years with many writers and an-
nouncers to clarify a lot of those things about Roberto's injuries,
but it seems to have gone right over their heads. Every time he was
injured—*every time*—you would read this hypochondriac bit, about
him always being injured, always being out of the lineup. Well, any
man that can hold the Pirates' all-time record for games played in
no way can be a hypochondriac. A hypochondriac is a man who is
constantly afraid of illness, who can't perform, and Mr. Clemente
performed, and he performed as well as, if not better than, any player
in this game's history.

He had a chronic back. You can talk to a hundred people who've
never had back trouble and they'll say, "Aw, you mean Clemente
can't play baseball with a body like he has?" But you talk to one
person who has a chronic back, like myself—I can't get outta bed
some mornings, it takes me maybe thirty or forty minutes, there's
no *way* I can play baseball. Any person with lower back trouble will
tell you what he went through. The muscles in his back used to get
so rigid and so tense that it took two and three days of constant
moist heat, and rubbing, and adjusting, to loosen 'em. I've seen him
go out on the field and play when he shouldn't have, when 99 percent of the players in both leagues wouldn't have gone *near* a ballpark.
But he did. He missed the All-Star game last year because of the
Achilles' tendon on his right foot. He played baseball *hard* and ran
as fast as he could. You overextend a tendon or a muscle and it's
gonna pull. Once the Achilles' tendon gets tight and sore, you should
not play until it goes back to normal. His was so tight it was in
danger of snapping. That's why he missed the All-Star Game in 1972.
But I defy any sportswriter in the country to tell me of a game
where they saw Clemente loaf. I defy them. I've seen him hit ground
balls to shortstop, to second base, to the pitcher, and run his *ass* off
to first, because there's always the chance the man'll hurry the throw
a little and throw it away. But I've seen other big stars hit ground
balls that maybe would be in doubt, and dog it to first base. That's
why on our ballclub we don't have players that loaf. I've seen one
young guy on another club who was great last year—he used to *fly*
down to first base. Now, he hits one and trots to first. Why? Because he's just acting the way the stars on his club act. But our kids

hustle all the time, because there's no other way. You've got to play Clemente Baseball.

How many people just shit on him because he was so nice? He couldn't refuse anybody. He used to rub down some of the players. At first he thought I'd mind, but I'd say, "No, you know more about it than I do!" Which he did. He studied about the spine, the muscles in the back. He was gonna open a clinic, and he told me, "I want you to come down and work for me in the wintertime." I'd say, "Bobby, please be careful, There's a lot of people who'll come to you, you'll work on 'em, and they'll claim that you hurt 'em. There's a lot of bad people in the world." He would never believe that! He couldn't believe that anyone would try to deliberately hurt him. He'd kid me, "Aw, don't worry, you dagos, you're always suspicious."

Bobby and Dr. Finegold, our team physician, were great friends, but they had their fights now and then. He had some back trouble and wanted to see Mister García in Puerto Rico. He had great faith in the man. How many people won't go to a specialist they have faith in? So he gets permission from Mr. Brown, the general manager, and leaves for Puerto Rico. Dr. Finegold was talking with one of the sportswriters off the cuff, and he felt very hurt about Bobby leaving. So he was quoted as saying "I'll never work on Clemente again." He might've said it, but he didn't really mean it. When Clemente gets back they show him the clipping from the newspaper and I think, "Oh hell, I hope Bobby don't get mad." He comes over and says to me, "What's this about Dr. Finegold?" He had that frowning look on his face and I say, "Aw, Bobby, you know how guys talk." He walks away and doesn't say a thing. "Jeez," I think, "I hope he's not mad." I see him with a marking pencil and a big piece of paper He's writing and writing. He was taping the paper up on his locker when I come over to read it. It said: "IN CASE OF AN ACCIDENT, NOTIFY A PRIEST OR A PUERTO RICAN DOCTOR." Everybody in the clubhouse cracked up, Finegold, too.

Another time, last summer, they had a full-size statue of Bobby. It's frightening because it looks so much like him. I don't know if it's right to tell this story now, with everything that's happened, but it was one of Bobby's favorites. He told it a thousand times and every time we were with some friends he'd say to me, *"Tell him the story, tell him the story."* Anyway, the statue had a cap, uniform, everything. Joe O'Toole, the assistant to the general manager, brings the statue in from the field and says, "Where can I put this?" "Put it in the back room," I say. So he lays it on the table in this dark room of the clubhouse at Three Rivers Stadium. He threw a blanket over it and all you could see was the right arm and the face. In the dark it looked *exactly* like Bobby. So I say, "Hey, Joe, let's stick Doctor Finegold." You see, Clemente had been sick with a virus for about three weeks, and he was still a bit sick. So Finegold comes walking in and I say, "Hey, Doc, goddamn, we gotta do something. Bobby's had a relapse. He's lying in the back room, with a blanket over him." Me and O'Toole walk back there with him. We open the door and the only light is from the clubhouse behind us. It's real dim. Finegold walks in and says, real loud, "Roberto, m'boy, how you feeling? Heard you had a relapse, eh?" He grabs his wrist to take his pulse, and this statue is made out of cold wax. "You'll be okay . . . oh . . . oh . . . oh . . . my God!" Me and O'Toole started *laughing*, and Finegold's heart was pounding like one of those old locomotives! Now, some of the guys take the statue and put it on the trainer's table. Clemente comes in from the field. He didn't care about the players or us joking about it. He was worried about the sportswriters. They were taking pictures of it, so finally I had to lock the statue up because it was getting out of hand. Clemente was really mad. I heard him tell Pagan in Spanish, "I'm gonna get a bat and break that fuckin' statue." So I hid it right away, because it's really beautiful. So now Bobby's mad. But two days later, I say "Hey, you still mad?" "Naw," he says. "Now I gotta tell you a story." So I told him all about Finegold, and he made me repeat that story right there about three or four times. He never stopped kidding Finegold about it.

On this club there's always been plenty of kidding, some of it pretty rough. It was nothing to hear somebody yell, "Hey, you nigger!" or "wop," or "dago." They authentically *liked* each other, and the tougher the insult the more affection there was behind it. It really started at the end of 1969, when they got close-knit. I never heard words like that before, but by the end of '69 they started to realize they had a good group of guys, and you never so much as heard one real argument. But if you walked by our clubhouse just before game time, you'd think they were going to *kill* each other! In 1971, when we won the World Series, there was all kinds of rumors about Richie Hebner being stabbed by Dave Cash, or Stargell and Clemente in a fistfight that was broken up by Robertston. All *kinds* of things. It got to a point where every time a strange sportswriter came into the clubhouse, someone in the corner would holler, "Fight! Fight! He's got a knife. He's gonna cut him!" I mean really. "Hey, kill that sonofabitch! That fuckin' nigger!" They jacked those sportswriters off all year about that. Hebner was sitting in a bar one night. There was this guy and his wife next to him, telling the bartender about Richie Hebner being stabbed by Dave Cash. The bartender knew Hebner, but Richie just sits there, listening. The bartender asks, "Where did Cash stab him?" "Right in the back," the guy says. "That's why he was in the hospital in Cincinnati." Actually, he'd been in the hospital with a viral infection of the heart lining. So Hebner finally gets up at the bar and says, "Do you know who I am?" The guy looks at him and says,. "Yeah! You're Richie Hebner!" Richie takes his shirt off and says, "Look, where's the hole again? Well, maybe he stabbed me in the ass. Want me to take my pants down?" He goes to do it and the guy yells, "No! No! My wife!"

We kidded around plenty on that club, and Roberto loved every minute of it. He would tell me, "My name, Clemente, is an Italian name! My great-grandfather, he used to make wine in Italy!" "Yeah, yeah," I'd say.

8

"I'm lucky to be alive. I could have been killed in that fall," Roberto said, referring to a freak mishap at his home in Puerto Rico in February 1968.

"My home is on a steep hill," he explained. "We have two patios. I was climbing down a wall from one to the other. I have these iron bars on the back of my house; they are about three inches around and four feet long. I called to my wife Vera that I was going to lift myself up to the back porch; just as she came out the back door, I grabbed the iron bar and it gave way. It almost fell on my chest, and crushed me. I fell backwards and somehow pushed the bar off and began to roll down the hill behind my house. I must have rolled seventy-five or a hundred feet until another wall stopped me. I went over on my shoulder several times, but the bar didn't hit me. If it had—"

After the accident, Roberto consulted with a doctor who told him he must wear a brace for three months, but he ignored the diagnosis. Nor did he call Joe Brown in Pittsburgh. "I didn't want you to worry," he later explained. When he reported late for spring training, the press was told that he was delayed because Vera's mother was ill. When he finally reached Fort Myers, he related the truth to Brown and to Larry Shepard, the Pirates' new manager. Nothing was said to the press, but his batting average spoke more eloquently than words. During spring training, Roberto went through a barren stretch of twenty-nine times at bat without a hit. After the season opened, sensitive to wisecracks over the years that he imagined his ailments, he refused to offer excuses. "No power, no power," is all that he said in those early weeks of April. "Do not write that Clemente is in pain. But when I swing a bat I feel weak." Finally, on May 3, he was benched for a few days, with a batting average of .216. The writers nagged him with queries about how a .357 hitter the previous year could nosedive so miserably. At that time, he told them about the fall.

By midseason, his condition had hardly improved; he was batting .245 and for the first time in nine years was not chosen to play in the All-Star Game. In addition to his aching shoulder, he was knocked flat by a siege of flu in June and lost eleven pounds. When reporters sought his comments, he obstinately replied, "I don't want to alibi. Anything I say will seem like an alibi." Only rarely did he let loose with a Clemente-style throw from the outfield. He brooded about his future. Dr. Thomas Tutko, a clinical psychologist who worked with the Pirates that season, said, "No one drives himself like Clemente. I've never seen a more intense person." During one breakfast interview with a reporter, he stared at his scrambled eggs and said with a sigh, "For two nights I don't sleep. I see the sunrise. I try to think nice things about my childhood, but my mind runs like a movie. I worry because I don't feel strong. I'm tired and I'm not hitting good. I'm not getting any younger." That night, after a plane trip to Saint Louis, he hurried to his hotel and tried once more to sleep. But, as he later related, after an hour's deep slumber he awoke, his body drenched with sweat, his ribs hurting. He had been dreaming about death. During the game that night, he hit two singles but sprained an ankle while sliding. In the clubhouse he pressed an ice pack against the sore ankle and asked *Life* magazine reporter David Wolf, "I wonder sometimes, is it worth the sacrifice? I know my wife wants to go out. My kids want to go to the zoo. But I got to say no. I got to rest. But this year—I don't concentrate the same way. I'm not getting any younger." Later, in his hotel room—it was practically morning—he flicked on the *Late Late Show*, holding the ice pack against his ankle, trying to relax. "Maybe I'm too serious," he philosophized. "People say I'm moody. But if I don't take care of myself, I'm stealing people's money. My conscience wouldn't stand that."

By mid-August, Roberto had raised his average to .277—still eighty points below his previous year. The future looked dim. "I won't play next year if the shoulder keeps hurting like it does now," he told a reporter in Pittsburgh. Despite his injuries, he managed to play in 132 games and boosted his average to just nine points shy of the .300 mark—a fine year for almost any player, but not for a four-time batting champion. That winter, at home in Puerto Rico, he sat down with Vera and talked about retirement. But Vera knew how much he loved the game and said, "Never quit when you're down. You have to give it another try. If you want to quit after another year, I won't say a word."

He relaxed at home, playing with the children, puttering around the house, toying with his hobby of ceramics. One day, while walking along a quiet stretch of beach, he found a large hunk of driftwood and took it home. Soon he had painted it, polished it up, and created an attractive adornment for his home. A few of his friends thought Roberto had gone *loco*. "They don't see what I see," he said. "They don't feel what I feel. They say it's just a piece of wood. The beach is full of pieces of wood, but no piece of driftwood is like another. You can take it and shape it and it is your own. It is you. You can make it part of your personality."

As late as February 1969, Roberto—approaching his thirty-fifth birthday—still entertained the possibility of retiring. But that month he flew to New York for a meeting of the Major League Players' Association, and sentiment won out over tired flesh. "As soon as I saw the other players and got talking about baseball," he said, "I knew I wanted to keep on playing." The players were embroiled in a dispute with the club owners over the proper share of the World Series receipts that should go to their pension fund. Marvin Miller, executive director of the Players' Association, had written to all players asking them not to sign their contracts while negotiations were underway. The chance of a strike seemed very real. Roberto, who was the player representative of the Pirates that season, joined with other stars, such as Bob Gibson and Dennis McLain, in supporting the Association's militant stand.

"There are rumors that the owners may decide to start the season with minor leaguers, but who is going to pay to see them play?" he asked. "They will play before empty parks, and that is not good for the owners . . . I don't know why they're so fussy about the whole thing. We just want our part of the revenue from the World Series TV proceeds. They make a lot of money out of that, and it all goes to their pot, nothing for us." The owners made a flat offer of $1 million to the pension fund, but the players demanded $2.9 million. "They can take all the money they get from radio and TV during the regular season," he said. "The World Series is all that matters to us. We want $1.9 million more than what they have offered, and if they do not give it to us, then we will not sign, or even go to training camp."

At the last minute, a compromise settlement was reached, and Roberto reported to Bradenton, Florida—the Pirates had chosen to train at a new site after thirteen years at Fort Myers. He felt fit, but on March 15—while giving the old Clemente try for a fly ball—he crashed into the right-field fence of the Bradenton ballpark and injured his left shoulder. Pirate physician Joseph Finegold recommended heat treatments and a few days' rest, but after a week Roberto was still hurting. He decided that his old friend Arturo Garcia in Puerto Rico should look at the injury. This upset Finegold, and in a fit of pique—as Clemente flew southward to San Juan—the doctor told a reporter: "Clemente better not complain to me about his shoulder again. He can just go back to that doctor in Puerto Rico. I'm sick and tired of listening to his complaints." Days later, Clemente and Finegold would renew their friendship, but the outburst made good copy and the sports editors played it for all it was worth.

After four days of having his shoulder warmed and kneaded by Garcia, Roberto flew back and rejoined the Pirates one Sunday in Miami. As he stood near the first base dugout before an exhibition game with the Baltimore Orioles, a television newswoman from Pittsburgh asked to interview him. The man started with a vague reference to recent accusations that Clemente was not being a team player. It was like throwing a lighted match on kerosene. What began as a quiet tête-à-tête soon brought the entire press corps running as Clemente in angry tones bellowed, "You say, maybe I'm no team player. I win four batting titles. I *kill* myself in the outfield. I try to catch everything in the ballpark. I play when I hurt. In fifteen seasons I never miss an opening game. What more do you writers want from me?" Scowling and spitting into the dark pocket of his leather glove, he asked, "Did any ballplayer ever come up to you and say I'm no team player? Who say that? The writers, right?"

As the reporters crowded around and a tape recorder whirred, he grew even angrier. "Well, I'll tell you one thing, the more I can stay away from the writers, the better I am. You know why? Because they are trying to create a bad image for me. You know what they have against me? Because I am black and Puerto Rican. I am *proud* to be Puerto Rican."

A reporter interrupted to say that some superstars played despite their injuries.

"They say American superstar Mickey Mantle . . . he's *limping*," Roberto said in mocking tones. "*Poor* Mickey, you put Mickey up like God in the sky. It's a lot of *bunk*. I play with four stitches in my foot, but nobody know about it. The American people have their idols. Look at Marichal, a Dominican. When Sandy Koufax was pitching, Koufax was best, and, maybe, Marichal was second-best. That wasn't true. Koufax was *never* the pitcher Marichal was, but he is the big star because he comes from this country. But who says Koufax is best? The damn press, that's who."

Clemente had cooled down after the game, but his temper flared again when a reporter asked whether he didn't regret this outburst, particularly since it was taken down on a tape recorder.

"I don't *care* about the tape recorder. I said those things because I believe what I said." Then, glancing with disdain over at members of a TV crew who were chatting in the clubhouse, he said, "There's a station in Pittsburgh which has said *three times* on the air that I'm not a team player. Now I ask you: What is a team player? That's a bunch of *bull*."

Was Clemente just being a "touchy Latin," as some writers said privately, or did his complaints have foundation? A poll taken by a major wire service asked fans nationwide to choose the Player of the Decade, baseball's most outstanding performer in the years between 1960 and 1969. Their first choice was Sandy Koufax. In second place was Mickey Mantle. Willie Mays was third, Henry Aaron fourth, and Roberto Clemente was a distant *ninth*. Hard-hitting Frank Robinson was even farther back.

Koufax, the winner, had a pitching record of 137 victories and 58 losses during the decade. Juan Marichal, the Dominican pitcher, won 191 games and lost 88 during the same period but was far back in the voting.

As for the hitters, here is how they fared during the ten seasons of 1960 through 1969:

	Runs	HR	RBI	B.A.
Clemente	916	177	862	.328
Aaron	1091	375	1107	.308
Mays	1050	350	1067	.299
Robinson	1013	316	1011	.298
Mantle	683	256	668	.282

By no criterion could Mantle—who had enjoyed his best years in the decade of the 1950's—be rated above the other batsmen in the 1960's. How could the fans have such a distorted view of what had really happened during the decade?

In an interview shortly after the results of the poll were announced, base-stealing champion Maury Wills commented: "A player is generally underrated only by the fans and by the writers—not the players, coaches, and managers. There are a lot of reasons. It helps to play in New York or on the West Coast, where the publicity trumpets blow the loudest." Wills was asked to select the nine most underrated players in baseball, and five of them—including Clemente and Marichal—were Latinos. Of the great Dominican pitcher, he said, "A lot of hitters don't talk up Marichal. They dislike him for making them look bad, almost humiliating them. Marichal stands out there on the mound with a kind of cocky smile on his face, like he's saying 'there's no way you can hit me.'" Clemente, Wills said, was as great a fielder "as anyone in baseball," and "when it comes to hitting, I think he's the only batter in our league who is a real match for Bob Gibson." He then asked, rhetorically, "Could it be that fans underrate Latins because the writers don't talk so often to the Spanish-speaking players, and therefore you don't read as much about them? And could it also be that the fans don't make heroes out of players from foreign countries because they can't identify with them?"

Early in the 1969 season, while Roberto's shoulder was still healing, he added a new injury during a game against the Mets at Forbes Field. While chasing after a foul fly, he smashed against the wall and pulled a muscle in his left thigh. A large lump formed on the thigh. Playing in pain a few days later, he heard his hometown fans boo him for the first time in many years. There were a few catcalls when he struck out in the first inning, and more when he grounded into double plays his next two times at bat. When he came to bat in the eighth inning—after letting a single bounce through his legs for an error a few moments before—the boos rang in his ears. Then he did a surprising thing. He tipped his cap to the crowd, and suddenly there was an explosion of cheers. They were still cheering when the umpire indicated "ball four" and he trotted to first base. "I wasn't trying to be smart with the fans when I lifted my cap," he said later in the clubhouse. "If my mother and father punished me when I was a boy, I would never raise my hand against them. The fans have always been kind to me. When I had trouble with my back in 1956, they were the ones who gave me the lift I needed. And if they figure I have it coming to me now, then they have the right to boo. I was just trying to show them that it was all right with me."

In the month of May, Roberto was hitting only .242 and still felt pains in his thigh and shoulder. Could anything else possibly happen to him? Yes. He was abducted by bandits in San Diego. The episode was so bizarre that it was not made public until a year later, but a suspicious reporter checked with San Diego police, whose records confirmed the incident. After a night game, Roberto strolled out of his San Diego hotel and saw teammate Willie Stargell eating a piece of fried chicken. When he inquired where he could buy some, Stargell directed him to a place a few blocks away. As he walked back to the hotel, gingerly holding the container of hot chicken in his hand, a car with four men pulled over to the curb and a man with a gun ordered him to get in. One of the men had a tic on one side of his face. "It made him seem like he was smiling all the time. I never forget that face, if I see it again." At least one of the thieves spoke Spanish. Fifteen minutes later, the frightened Roberto saw the car stop in an isolated mountainous area. The men ordered him to remove all of his clothes except for his undershorts. They took his All-Star Game ring and his wallet with $250 in cash, most of it the winnings from a recent trip to the racetrack.

"I figured they were going to shoot me. They already had the pistol inside my mouth," he recalled.

Fearing for his life, Clemente told them he was a major league ballplayer and asked them to look in his wallet for his membership card in the Baseball Players' Association. Perhaps the thieves were fans of his. Whatever the reason, they returned his clothes. "Don't forget to put on your tie, we want you to look good," one of them said. Minutes later, they deposited him on the sidewalk near the hotel. As he headed toward the entrance, he heard a car approach. Them again.

"I started looking around for a rock, but I couldn't find one."

The car pulled up next to him, and one of the thieves said, "Here, we forgot this." It was the container of fried chicken.

Roberto regained his batting eye at about the time of the San Diego abduction, and in the final 111 games of that season he sustained a torrid .373 average, helping the Pirates to climb three notches to third place in the league.

By August, he was swinging his heavy bat like a young man again. He walloped three home runs in a single game. Indeed, he might have won his fifth batting title were it not for a two-week stretch in September when he developed a severe sinus infection that left him weak and bleary-eyed. The Pirates had played in the rain one afternoon and he was soaked to the skin. The next morning his head throbbed and he was running a fever. "Go see a doctor," Vera advised. "I'll see the doctor at the ballpark," he told her as he left. Expecting her husband to be home soon, Vera flicked on the radio and was surprised to hear that he was in the lineup. "How can you play?" she asked when he came in, sniffling, several hours later. "They say try, so I try," he said, shrugging his shoulders. Between September 6 and September 20, as he and Pete Rose of Cincinnati were locked in a two-man race for the batting championship,

Roberto managed only nine hits in 44 times at bat. His morale was not lifted when he heard recurring rumors that manager Larry Shepard favored the idea of trading him to another club to secure a few younger players. (It was Shepard, however, who would be released during the last week of the season.) With just one week remaining in the season, Cleon Jones of the New York Mets led the league in batting with a .346 average. Tight on his heels was Pete Rose of Cincinnati with .344. And Roberto was a relatively distant third, with .335. But, aroused by the vision of his fifth batting crown, he got three hits in a doubleheader against Philadelphia and six more in three games against Chicago. This moved him past the fading Jones with just two games left in the season. On October 1, against the Montreal Expos, he got two more hits. The next day was the final game of the year, with the Pirates playing against Montreal and Cincinnati ending up in Atlanta. Only a miracle could gain the championship for Roberto. He got three hits, giving him an astounding .538 average over the final seven games, and a .345 average for the season. But this left him three points short of the hustling Rose, who on his final at-bat of the season bunted for a single.

Throughout that long summer of 1969, despite the fact that Roberto had re-established himself as one of the game's finest hitters, he insisted that he was not afforded the same lofty status as white star athletes.

"Things are changing a bit," he conceded to Phil Musick, a Pittsburgh writer, "but I still feel that we—Latin players, American Negroes—are foreign to white American writers." To illustrate his point, he said, "When Martin Luther King died, they come and ask the Negro players if we should play. When President Kennedy dies, I cry in my heart. But King is a great leader, too. When they come to me I say, 'If you have to ask Negro players [that question], then we do not have a great country.'"

Despite Roberto's anguish over the state of American journalism, racism, and other broad social issues, his personal relationships with members of the Pirate team became warmer, deeper, and more rewarding. He was years past being the uncertain rookie and was now the rock-solid center of the team. He had close friendships with some of the players, and at least some kind of comic "bit" going with virtually everyone on the team.

One of his favorite Pirates was Steve Blass, whom Roberto affectionately called *loquito*, the little crazy one. Blass, who claims to be not only the *first* major leaguer from Falls Village, Connecticut, but also "the *only* person ever to leave Falls Village," became a full-time Pirate in 1966, and soon developed into one of the club's finest pitchers.

"I always used to kid Robby about how I'd pitch to him if I ever got traded," he recalls. "'Robby, I'd throw to you inside and take my chances, 'cause I *know* you're going to hit .350 if I throw outside, where everybody else does.' He'd point his finger at me and say, 'Blass, if you pitch me inside, I will hit forty-three home runs a year, thirty-seven of them off you!'"

"A lot of people didn't realize the fun Roberto had, especially in the last five years of his career," Blass says.

"Maybe some of his own sensitivities relaxed a bit; maybe it was because we were finally becoming a good ball club. On the airplane trips, we'd play cards a lot. The six or seven of us that played would confiscate a few rows of seats and get out the blankets, and everybody had to bring change. The guys who played that afternoon would get the most comfortable seats, facing ahead, and us pitchers who hadn't worked had to lean over the other seats, facing down. From Pittsburgh to Los Angeles that can get a bit tiresome! Robby would invariably have a corner seat. It was really something to watch him trying to eat dinner and play seven-card stud at the same time, getting his money out, trying to drink a cup of coffee and, every once in a while, he'd interrupt the game and give us a clinic on how we should have played a particular hand.

"I think his favorite time of day in the ballpark," says Blass, "was the time between when we finished infield practice and when the game started. For night games, that would be between 7:35 P.M. *and* 8:05 P.M. He'd lie flat on the trainer's table, and I'd sneak under there when Tony was rubbing his back and do a 'Mission Impossible' tape, just a lot of nonsense, like, 'Good morning, Mister Clemente, this is your neck. Your assignment today will be to go three-for-four against Jack Billingham with a bases-loaded double, and throw out two runners at third base. In five seconds, this tape will self-destruct. Phssssssssst!' He knew it was me all the time, but he'd look around, making believe he was trying to figure out where the noise was coming from.

"We sometimes got pretty light-hearted, and when Robby got involved there was always a crowd. You knew something really funny was happening. But I never saw anybody so much aware of who came in that clubhouse door. He was concerned that if media people were there, it could be taken out of context and the feeling between the players would be lost. But when we were alone, oh, gee, he and Tony would agitate each other back and forth and then Giusti would come in and they'd get going about the Puerto Ricans versus the Italians, *screaming*, and just loving every minute of it. But despite all the kidding, Roberto always insisted that you must never lose your dignity. 'Tony,' he'd say, 'lose everything else, but never lose your dignity.' He'd say it in a half-kidding tone, but you *knew* he meant it."

"We were always friendly," says Bill Mazeroski, who joined the Pirates in 1956, "but we became really close in the last few years. He liked to talk about some of the long balls he'd hit, and he'd always tell the younger kids, 'Ask Maz, he was there.' They'll ask, and I'll say, 'Nah, he didn't hit that one very good.' And he'll go grumping around about that 'dumb Polack doesn't know what he's talking about.' "

The Pirates added some promising new talent to the club in 1969. There was Richie Hebner, a voluble hard-hitting infielder whose father supervised an old Jewish cemetery outside Roxbury, Massachusetts. "In a good winter I'll dig fifty graves. It's good work. I get twenty-five bucks a grave." He told of one winter day when the ground was so hard that he decided, "Aw, that's deep enough. There's a law that a grave's got to be so deep, five feet or some-thing, and the rabbi says, 'That's not deep enough.' So I ask him, 'Did you ever see one get out?' "

When he first came up, Hebner recalls, "Me and some of the other new guys were probably making the minimum, $12,500, and here's Clemente, a guy making $150,000. Some guys who make this money might dog it a bit, but when *he* hit one back even to the pitcher he'd run to first like the cops were chasin' him! I remember thinkin' to myself, 'Hell, if *that* guy can do it, I'm gonna do it.' Let me tell you, it's hard to go out there every day, but once Clemente crossed over the white line onto the field, I think his philosophy was: If you're going to go half-ass, no sense doing it. Maybe he made mistakes when he was younger, but in my years with him I don't think he made a handful of mental mistakes. He threw to the right base, hit the cut-off man, took the extra base when he should, hit behind the runner, sacrificed himself at the plate. Guy on second, he'd hit the ball and move the runner along. Next thing, there's a wild pitch or a sacrifice fly and we win the game. A lot of people leave the ballpark and say, 'Well, Clemente didn't do nothing today.' But Clemente was the guy who hit the man over to third. And out in the field, not many guys tried going from first to third on him. He'd fire it in accurate, right on the bag. I tagged plenty of guys with two minutes to spare! In the clubhouse, where he knew everybody, that's where you saw his sense of humor. He was in the Marine Corps Reserve for about six months, and he'd get to talking about how tough the Marines were, and oh, he was funny. Strange thing is, he *still* knew the names of his three Marine drill instructors! Tony would get him on the rubbing table and he'd talk and talk. There'd be twenty-five guys in the room, crowded around, and if you wanted to put in a couple of words, 'No! I haven't finished yet!' He could talk for an hour. The game would start at eight and he'd be in the trainer's room at five minutes of, with no uniform on. Eight o'clock he's out on the field. Got dressed faster than any player I've ever seen. Then he'd get up the first time and hit a line drive you wouldn't believe. He had three hits before he got up in the morning! Fantastic."

Another rookie that year was Manny Sanguillen, a muscular Panamanian who was fast becoming one of the finest catchers in baseball. Sanguillen grew up in a tough *barrio* and didn't touch a baseball until he was nineteen, when he heard a pastor preaching sermons on a street corner, joined the Evangelical Baptist Church, and became a member of the church team. Two years later he was signed to play professional baseball. Sangy, as the Pirates call him, worshipped Roberto, calling him "Mr. Clemente" when he first joined the Pirates. Soon they became like brothers. Like Clemente in the early years, Sangy was a stranger in America, and his "big brother" took him in tow, inviting him out to eat, counseling him, boosting his confidence. He recalls, "Once we were in Fort Myers, I think it was 1967 when I was still in the minor leagues, and we wanted to eat in a Howard Johnson. There was Clemente, Manny Mota, Mateo Alou, José Pagán, and me. They made us wait for more than an hour because we were colored and speaking Spanish. Finally, I think they recognized Roberto and sent a waiter over. In 1968, I tried to stay at the Howard Johnson in Bradenton and they told me I had to have a letter from the governor of the state. But Roberto has fought a lot for the rights of the Latins. He knows that we don't get any credit. We also had a lot of fun together. Especially in the clubhouse. He'd tell me, 'Hey *negro*,'—in Spanish *negro* is a word of affection—'hey, *negro*, you say you're strong. I'd like to see you try something on me!' He would say that he had 'declared war' on me and we would have contests to see who hit the longest ball. He would always yell, 'Don't let that *negrito* near my locker! He's bad!' There were days that nobody could make him laugh except me. And some Sundays in the clubhouse before the game we would sing religious hymns— him, Tony the trainer, Pagán, me, and some of the other guys. He taught me one of them, 'Only God Makes a Man Happy.' I didn't know it. He loved those hymns. He said that he felt Baptist, and that when he died he wanted people to sing hymns at his funeral."

"Three Hundred Thousand Signatures"

Juan Esteban Jiménez is a small man who thinks big. In 1970, when Roberto Clemente was given a special "night" at Pittsburgh's Three Rivers Stadium, Jiménez mobilized a massive campaign to honor Puerto Rico's superstar. He flew to Pittsburgh with a huge scroll of congratulations, signed by 300,000 of Roberto's countrymen. Jiménez is a dynamic young businessman who has launched a series of ventures in Puerto Rico—including a kosher-style delicatessen for tourists. He has arrived late from work and sits now in the rear den of his white stucco house in San Juan's Miramar section, eating his supper from a small tray, watching the news on television, and telling how his zest for promotion coincided with a dramatic moment in Clemente's career.

In the summer of 1970, it was announced that Pittsburgh's new Three Rivers Stadium would be inaugurated with a "Roberto Clemente Night." This was the first time that Clemente or any other Puerto Rican athlete had been so honored—it was all over the local sports pages—and the people here were very enthused. One of my employees, "Baby" Ocasio—he started out as night cashier and later became manager of my restaurant—came from Carolina, Clemente's hometown, and was his friend. All he kept talking about was the big day for Clemente in Pittsburgh, and it occurred to me to do something. This was about thirty days before the activity, which took place in June. I decided to start a movement called *Puerto Rico Felicita a Clemente*, "Puerto Rico Congratulates Clemente." Banco Popular was going to transmit the special night on satellite TV, they were going to fly Roberto's parents up there, and every business you can imagine was going to arrange for plaques, testimonials, gifts—they wanted to jump on the bandwagon, for publicity. I thought to myself: What can I do that will be different, and significant? Only a limited number of Puerto Ricans could travel to Pittsburgh, but on such a day I knew that the whole island would want to be with Clemente. So I made a huge scroll where all of his *compatriotas* could sign it, and be with him symbolically. Next, I thought, what gift can we give to Clemente, a man who has everything? We decided, the best gift was something that *he* could give. Let him serve as an example for underprivileged children, who can see in him the greatness that a man can achieve, despite his race or economic status.

I went to the Police Athletic League, which has an island-wide network, and created a task force to collect the signatures. IBM lent me a number of continuous paper forms for the job. Well, we went out and when we were done we got *three hundred thousand signatures!* You can imagine what that means on an island of less than three million people. *Everyone* wanted to sign! Then we began to choose a number of poor kids who would go to Pittsburgh on Clemente Night. We took six or seven from the Police Athletic League, some from the Boy Scouts, from Boys' Town, from the Deaf-Mute Asylum, and there was one blind child, too. In addition to the fifteen underprivileged children, the only others were my son and "Baby" Ocasio's son.

One of the kids lived in a foster home and his foster parent composed a hymn to Clemente. It went: "*Ro-BERTO Cle-MENTE, Or-GULLO de Puerto RI-co,*" et cetera. The Pride of Puerto Rico. The kids sang it, and it was used on TV here. We also sent tapes to all the radio stations in Puerto Rico and New York. The idea was that this would be a dream trip for the kids. All they needed was a toothbrush; the rest—a brand-new outfit, et cetera—would be supplied by different companies.

We left Puerto Rico on a Thursday, the day before the homage to Clemente. Eastern Airlines flew us up. Imagine, this was the kids' first time on a plane, and they were dressed to kill. There were other delegations on the plane, including one from Carolina, Roberto's home town, that was organized by "Baby" Ocasio. Two hours from San Juan, the pilot said there was a threat of a bomb on board, so we landed at Nassau, which meant that we would miss our connecting flight from New York to Pittsburgh. I got angry over the delay and talked with the Associated Press man in Nassau. After they searched the plane, we flew to New York; a battery of photographers and reporters were waiting for us—it was like a hero's welcome for the kids! The climax of our visit to Pittsburgh was going to be a banquet in the Pittsburgh Hilton. I called the New York office of the Commonwealth of Puerto Rico, to see if they could set up a free rum cocktail party. A *gringo* who headed the office of rum promotion tells me, "Cocktails for guys like Clemente and Jiménez are a dime a dozen." Imagine, this guy is on the payroll of the people of Puerto Rico and he didn't even know who the hell Clemente was! In New York, we went through the "classical" experience of being Puerto Ricans abroad. Since we'd missed our connecting flight, Eastern wanted to send us to Pittsburgh in a *bus*. That's a hell of a long ride. I got angry and said, "Look, *señor*, we're not going on any bus. We're going to stay in a first-class hotel, and in the morning you're going to fly us to Pittsburgh."

The next day we flew to Pittsburgh and got to the Hilton, right across from the stadium, a little after 11 A.M. The game was that night. By half past noon, we already had a cocktail party for the press. Some of the kids played the hymn to Clemente on their guitars. We had a big pennant showing a Puerto Rican *jíbaro*, a rural peasant, shaking hands with a Pirate, with the map of Puerto Rico in the background. By now the hotel was filled with visiting Puerto Ricans, and they were having one hell of a time! At the press cocktail party I met a man who was co-chairman of Clemente Night, George Smith. While still in Puerto Rico, I thought, it would be nice to give something to the organizers of Clemente Night. Since our budget was tiny, and I'm no big capitalist, I went to the Institute of Puerto Rican Culture in San Juan and got a small reproduction of a *cemí*, an icon worshipped by the Taíno Indians, who lived on the island before Columbus came. I went up to George Smith and told him that the people of Pittsburgh had been so noble to honor Clemente that we wanted to give him a symbol of our ancient, indigenous culture, et cetera. His eyes clouded over, and he said, "I'm honored, but I would prefer to accept this tonight at the stadium, when the other co-chairmen are there." So I took my little *cemí* back for the time being.

That afternoon, I rushed around and got 500 copies printed up of the Hymn to Clemente; I got a big plastic urn to hold the the 300,000 signatures, and I got a scroll lettered in Spanish. All in a few hours. Some of the shops were closing, but the minute I said "Puerto Rico" the people would yell "Clemente!" and that was that. The police even provided us with a special bus to drive the kids to the stadium, and to take them on tours. All I had to do was say "Puerto Rico," and it was explosive. *Anything* for Clemente.

It was an hour before game time, and the first part of the ceremony was for all the delegations from Puerto Rico. I went down to the field with one of the kids—the rest were sitting in box seats up front—and George Smith introduced me to everyone. They began to announce the co-chairmen. George Smith goes up to the mike and all he says is, "Ladies and gentlemen, I wish to introduce THE REPRESENTATIVE OF THE PEOPLE OF PUERTO RICO, JUAN JIMENEZ!" Mind you, this was on satellite TV, and everything was timed to the second. All the coordinators started looking around, asking "Juan Jiménez? Who's he?" The whole program was out of kilter. So there I went with my little *cemi*. "ON BEHAAAAAAALF OF THE PEOPLE OF PUERTO RICO, WE WISH TO PRESENT—" Well, we gave out the *cemi* and presented the 300,000 signatures, and the scroll, and out of the one-hour show, including commercials, I was on for six minutes! Later, when it came time for the presentations from Pittsburgh, they gave him so many things, and said so many nice things—when all those thousands of people stood up and cheered, well, Roberto let loose with a torrent of tears. And when he spoke, everyone else cried. There was complete silence, and in quite good English Clemente thanked them all. When he finished, I thought the stadium would collapse from the cheers and applause.

Finally, the game began. The kids are stuffing themselves with hot dogs, Crackerjacks, soda pop. From Clemente's hometown alone there must have been 300 people. Roberto was in right field, close to where most of the Puerto Ricans were seated. All during the game they're singing, *"Ro-BERTO Cle-MENTE, Or-GULLO de Puerto RI-co!"* They're all wearing *pavas*, big straw hats, and singing, and the people from Pittsburgh were joining in, too. It was a very lovely moment, two communities—Pittsburgh and Puerto Rico—sharing a common son.

That night, we got back to the hotel, and as you know we Puerto Ricans don't need much of an excuse to have a *fiesta*. The hotel had parties going in almost every suite. Even outside, taxi drivers, when they heard you were from Puerto Rico: "Clemente!" They'd stop the cab, buy you a drink, and wouldn't charge for the ride. The brotherhood was overwhelming.

Next day, we took the kids on a tour of the town. Wherever we went people said, "Ah! There go Clemente's kids!" It was a thrill, just watching the kids enjoy themselves. One of the high spots for them was at the zoo, where a big ape took a mouthful of water and bathed a police lieutenant. That night, people from Clemente's hometown had a private banquet for him, just off the lobby at the Hilton. There were only childhood friends and "Baby" Ocasio and me. People spoke to him not as an idol, but as a childhood buddy, *tú a tú*, very intimately. When it came time for Roberto to speak, the whole salon was paralyzed; even the waiters stopped, and the cooks peeked out from the kitchen. Clemente wasn't eloquent in the sense of a professional speaker, but he had a way of expressing great sentiment, because of his sincere emotions. He covered many topics, but mainly two things filled Roberto with pride: representing his native land of Puerto Rico and—although it's not so widely known— his great pride in being a black man. When he finished, you could hardly hear a fly breathe. Just then, a man in the back of the room, in a very subdued voice, begins to sing, *"Laaaaa tierra de Borinquen—"* The Puerto Rican anthem. Let me tell you, the tears flowed, and everyone sang.

As if that weren't enough, after the banquet Roberto headed for the suite of the mayor of Carolina. Just when we reached the lobby, the police bus pulls up and the kids pour out. For the first time, the kids meet Roberto face to face. A big circle formed around Clemente, his wife, and the kids. Some of the little kids were quite talented. One boy, a twelve-year-old orphan from Ponce, had written a poem and began to recite it. It was about an orphan, telling when his mother dies. Then a little boy from Ciales, who plays guitar and has an angel's voice, began to sing the song that perhaps means most to a Puerto Rican far from home, *"Soñando con Puerto Rico,"* "Dreaming of Puerto Rico." Well, I'll tell you, Clemente starts to cry, his wife starts to cry, the kids start to cry, about a hundred fifty Puerto Ricans gathered around, they *all* start to cry! There was a fellow, a millionaire who owned a ball club on the island; in his euphoria, all he could think to do was stick his hand in his pocket and hand out hundred dollar bills to the kids!

It was a marvelous surprise to find ourselves in a part of the United States where, *by virtue of being Puerto Ricans*, we were some-body! On the streets, in the bars, *everywhere*, the camaraderie was tremendous. It shows how little difference there really is between people. All you need is a kind of catalyst to find that common de-nominator, to join them together. And Clemente was that catalyst.

9

oberto looked remarkably fit for a veteran of fifteen seasons as he stood near the batting cage in Bradenton. For the first time in seven winters he had played nearly a full schedule in the Puerto Rican league. Swinging a heavy leaded bat under the Florida sun a few days before the opener of the 1970 season, he told the writers that he had devised a "three-year plan."

"I need 441 hits to reach the 3,000 mark for my career," he said. "If nothing happens to me, I can do it. In fact, I could play four more years if I feel like I do right now."

With manager Shepard's dismissal, the Pirates turned again to Danny Murtaugh, and after the doctors examined his heart and gave him a clean bill of health the doughty Irishman accepted. The rancor between Danny and Roberto had long since subsided, but the press corps, sniffing for a spicy lead, scratched at the old wounds. The thirty-five-year-old Roberto, now the confident leader of the team, was conciliatory. "We once didn't communicate, but I think I'm a different person now and as a manager I think he's different. I think he's a good manager." Murtaugh, an old hand at parrying such jabs, shifted the big brown wad of Beech-Nut tobacco to the other cheek and said, "Clemente is Clemente. He's the best player I've ever seen. I'm old enough and I think smart enough to get along with anybody on our ballclub, especially if he's a .350 hitter."

Roberto showed no sign of being in the twilight of his career. He hit, ran, and fielded with the zeal of a rookie and the finesse of a maestro. At home games, his wife kept him company in a box seat.

Robertito and Luis frisked about next to her, and Enrique, still an infant, dozed in her arms, a tiny fist tucked under his cheek. Robertito was already chirping to reporters that he would be a pitcher and Luis solemnly affirmed that he would catch. As the fans cheered her husband on, Vera said, with quiet pride, "I never imagined how people felt about Roberto until I came to Pittsburgh." He had learned to relax more. For a brief stretch early in the season, he was hitting poorly and protested a call by the umpire, who ejected him from the game. "The way you're goin'," the umpire cracked, "you'd be better off out of the game anyway." Roberto walked into the dugout, chuckling. He remarked to a teammate, "When he told me that, there wasn't anything left for me to say." Later that summer, he helped to calm a potentially ugly brawl between the Pirates and the Chicago Cubs. While the Pirates' outspoken pitcher Dock Ellis stood at bat, he was apparently being razzed, and fired back a remark about the age and lineage of Cubs manager Leo Durocher, who had not acquired his nickname of "The Lip" for no reason. The sixty-three-year-old Durocher stepped angrily onto the field. The umpire stopped him, but by then both teams were advancing upon each other like opposing ranks of infantrymen, and a few Chicago fans scaled the wall, presumably to engage in guerrilla tactics. Ellis, bat in hand, stood a few feet from home plate as several players began to jostle each other. Plate umpire Nick Colosi, hoping to defuse the tense situation, urged him, "Go ahead, get up there and bat, c'mon now, it's all over." Ellis hesitated, but Roberto walked over and said calmly, "You listen to the umpire. He's right. Go up there and bat." Ellis dug in and soon the players, flipping insults over their shoulders, retreated to the trenches. The uproar set Danny Murtaugh's heart to beating at an alarming rate, and that night he went to a Chicago hospital for a checkup. There he found three of the umpires visiting a colleague who had suffered a broken ankle during the game. "I want to tell you something about Clemente," Colosi said to Murtaugh. "He helped us out when we needed it most. He said exactly what he had to." Mel Steiner, another umpire, added, "Tell him thanks for us." It was ironic, perhaps, that the only man Colosi had ejected from a game that season was Roberto Clemente.

But Roberto could still reach the boiling point when he thought his dignity was offended. Earlier that spring, *New York Post* columnist Milton Gross interviewed him and wrote a story, trying, in his words, to correct some of "the unfair raps that he was a malingerer." A few days later he received an angry letter from Clemente: "I give you two hours of my time, and you write a horseshit story about me. I don't want to talk to you no more if you write horseshit stories." Gross was bewildered. He wrote back, asking for Roberto's objections, but got no reply. When the Pirates next visited New York, he found Roberto at his locker in Shea Stadium and asked, "Did you get my letter? Why didn't you write me and tell me what was horseshit?"

"I don't read the story," Roberto admitted. "A friend called me and tell me what you wrote. I'm angry, so I sit down and write to you."

"Now *I'm* mad. Don't ever talk to me or complain again until you've read that column," Gross said, walking away. Weeks later, Gross had forgotten the incident, when Roberto approached him and said, "I call my friend and tell him *he* is horseshit." Noting Gross's perplexed expression, Roberto explained, "You remember you tell me I have to read your story before I talk to you and complain? I read the story. So now I apologize for the letter and I tell my friend he is no longer my friend because he does not tell me the truth."

Gross later recalled, "It was a rare moment in my years in sports: a player admitting that he may have been wrong. Clemente was not an easy man for non-Latin sportswriters to know, but he was worth the effort."

More and more, stories surfaced about Clemente's warm personality. Not that he had ever been a misanthrope, but the writers—perhaps pricked by guilt for past omissions—began to take notice. In Houston one afternoon, he stood outside the Astrodome signing autographs and chatting with Mrs. Loretta Miller, a housewife; her two teen-aged sons; and two women friends of Mrs. Miller. "Somebody was supposed to pick up Clemente but hadn't shown up," she said later. "Suddenly he turned to us and asked which way we were going home. We were thrilled to be even talking to him, and when we drove him to the Marriott Hotel he asked if we would like to come in for a drink." For two hours they sat in the hotel lounge, together with three sportswriters; according to one of the writers, Luke Quay, "Roberto was the gracious host and really captivated his Houston admirers. At one point he excused himself to make sure everything was all right with Mrs. Miller's two sons, who were busy in the lobby collecting autographs of Pirates players."

"He wants to make sure the boys are okay—my boys!" Mrs. Miller said with delight. "I can't believe this is really happening. We've never heard anything good about Clemente. But he is really one of the nicest men I've ever met."

Describing Clemente as "one of the few big stars willing to satisfy as many autograph seekers as humanly possible," Quay recalled another time in Houston when Pirate announcer Nellie King took Roberto over to the stands to meet Jamie, a fourteen-year-old deaf child. After he returned to the dugout, Roberto autographed one of his bats, went up into the stands, and walked about fifteen rows into the reserved seat section to personally deliver the souvenir to the boy.

His social circle expanded, and he and Vera acquired a number of friends in the Pittsburgh area. One of them, Henry Kantrowitz, recalls that he sometimes felt embarrassed by Clemente's selfless hospitality when he visited the baseball star in Puerto Rico. "Roberto couldn't do enough for me and my wife. Every time we wanted to go somewhere, Roberto was there to drive us—morning and night. Believe me, I'm not accustomed to a $100,000-a-year chauffeur!"

Roberto was asked by a television company to tape a film that warned teenagers of the evils of drugs. When he saw that the brief film was only to be done in English, he reminded them that many Spanish-speaking youngsters were also on drugs. A TV man told him, "But the commercial is only written in English. Who's going to translate it?" "I am," he said, whereupon he sat down for an hour, laboriously preparing the Spanish script, throwing one false start after another into the wastebasket until he was satisfied.

It was even rumored that Roberto might run for mayor of his hometown or seek some other political office. But, with his usual candor, he said, "I am afraid people will vote for me because I'm a ballplayer, not because I would make a good mayor. I'm not just a series of records. I am a man, and they should look at me like that. Because of this, I don't know whether I will run for office."

There is nothing like a winner to put a man's mind at ease, and this, too, buoyed Clemente's outlook on life. The Pirates, with a fine mix of youth and experience, were now top contenders in the league. The cordial mayhem that took place in the Pirates' dressing room was also becoming legend. "A ballclub ought to be happy," said manager Murtaugh. "Or maybe 'happy' isn't the word." Then, borrowing a page from his colleague, the fabled lexicographer Casey Stengel, he added, "This club doesn't have any disgruntlements."

They were quite a sight as, young and old, white, black, Latino, paraded out of the clubhouse after a game, with their Ivy League suits, see-through shirts, jeans, dashikis, planter-style straw hats, huge floppy caps, bell bottoms with wild designs, thick heels, sandals, and leather boots. Roberto had become a bit more "mod"— the sideburns of his close-cropped hair now crept down close to the ear lobes. But he was still the traditional man who wore well-tailored suits and shirts with cuff links.

They were a club with no "disgruntlements," who, when they were not heaving racial slurs back and forth across the locker room like meringue pies on a vaudeville stage, liked to sneak up behind a teammate and lift him violently off the ground, just for the hell of it. Sangy loved to grab tiny reserve infielder Freddie Patek and let him dangle helplessly in the air. One of big Bob Veale's favorite victims was Blass, who hung there half out of breath, kicking and gasping, "Now, *wait* a minute!" When the Pirates went on the road, the innocent clubhouse boy assigned to them was often the target for their shenanigans. One time in Atlanta, trainer Tony Bartirome, in braggadocio tones, offered to bet one hundred dollars that he could lift three men at once, providing "the lightest guy stands in the middle." After much mock ceremony, Willie Stargell and Dock Ellis were chosen, and Bartirome asked the clubhouse boy to stand in the center. The two big players locked their arms and legs tightly around the young fellow as Bartirome made an elaborate show of flexing his muscles. Suddenly, he zipped open the fly of the surprised novice, and a flock of whooping Pirates filled his trousers with shaving cream and ice-cold soda. "Oh!" shouted one player, "we gotta do this in Montreal. That French boy who can't speak English, he'll go 'wallawallawalla!'"

By now, the topic of Clemente's physical condition had become fused with his image, much like Jack Benny's reputation as a tight-wad. Dock Ellis, Sangy, and others often aped him, limping around the clubhouse, moaning with pain, as he shook his head and laughed. Almost daily, new anecdotes were added to his growing legend: "He has a favorite Saint Louis chiropractic clinic now, and carries a chart showing where chiropractors trained by that clinic can be found all over the country."

As the club's elder statesman, Clemente's expert opinion was now much in demand. Dave Giusti came in a trade from Saint Louis largely on Roberto's recommendation. "I always liked Dave," said general manager Joe Brown, "but I wanted to find out what some-one who had faced him at the plate thought. I finally called Roberto at his home in Puerto Rico. He said he always had trouble with Giusti's palm ball and thought we should take him."

"The first time I saw Roberto is when I played for Houston and Saint Louis. Needless to say, I respected him. He had as much power as *any* batter," says Giusti, who became the Pirates' chief relief pitcher in 1970.

That June the Pirates played an exhibition game against Kansas City, and Orlando Pena, thirty-three-year-old Cuban, was throwing batting practice. He had been released from his last major league contract and planned to quit the game rather than drift to the minors. "Joe Pagán, Luis Alvarez, and I were standing at the batting cage, watching him throw his fork ball," said Joe Brown, "and Pagán mentioned he always thought Pena was a fine pitcher when he faced him in the winter leagues." Brown needed another right-handed reliever to back up Giusti, and he went to Clemente, who affirmed that "he can help you." As the Pirates showered and dressed to continue their road trip, the press was told that Pena had been obtained in a lightning deal. During the rest of the season, he pitched more than twenty times, helping to save several clutch games.

The Pirates inaugurated Three Rivers Stadium on July 16, 1970, and left behind six decades of memories at Forbes Field. The new $35-million park at the juncture of the Ohio, Allegheny, and Monongahela rivers is an impressive monument with a symmetrical playing field, synthetic green Tartan Turf, seats for 50,235 fans, a huge Disneylandish scoreboard that explodes with moving words and cartoon figures, and a glassed-in, chandeliered dining room and bar called the Allegheny Club, which occupies a good part of the third and fourth tiers behind first base.

Artificial turf on playing fields was fast becoming common-place, and, announcer Bob Prince recalls, "Roberto began to think of ways to cope with it. He soon perfected one technique that I've *never* seen another player do. A hard ground ball hit to the outfield on synthetic turf often gets through for extra bases. Roberto would run after the ball and, instead of trying to backhand it and throw, he would *slide* on his left side, his feet extended, just like he was slid-ing into a base. As soon as he'd intercepted the ball, he'd immedi-ately pop back into a standing position and get rid of the ball. It was unbelievable! Oh, I've seen Roberto make so many plays I could talk about them forever. In old Forbes Field, the right-field line went down 300 feet and then angled out quickly. Billy White of the Cardi-nals once batted a ball over first base fair, it hit something, and skit-tered into the bullpen area behind the stands. White was already rounding second on his way to an easy triple. Roberto charged over from right field, slid into the gravel, grabbed the ball, kicked off the wall with his foot, and threw a perfect strike to third base. Roberto couldn't even *see* third base when he threw—he was in behind the lower stands—but the ball zoomed over the pitcher's mound and reached third on a fly. White was out by six or seven feet. Most remarkable throw I've ever seen him make."

Roberto had suffered a bruise on his palm in mid-July. He was benched on July 25 and did not appear again until August 8, when the Pirates came up against the Mets in a crucial game. Sitting with reporter Pat Jordan of *Sport* magazine, he rubbed the palm against his wooden stool in the locker room, wincing as he said, "The rub-bing gets the bad blood out." A solicitous Manny Sanguillen came over, held Roberto's hand, and massaged it gently. "We all try to help Roberto whenever he's got an injury," said six-foot-six pitcher Bob Veale. "I give him rubdowns whenever his back is bothering him. I'd do anything to get that guy out on the field. You've gotta wind him up, both mentally and physically." Moments later, Roberto heard that he was not in the lineup, but he spoke privately with Murtaugh and his name was penciled in. Each Pirate, in his own way, demonstrated affection for Roberto. Dock Ellis's approach was a bit different, but it rarely failed to elicit a grin from Clemente. "Hey, Roberto," he said, as he paced quickly back and forth in front of Clemente's locker, "did you see that Johnny Bench did a Vitalis commercial! He's only been in the league three years. How long you been in the league, Roberto? You ever do a Vitalis commercial? Hah!"

The rest, the massages, and the friendly barbs apparently helped. In August, he hit better than ever. During a pair of games in Los Angeles, he got ten hits, the first time in modern baseball history that a player had done so. As the summer waned, Clemente led the league with a .363 average and had his eye on a fifth batting championship. But on September 4, in the fifth inning of a game against Philadelphia in Three Rivers Stadium, he swung hard at a pitch and felt a familiar, ominous twinge in his back. He would not play again for two weeks. Clemente's vertebrae were out of place again, and after spending two days in traction in Pittsburgh he flew to see his old friend Arturo García.

"The superb athlete, with one of the best physiques of any human being, looked like an old man when he walked, hunched over," said Tito Stevens of the *San Juan Star*, who was there when Roberto drove up to García's home in the Round Hills section of San Juan.

"Last year when I hurt my shoulder," he told Stevens, "I couldn't hit high pitches, but they kept throwing me low and away and I could hit that pitch without much pain. 'Look, he gets three hits, but he says he's in pain,' they say, but they don't know that I can't go for the high pitch, and I'm not about to tell them!"

He was still not fully cured when he returned to Pittsburgh. "My back hurts me when I sit down. It hurts me when I stand up. It hurts me even when I breathe sometimes." His chances for a batting title were fast slipping away, but he said, "Right now, I don't feel as bad as if we were losing. Maybe my being hurt helps the team. Lots of times they don't see me playing, they push themselves more."

None pushed harder than Willie Stargell, a 215-pound bear of a man who was the Pirates' left-handed cleanup slugger. He had joined the club in 1962 and since 1965 drove in more than one hundred runs per season. Only two fair balls have been hit out of the Dodger ballpark in Los Angeles, both by Stargell. The owner of a prospering fried chicken restaurant in Pittsburgh's Oakland section, Stargell is a thoughtful, concerned man who presides over the Black Athletes Foundation, leaders in the fight against sickle cell anemia. He also has a keen, offbeat sense of humor. One night, after he smashed one of his Promethean homers—he calls them "long taters"—a friend asked, "Were you mean out there, Willie?" He responded, "*Angry*, like a tiger in heat." As Stargell lumbered around the clubhouse, Manny Sanguillen, seated near his own locker, would often flash a grin, raise a two-fingered "peace" sign and say, "Hey, I have always like you."

"Back in 1962," Stargell recalls, "probably the most exciting thing for me, besides going to a big-league camp, was to be able to say hello to Roberto Clemente. As the years went by, I respected a hell of a lot the way he did various things. It made him shine just a little bit brighter than most men. He worked like a dog and took an awful lot of pride in his work, but never got proper recognition. It *had* to be discrimination. I've always felt that blacks get the trophies and whites get the money. It's really pitiful. Whenever Clemente spoke out on these issues, the things he said were always taken and twisted around. Roberto knew the need and he spoke out."

As the 1970 season came to a close, the Pirates—sustained largely by Stargell's murderous hitting—still held a slim lead in the Eastern Division. On September 20, an impatient Roberto said, "I am going to play today. I can't wait any longer. I have to find out if I can help for the rest of the season." Before the game, Roberto griped loudly about the quality of the clubhouse coffee, and Bob Veale, riding him hard, said, "Ah, you want Puerto Rican coffee, eh? Guys like you and me, who don't play, shouldn't ask for things. Get your butt back in the lineup, then you can have Puerto Rican coffee!"

"Screw you," said Clemente, as he walked into the trainer's room and stripped for his rubdown. As he lay on the table, Veale came in and said, "Hey, I'm sorry I got on you out there. I didn't know you were playing today."

"I don't hear anything you say," said Roberto.

"I apologize, okay?"

"No," said Roberto, winking slyly to a newsman nearby.

He struck out three times in the game but also drove in Mateo Alou with a double and scored on Stargell's sacrifice fly, accounting for both Pirate runs in their 2-1 win over the Mets. Holding his back, he walked to the shower and said, "The only thing that keeps me from feeling terrible is that the Pirates have been winning."

The Pirates did win the Eastern Division title but never reached the World Series, because the Cincinnati Reds beat them three straight in the playoffs. Willie Stargell tore the Reds' pitchers for six hits in twelve times at bat, but most of the famed Pirate cannonry was silent. Roberto, still ailing, managed only three singles in fourteen chances.

That season, Henry Aaron—who had begun his career one year ahead of Roberto—connected for his 3,000th hit in May, and Willie Mays—who joined the National League three years before Roberto—reached the magic figure in July. Roberto's 145 hits, giving him a .352 batting average, left him only 296 hits short of the goal.

Except for the final Pirate defeat at the hands of the Reds, it had been a satisfying year for Roberto. During his long career he had thirsted for recognition, but in July of 1970 he was moved to tears by the stirring tribute on "Roberto Clemente Night." More than 43,000 fans, including a large contingent from Puerto Rico, were on hand to honor him and give him an automobile and a dizzying assortment of gifts and trophies. An even greater gift, they announced, was that they had arranged to fly his parents up for the special homage (*don* Melchor had never been on a plane before). As the day approached, Roberto urged those who planned to give him gifts to donate cash, instead, to Pittsburgh's Children's Hospital, and several thousand dollars were raised for that institution.

It would be understatement to say that it was an emotional evening. Out on the field, seated in wooden folding chairs, were Vera and his three children, his parents, Heriberto Nieves (the mayor of his home town), representatives of Puerto Rico's government and sports world, and dozens of prominent admirers from Pittsburgh. The program was being televised to Puerto Rico via satellite, where tens of thousands of his countrymen were tuned in. Before the "Star Spangled Banner," the crowd hushed to hear "*La Borinqueña*," Puerto Rico's anthem. Among the many awards was a plaque from 175 Puerto Rican soldiers who had served in Vietnam. Roberto, seated with his tiny son Enrique in his arms, felt the emotion well-ing up. As the photographers crowded around, he snapped, quite nervously, "I don't have much more time for this. I'm here to play baseball." Finally, he was asked to speak to his people in Puerto Rico via satellite, and he rose and walked to the microphone. In a low voice, his chin resting against his chest, he said in Spanish: "Before anything, I want to send an *abrazo* to my brothers—" And he couldn't speak any more. Finally, after announcer Ramiro Martínez cheered him up with a few words, he continued: "I want to dedicate this triumph to all the mothers in Puerto Rico. I haven't the words to express my gratitude. I only ask that those who are watching this program be close to their parents, ask for their blessing, and embrace . . . and those friends who are watching or listening, shake hands, in the friendship that unites all Puerto Ricans. I have sacrificed these sixteen years, perhaps I've lost some friendships because of the effort one must expend to be outstanding in sports, and especially the arduous labor that we Puerto Ricans and all Latins must expend in order to triumph in the big leagues. This triumph of the Latins is a source of pride to all Puerto Ricans, and to all those in the Caribbean, because we are all brothers. I haven't got the words to express my gratitude, and especially to see my parents, who are old now, and the emotion that this offers them—"

As one witness said later, "With tears streaming down his cheeks, Roberto looked over at *don* Melchor and *doña* Luisa with such tenderness that those nearby had to lower their heads."

Minutes later, the game began, and with Dock Ellis pitching flawlessly, an inspired Roberto led the Pirates to an 11–0 victory over the Chicago Cubs. Roberto made two hits, a sensational sliding catch, and late in the lopsided game—when it really didn't matter—made a diving catch of a foul pop-up.

"It's the only way I know how to play baseball," he told reporters in the clubhouse afterward, as blood oozed from the damaged knee. Surrounded by friends from Puerto Rico, during an impromptu press conference, he was asked about his tears earlier that evening. He responded very quietly, "In a moment like this, you can see a lot of years in a few minutes. You can see everything firm and you can see everything clear. I don't know if I cried, but I am not ashamed to cry. I would say a man never cries from pain or disappointment. But if you know the history of our island, you ought to remember we're a sentimental people. I don't have the words to say how I feel when I step on that field and know that so many are behind me, and know that so many represent my island and Latin America."

"He Was So Darn Sincere"

"Clemente's death hit this island like an H-bomb," said a husky, hoarse-voiced man who works with Bob Leith. "With so many bums walking around alive, a guy like that should live for a hundred years, but I guess when your number's up, it's up." He shook his head and rose from the couch in the reception area to answer a ringing telephone. Leith was still busy inside his office. Born in the United States, raised in Puerto Rico, Bob Leith has a shipping business near San Juan Bay. But he is better known as a sportsman, as the promoter of world championship boxing matches on the island, as the owner of a baseball club in the winter league. He pops out of his office, excuses himself for being still busy, and the interview begins downstairs in his chauffeur-driven car, en route to an appointment in an office across town. After he dashes out toward the building—"I'll be back in a jiffy," he says—and as the car idles in a curbside parking space, his elderly chauffeur turns around to the back seat and says quietly, "Mr. Leith, when he learned about Clemente's death, he cried."

When I bought the San Juan baseball club in 1960, Clemente was on the roster. He had started out with Santurce, they sold him to Caguas, and Caguas sold him to San Juan. I was new at the time, and by June 1 you had to send out contracts to all the players on the club. I guess I got too busy and didn't send them out—or at least I didn't send Roberto's out. So by law he was a free agent and could have gone anywhere, asked any price. I'd bought a club and all of a sudden I found myself without the star! But I sat down with him and explained the situation. We got together, and that was the year we won the pennant.

Later, when we went to Caracas for the Caribbean Series, some of the American players on the club kind of tried to renegotiate their contracts with me in midstream, and some even refused to play. Clemente asked me to step outside of the dressing room. Some of these guys were big leaguers, even better known than he was at the time, but he must've given them a real dressing down, because they played.

I think my biggest mistake with him was in the mid-1960's, just at the height of the Vietnam War. I belong to the Santurce Rotary Club, and they were planning to dedicate one of their banquets in honor of Clemente and Orlando Cepeda. He had made a speech somewhere and been quoted in the Associated Press as saying something to the effect that if Communism were good for Puerto Rico, then he would welcome Communism. It's all right to say something like that in private, but I got mad at him for saying it in public. After all, some people might be on the verge of deciding whether or not they want us to go Communist, they hear him make a statement like that, and figure, "Well, if Clemente says it's good. . ." I got so mad that I passed a motion that the Rotary Club shouldn't honor a man who made such a statement; they put it to a vote and they withdrew the invitation. Later on, I spoke to him and he explained that he was such a fanatic about doing good for his people that no matter *what* it was, as long as it was good for his people, he was in favor. I thought he chose a horrible example, especially at a time when we weren't trading with Russia or China, and Cuba was exporting its revolution all over. Actually, Roberto wasn't very interested in politics *per se*, but he wanted the best for his people.

One thing I remember particularly about Roberto is the way he adored his parents. I've never in my life seen a man adore his parents so much. When he was a free agent, I did more talking with his folks than with him about the contract. Lots of people in the states think this doesn't exist any more—the old-fashioned respect between a son and his mother and father, but it did in his case. He was also very much of a fun-loving guy. He and Vera did lots of entertaining at their home. And the way he tucked all those trophies away down in the room next to the garage, you didn't even know they were there. The greatest year was after the 1971 World Series; he got a big electric organ from an outfit in Pittsburgh, for an endorsement he had made. How he could flip those buttons and make the rhythm section go! He picked up everything by ear, and we had some wonderful times. Actually, I think he was even more popular in Pittsburgh than in Puerto Rico. The local fans are very demanding—they wanted to see him hit a homer every time he came to the plate! The fans in Puerto Rico never got to see all his great years in Pittsburgh, and he'd only play part of the time in the Winter League. But in the off-season down here he'd be busy, busy all the time. And when it came time to leave for spring training, he still wouldn't be packed! One thing that kept him busy was his free clinic for people suffering with ailing backs, right in his own home, down in the basement. After the 1971 season, I believe he treated more than a hundred people, including one old woman who was bent over like a question mark. He'd put them down and start hitting those pressure points, and, by God, it was unbelievable! Last winter, my wife and I went to see him at his house. She's had back problems for years, and before the evening was out the four of us— Vera and Roberto, my wife and me—went into the bedroom. My wife laid down on the floor. Roberto put some Vaseline on his forearm and used it like a rolling pin, up and down her back. When she was lying there, he said, "She has one leg longer than the other." By the time he was done both legs matched, and to this day she's never had more trouble with her back. It's the honest-to-God truth. Another time, we went to see Governor Ferré at the governor's mansion in San Juan, because Roberto had been named the outstanding athlete of the year. We were accompanied by Dora Pasarel, the head of the Parks and Recreation Administration. While we were waiting out in the hall to see the governor, he cured Dora's migraine headaches. "There's no such thing as a migraine headache," he said to her, and by just pushing on some pressure points she felt like a million dollars. It didn't take two minutes to start him talking about the body and ways to cure pain. I think he talked more about that than his batting average.

In September of 1971, the Puerto Rican fans gave him a beautiful gold Cadillac as a gift. There was a dock strike at the time and I had the only company operating out of Miami. "What can I do?" he asks me. "You're lucky," I said. I explained that I was going up to Washington for Thanksgiving to see my daughter and I intended to take a car from there to Miami to see Disney World. So I told him I'd go through New York, hitch his car to the back of my Camaro, haul it to Miami, and put it on the ship. So I picked up my wife and daughter and a friend in Washington and we started out. Somewhere through Richmond, Virginia, one of the tow hooks slipped out of place and the car almost got loose. I stopped at a bus station, talked to the dispatcher and found an off-duty bus driver. I gave him one hundred dollars to drive my Camaro to Miami and take a bus back. Well, we finally shipped the car from Miami, and when it reached Puerto Rico, Roberto had to pay an excise tax of $5,250 to get it on the island! As you know, we have some pretty stiff excise taxes here, especially on luxury vehicles. Well, that really hurt Roberto. "How come I've gotta pay for a gift?" he asks me. "Roberto, you're like anybody else, you've got to pay the tax, gift or not." But I went to Manny Casiano, head of the government's Economic Development Administration. We made a deal that Manny would give Roberto a contract for $5,250 to make several speeches in the United States on behalf of Puerto Rico, and that would more than make up for that amount. The funny thing is, he made the speeches, he paid the $5,250 in excise tax, but he never sent the bill to the government to get his money back. The mere fact that he thought he could get it was enough. It was the question of *dignidad*. I don't think that people in the states quite put the value on dignity that he and a lot of other people here do.

He also felt that his dignity was offended when he didn't get offers for commercial endorsements. It was only near the end of his career that some offers came in. Coca-Cola wanted to talk to him about a big contract, and after he got through playing he would be set up for life as a vice president of public relations. A lot of doors opened after the 1971 World Series.

Sometimes, he was so darn sincere that it hurt him. Like the time we were trying to get a contract for him with Coca-Cola and he turns around and tells some reporter that he's thinking of retiring. I tried to explain to him that such contracts run for two or three years, and that talk of his retiring could reduce the value of the contract. It was the same with his playing. He would tell people right out that he had a strong arm, or was a heck of a hitter, and he was. Some people thought he was bragging, but he was just being himself.

10

In October, 1971, more than 60 million baseball fans who watched the World Series on television learned what the people of Pittsburgh had known all along: Roberto Clemente was an outrageously talented man.

Of that series, Roger Angell would write in *The Summer Game* that Clemente played "a kind of baseball that none of us had ever seen before—throwing and running and hitting at something close to the level of absolute perfection, playing to win but also playing the game almost as if it were a form of punishment for everyone else on the field."

No one could predict such a ringing triumph during the spring of that year, but everyone knew that the Pirates, with a frightening array of batsmen and a strong pitching staff, were as "ready" as any team had ever been. In Florida that March, Roberto toyed around on the sidelines, heaving knuckleballs to Manny Sanguillen. "I've got a good knuckleball," he joked. "I could hang around another six or seven years with it." The writers, already concocting in their heads the now-stereotyped feature story about Clemente's perennial ailments, were disappointed to hear him say, "I feel good. No aches, no pains, no back problems, no shoulder problems." They perked up, however, when he mentioned that during the winter he had managed the San Juan club to a second-place finish in the Puerto Rican League. Would he like to be the first black manager in the major leagues? "I don't think about it now. I worry about it when the future comes. The first black man to manage, he must be absolutely ready. I am not that ready yet." He would be a tough manager, said teammate Dave Cash, who had seen him in action: "If he has any fault, it's that he demands that his players do things as well as he does." Mike Cuellar, the veteran Cuban pitcher of the Baltimore Orioles, was less diplomatic: "I pitch too many years for Clemente to tell me how." He had quit the San Juan club in midseason. In rebuttal, Roberto said, "The guy was getting good money for pitching down there, but he was trying to get the batters out with stuff that wouldn't even be any good in the Little League." Cuellar and Clemente would see each other again in October.

It was now almost a standing joke that Roberto performed best when he was hurting, and events early that season only served to perpetuate the story. Feeling fit, he had a dismal beginning, and some believed that the Pirates' star—who would be thirty-seven that August—was through. In mid-May, hitting a mere (for him) .280, he was booed by the Pittsburgh fans when he struck out with the bases loaded in the third inning of a game against Montreal. The fans cheered in the ninth, when he won the game with a two-out triple, but afterward, as he sat in a whirlpool bath, the catcalls rang in his ears. "They pay for their tickets, so let them do what they want," he said, but then, his temper rising, he added, "If I don't hustle or something like that I'd say it would be good for them to boo me. But the fans want you to start every year right on top, boom, boom, boom. Now I start a little slowly, so they boo. I get mad. One of these days, I'll leave my uniform on the field and keep on walking." But he was soon up above the .300 mark, and if applause and cheers lifted his spirits, he would hear enough in Houston on June 15 to last most people a lifetime. He saved Steve Blass's 3–0 shutout in the eighth inning with what one Texas sportswriter called "an unbelievable theft that probably surpasses any other defensive play ever made in the Astrodome." Actually, Roberto made two splendid plays that inning. With a Houston runner on first, one out, and Pittsburgh ahead by 1 to 0, César Cedeño hit a short line drive and Clemente dashed in to make a sliding catch inches above the grass. But that was just the appetizer. Bob Watson then hit a powerful shot to the right-field corner. There is a yellow line on the wall, ten feet above the warning track that circles the outfield, and the ball looked as though it might clear the line for a home run, putting Houston ahead 2–1. At the very least, it would go for extra bases and drive in the tying run. Eyewitnesses swear that Roberto actually outran the ball, leaped, and caught it just as he collided with the barrier. "He hit it wide open. He never slowed up. It was the greatest catch I've ever seen," said Houston manager Harry Walker, who has spent more than three decades in baseball. A Houston writer agreed. "I wasn't more than seventy feet away and heard—you might say *felt*—the impact. The *guts* it took to go bluntly into that wall! He was stunned when he bounced back onto the warning track." The 16,000 fans in the Astrodome were also stunned. Roberto had just robbed their team of a chance to win, but they gave him a standing ovation and stood once more to applaud when he next came to bat. After the game, as Roberto sat near his locker, there were cuts on his left hip and knee; his left ankle and elbow were in ice packs. "I didn't think I could get the ball," he said, "but I had to try."

That reminded one Houston sports columnist of a statement Roberto had made in January at a dinner of the Houston Baseball Writers, where he received the Tris Speaker Award "in recognition of his illustrious career." The acceptance speech, made before 800 listeners, was "one of the most inspirational we've ever heard," the writer recalled. At the end of his talk, Roberto had said, "Accomplishment is something you can't buy. If you have a chance and don't make the most of it, you are wasting your time on this earth. Win or lose, I try my best."

There were stacks of letters around Roberto's locker in Three Rivers Stadium on August 18. Many were routine requests for autographs, but there were also hundreds of cards to congratulate him on his thirty-seventh birthday. "A lot of people write me telling me not to quit baseball. They say a lot of nice things." This was no time for quitting. The Pirates had built an eleven-game lead by the middle of July and, though they seemed to slump a bit, still held a firm grip on first place. Roberto and four of his teammates were hitting above .300. His friend Willie Stargell, now thirty, had finally come into his own and by season's end would lead the league with 48 home runs and 154 runs batted in. As Roberto liked to say, it's fun winning.

"We'd cut up all the time," says pitcher Nelson Briles, who had been traded from the Cardinals at the end of the 1970 season and spent winters polishing a second career as a nightclub entertainer. "We used to psyche him up for a game by kidding him about being a hypochondriac. 'Hey,' we'd say, 'did you hear what so-and-so wrote about you?' *'Who? Where'd he write it?'* Sometimes, on buses to the airport, I'd use my impersonations to loosen up the club. Impromptu songs, with just the *rankest* of lyrics, the ranker they are the funnier it becomes. I'd do it sometimes when the club was uptight. Not too many people notice when you do things, but Roberto came up to me once and said, 'You do things when they're needed.' "

Roberto also did things when they were needed. Jackie Hernández, a Cuban shortstop, had been obtained from Kansas City the previous winter. As the Pirates drove hard for the division title, regular shortstop Gene Alley injured his knee and Hernández replaced him. Jackie, a sensitive man, booted a few ground balls in key games, and one night he sat near his locker almost in tears. "I was mad, mad because I hadn't made the plays," he says. "I felt like spending the whole night in the clubhouse. I didn't want to go outside." Roberto came over, put his arm around him and said, "These things happen in baseball. You have another game to play tomorrow. C'mon, tonight you're going out to dinner with me." During the next few weeks, Hernández fielded brilliantly.

As for Clemente, by early September he was challenging the league's top batters with a .350 average—during one fifteen-game stretch he hit .523. Later that month, his Puerto Rican admirers filled Shea Stadium in New York and, in a ceremony prior to the game against the Mets, gave him a Cadillac. At first, Roberto was reluctant to accept the huge luxury car, protesting, "If I want a car, I can buy it myself." But then he said, "This is not something you can refuse. I know that the Puerto Rican people, to give me this honor, have had to go through hell." Moved by the tribute, he repaid the 35,936 fans that chilly night by driving in two runs, including the one that gave Pittsburgh a 3–2 victory.

East met West in San Francisco on October 2, when the league's two division champions—the Pirates and the Giants—played the first game of a post-season playoff to decide the National League pennant. Pittsburgh lost the opener but swept the next three games and earned a chance to meet the Baltimore Orioles in the 1971 World Series. In the final playoff game, the Giants scored one run in the top of the first inning but were stopped from adding more thanks to a brilliant throw by Roberto that held a runner at third base. The Pirates got two men on base during their turn at bat in the first. Clemente, after fouling off four two-strike pitches, drove them both in with a single. With the score tied 5 to 5 in the sixth inning, he again whacked a single up the middle to drive in Dave Cash with the deciding run. Moments later, he dashed to second on a passed ball, and—with first base open—the Giants gave Stargell an intentional pass. Al Oliver slammed a long homer to insure the victory. The Pirates were on their way to their first World Series since 1960.

They raised hell in the clubhouse, splashing each other with champagne, milk, beer, soda—but Roberto sat quietly upon a rubbing table in the trainer's room, his favorite spot. "I am happy, *very* happy, but I don't have to jump up and down. Some people think I am strange because I don't jump up and down." For similar reasons, he explained, people thought him sad because he was rarely seen smiling. "But I am happy inside. It's just how a person's face muscles are. Now you take Sangy, the way the muscles in his face work, he looks like he's always smiling, even though he may feel sad." Pirate owner John Galbreath wedged through the circle of reporters and shook Roberto's hand effusively. "You're everything we think you are. You never let us down. You come through every time—you're the greatest."

"Do you really think you're the greatest?" asked one reporter.

Reflecting for a moment, Roberto replied, "How do you measure a man? How can you compare one man with another unless you've seen them both? I cannot tell about other men who played long ago." Then, thinking of an old friend and rival, who was in the twilight of his career and had not enjoyed a great playoff series, Roberto said, "I saw Mays. To me, Willie Mays is the greatest who ever played. But he is forty and has had his days. He is tired. San Francisco is all tired. For them it was not easy. For twenty days they were in a tight pennant race and don't know where they are. Mentally, they were going to be tight. You could see Mays is tired." Another writer asked about Mays's ineffective bunt in the final game. Roberto looked him in the eye and said, coolly, "If he bunts good, you say it is a great play. He bunts bad, so you say it is a bad play. Tie game I think maybe I bunt, too."

A grinning Pirate approached, arm poised to douse him with beer. "No, no, I got a bad eye!" Roberto protested, prompting a burst of laughter from the group. Dave Giusti and a few other teammates, all of them soaked from the victory celebration, peeked into the trainer's room. "Get out, Giusti," Roberto said. "You know I don't like Italians." But big Bob Veale, all six-feet-six of him, gently hoisted Roberto atop his shoulder and, while Giusti applauded, carried him to the shower. "As you can see," Roberto said in parting, "there are no privileges on the Pirates."

"He called me 'Hully'—that's my nickname," said the Pirates' equipment manager John Hallahan, who started out with the team as a batboy more than thirty years ago. "Sometimes he'd call me John, and I'd say, 'Well now, don't get too personal there, Herschel.' For some reason Roberto kidded me about being a Russian Jew, even though I'm not, and then he'd claim *he* was Jewish, too! So I'd call him Herschel, and he loved it. I always told him that someday I wanted to buy a home, and he'd say, 'Stick with me Hully and I'll put money in your pocket.' Then he'd kid around and say, 'We're gonna put some *ham* in that refrigerator, no more plain baloney.' Sure enough, when we won the 1971 World Series, I got a full share of the winnings and right away I put $10,000 down on a house. He was so tickled about me getting the house. I remember, during that Series, when he was at bat, I'd yell, 'C'mon, you sonofabitch! C'mon Herschel, hit one for me!' "

Just before the Series, Jim Russo, the Baltimore Orioles' "superscout," briefed the team in their clubhouse at Memorial Stadium. "Roberto Clemente's weakness, whatever little he has," he told the Oriole pitchers, "is so close to his strength that you are always in danger. There's only one way to pitch to him, and that's low and away, but he's going to make you throw strikes on that part of the plate. If you make a mistake he's going to hit it out of sight to right field."

The writers and the bookies had a low opinion of Pittsburgh's chances against Baltimore. Just as in 1960, when they upset the Yankees, the Pirates were the overwhelming choice to lose. "The way everyone talks, we should be playing in the Little Leagues," said Roberto. Pittsburgh had terrorized the National League with a slew of home runs and a .274 team batting average during the season, but the Orioles were a cool, well-balanced team with four twenty-game winners on its pitching staff. Furthermore, they were hot, having won their last eleven games in the regular season and three straight against Oakland in the playoff. Thus, few of the 53,229 Baltimore fans were surprised when their favorites slapped three Pirate pitchers around for ten hits in the first game of the Series and won 5 to 3; Oriole pitcher Dave McNally allowed only three hits and set down twenty-one of the last twenty-two Pirate batters. Roberto made two of the team's hits, including the only double of the game. "We respect the Orioles, but we're not intimidated by them," said manager Danny Murtaugh. "We'll be back tomorrow."

"Tomorrow" it rained, as it had all night. About ninety minutes before game time, baseball commissioner Bowie Kuhn, a black umbrella held over his head by a member of the Baltimore ground crew, sloshed through the rain-soaked grass at Memorial Stadium, checking the terrain, consulting with the umpires. Finally, Kuhn decided to postpone the game until the next day, Monday, at 1 P.M.

A day's rest was of no help to the Pirates. Mrs. Richard M. Nixon threw out the first ball, "with more accuracy than the Pirate pitchers have displayed," wisecracked one observer. The Orioles manhandled half a dozen Pirate pitchers for fourteen hits and seven bases on balls, scored six runs in the fifth inning alone, and finally won the uneven contest by 11 to 3. "The World Series is no longer a contest," wrote one columnist. "It's an atrocity; it's the Germans marching through Belgium." During the slaughter, Roberto played the only way he knew, hitting a hard single and a double against the right-field wall, and making—in the words of Andy Etchebarren of the Orioles—"the greatest throw I ever saw by an outfielder." The most notable aspect of that throw is that it was made in the midst of Baltimore's six-run splurge in the fifth inning and got absolutely no one out. It changed the outcome of the game not one iota. But it was simply there, in all its irrelevant splendor. With Merve Rettenmund on second base, Frank Robinson hit a long fly ball to right field. Rettenmund crouched at the bag like a sprinter, ready to advance to third, which appeared to be an easy feat. Roberto caught the ball on his glove side, whirled around in midair and fired a perfect strike to third base, missing the speedy runner by inches. After the game an admiring newsman said, "You'd of had him if it weren't Rettenmund." Roberto, who had been playing with a sore shoulder since July, said, "If I have my good arm, the ball would get there a little quicker than he does." In the gloomy Pirate clubhouse, Roberto complained loudly about the ragged playing surface of Memorial Stadium. The field had been chewed to bits in recent days by the football cleats of the Baltimore Colts, and the groundskeepers had actually painted some of the bald spots green for the benefit of color-television viewers. Then, trying to cheer up his teammates, he said in a loud voice, "Don't worry. I'll get you up when we get to Pittsburgh. I will hit those Baltimore pitchers like we are taking batting practice." But on the flight back to Pittsburgh each Pirate knew that the team was in deep trouble. Since 1903, only five teams had managed to bounce back after losing the first two games of a Series. Murtaugh said soberly, "Now our backs are to the wall."

In game three, played under a cool October sun on the smooth Tartan Turf of Three Rivers Stadium, the Pirates went with right-hander Steve Blass against one of the Orioles' twenty-game winners, Cuban left-hander Mike Cuellar. They got off to a 2 to 0 lead on Clemente's ground ball that allowed a runner to score from third and Pagan's single that drove in Sanguillen. After Baltimore's Frank Robinson narrowed the advantage to 2–1 with a solo home run in the top of the seventh, the Pirates broke the game wide open in their half of the inning. It all began harmlessly enough. Clemente, swinging hard, topped the pitch and dribbled an easy grounder to the pitcher's mound. When Cuellar turned to make a leisurely throw, he was astonished to see Roberto running full speed; so astonished that he threw the ball wide, pulling first baseman Boog Powell away from the bag, and Clemente was safe. Upset, Cuellar walked Stargell on four straight pitches, and up came Bob Robertson. With the count 1-and-1, a bunt signal was flashed from the Pirate dugout, but the 205-pound Robertson, who hadn't been asked to bunt all season, missed the sign completely. Clemente had spotted a signal but wasn't sure whether it was to bunt or to hit-and-run. As he led off second base, he waved his arms frantically at the umpire, trying to call time, but Cuellar was already in his windup. Robertson smacked the pitch over the right-center field fence for a three-run homer. As he trotted toward home, grinning broadly, a straight-faced Stargell patted him on the rear and said, "That's the way to bunt the ball." The Pirates won, 5 to 1, but more important was the psychological effect of breaking Baltimore's sixteen-game win streak. Watching the game from a box seat was Joe Torre, the Cardinals star who would be voted the league's Most Valuable Player that season. He said, "It all began with Clemente hustling to first. He knows only one way to play this game."

The outstanding player of the Series would receive a Dodge Charger automobile from *Sport* magazine, and already—after only three games—*Daily News* columnist Dick Young wrote: "The best damn ballplayer in the World Series, maybe in the whole world, is Roberto Clemente, and as far as I'm concerned they can give him the automobile right now." But there was more to come.

The fourth game was the first in the sixty-eight-year history of the Series to be played at night. In addition to the record total of 51,378 fans who squeezed their way into Three Rivers Stadium, an estimated 61 million people huddled around 21 million TV screens to watch the game. The marketing experts at NBC boasted that about half of all the nation's sets were tuned to the game, making it the largest audience ever to view a sporting event during "prime-time" evening hours. The Orioles rushed ahead 3 to 0 in the first inning but were handcuffed thereafter by a skinny twenty-one-year-old rookie, Bruce Kison, who throws vicious sidearm fastballs that sometimes get away and settle in a batter's ribs. Kison toiled under a double burden—he was scheduled to marry a young lady by the name of Anna Maria Orlando on the evening of October 17, right after the seventh Series game, if one was necessary. The Pirates nearly evened the score in their turn at bat as Stargell, shaking off a long hitting slump, lined a double to score Cash and scored himself on Oliver's single. In the third inning Roberto Clemente came to bat with Richie Hebner on first, and the organist at Three Rivers Stadium broke into a peppy rendition of "Jesus Christ Superstar." Roberto leaned across the plate for an outside pitch and sent it streaking down the right-field line, over the wall. But umpire John Rice ruled it foul by inches, sparking what promised to be a small riot, with Clemente as one of the central agitators. When Roberto finally calmed down, he dug in and punished another pitch, which landed fair in right field for a single, sending Hebner to third base. Al Oliver lined a hit to right, and Hebner scored to make it 3-all. The Pirates threatened again in the fifth, when Clemente bounced a grounder through the pitcher's box—his seventh hit of the Series—Stargell singled, and both men advanced on a bad throw, leaving first base open. Al Oliver was given an intentional pass, but the inning ended with a force play, where Oliver threw himself so hard into a flying block at the Oriole second baseman that both men rose from the dust and put on each other's caps. In the seventh inning, with Pirate runners on first and third, young reserve catcher Milt May, the son of former big leaguer "Pinky" May, pinch-hit for Kison. He drove in the winning run with a single, to even the Series at two games apiece. Pittsburgh's momentum carried it to a third straight victory at Three Rivers Stadium as Nelson Briles—throwing with such a hard, fluid motion that he landed flat on his face three times during the game—pitched a stunning three-hitter. Robertson's 400-foot homer over the center-field fence gave Briles a 1 to 0 lead, which is all that he required. Clemente drove in one of the Pirate runs in the 4 to 0 victory with another hard single through the mound, giving him a string of twelve straight Series games—dating back to the 1960 Series—in which he'd gotten a hit. Now Baltimore had *its* back to the wall. Pittsburgh's famed offense was finally on the move, and its pitching staff was proving to be a marvelous *lagniappe:* Messrs. Blass, Kison, Giusti, and Briles had allowed only ten Baltimore hits in the past three games.

With five games elapsed, Roberto—with nine hits and a .429 batting average—was being called "the towering figure of the Series." Oriole third baseman Brooks Robinson shook his head, saying, "I thought he was great, but now that I've seen more of him he's even greater than I thought." Baltimore's worried scout Frank Russo groaned, "All I see is Clemente coming up to bat every time I look up. So far he's been unbelievable." As the team prepared for the return trip to Baltimore, Roberto told a reporter, "I'm thirty-seven and may not play in another Series. Money means nothing to me, but I love competition—to me to compete is to compare, and that's everything."

The Pirates were in a happy mood before the sixth game. One more, and that's all. But one more might be hard to get. No team had lost on its home ground. The sixth game, and the seventh if necessary, would be played in Baltimore. The pattern remained intact in the sixth game, as the Orioles won a ten-inning thriller, 3 to 2. Even in defeat it had been a great day for Clemente. He got his tenth Series hit in the first inning, a shot against the left-center field wall that he stretched into a triple with a surprising burst of last-second speed. Two innings later, Jim Palmer threw him an outside pitch and he sent it soaring into the right-field bleachers for his first Series home run. This gave Pittsburgh a 2-to-0 advantage, but the Orioles struck back with single runs in the sixth, seventh, and tenth innings. Clemente prevented an Oriole victory in the ninth inning with a mighty throw from the right-field corner that held a runner at third base. Danny Murtaugh was angry over some of the umpires' calls during the close game, but back in the clubhouse he sat calmly sipping a cup of skim milk and told the press, "Well, the next one tells it all." In one corner of the Pirate clubhouse a black canvas was draped over a television camera; lights and thick electrical cables hung from a pipe near the ceiling. In anticipation of a Pittsburgh victory, the TV network crews had prepared to cover the clubhouse celebration. Now, the harried fellows from NBC had to build an identical set-up in the Baltimore clubhouse, just in case.

For splendor and tension, no sporting event can match the seventh game of a World Series. Played under a cool October sun that etches the combatants in sharp relief against the green turf, fed by a rich folklore that dates back to the early days of the century, buoyed by the partisan enthusiasm of millions of fans, this is "it"—the winner-take-all climax between two champions.

In the bus that took the Pirates to Baltimore's Memorial Stadium that Sunday, announcer Bob Prince was flipping through a newspaper. "I spotted a column claiming that Roberto wasn't a complete ballplayer because he couldn't pull the ball to left and hit home runs. I casually said to one of the players—Dave Giusti, I think it was—'Hey, did you see what this guy wrote?' Roberto's ears pricked up. He read the column and was screaming right and left. By the time we got off the bus, I said to myself, 'I pity whoever's pitching today.'"

Mike Cuellar was pitching for Baltimore, and the veteran left-hander from Cuba had a score to settle with Roberto that dated back to the previous winter. The Pirates selected their ace, Steve Blass, to take the mound. Blass was so nervous that during batting practice he sought refuge in comedy to stay sane. After hitting a ball that fell into the first row of the left-field bleachers, Blass—a .120 batter—did a perfect imitation of Clemente, arching his back, rolling his head around a few times, and glaring out at the pitcher for the next throw.

But all humor was set aside moments later, as Secretary of State William P. Rogers threw out the first ball, and the crowd of 47,291 people roared in anticipation of a thrilling duel.

Blass was rattled slightly in the first inning, when Oriole manager Earl Weaver protested that his foot was not making proper contact with the pitching rubber as he released the ball. Extra careful, he gave a base-on-balls to Don Buford. But the incipient threat ended when Clemente made a good running catch of Frank Robinson's fly ball. Cuellar was in fine form and retired the first eleven Pirate batters—until Roberto walked up to the plate with two outs in the fourth inning. He swung on the first pitch and sent it zooming over the 360-foot sign on the green fence in left-center field. Pittsburgh was ahead, 1 to 0.

No more runs were scored until the eighth inning in the tense pitcher's battle, as Blass and Cuellar set down the hitters with puzzling assortments of curves and speeds. After Willie Stargell grounded a single to the left of second base, up came José Antonio Pagán, a veteran infielder from Barceloneta, Puerto Rico, who had sat out much of the summer with a fractured wrist. Juan Marichal once said, "I think Pagán must have been born under some sign of the zodiac that makes him the forgotten man." Pagán had played for so many years, with such steady competence, that he was taken for granted. Few fans remembered his clutch home run for the Giants in the 1962 Series. The one day in his long career that he hit two homers, Willie Mays overshadowed him by hitting four. Pagán had been swinging out in front of Cuellar's pitches all day, so he set aside his favorite 38-ounce bat and chose one two ounces heavier. On a 1-and-1 pitch, he drove it deep against the fence in left-center and Stargell slid across the plate with Pittsburgh's second run. It was needed. In the eighth inning, with only Baltimore six outs remaining, Elrod Hendricks hit one of Blass's pitches for a single over second base. Belanger hit another to almost the same spot. Tom Shopay, batting for Cuellar, advanced both men with a bunt, putting the tying run at second base. The Baltimore fans were in a frenzy; the crowd was like a monster with 47,000 mouths and pairs of arms, urging on the kill. Buford hit the ball to first base and Bob Robertson beat him in a race to the bag, but Hendricks had raced home, making the score 2 to 1. Dave Johnson, a dangerous batter, extended the count to 2-and-2 and hit a hard grounder to deep short, but Jackie Hernández made a flashy stop and threw to first, snuffing out the threat.

In the ninth inning, Blass needed just eight pitches to retire three batters. When Hernández fielded Rettenmund's grounder and threw him out to end the Series, the Pirates—each of them about $18,000 richer and champions of the world—simply went insane. Blass kept jumping up and down near the pitcher's mound, and Manny Sanguillen, wearing his catcher's gear and holding his mask in one hand, swooped around the infield, his arms outstretched, like a happy bird.

Earlier that afternoon, before the final game, as Roberto tied the laces on his spiked shoes, he saw Pirate scout Howie Haak strolling about the clubhouse and called him over. Haak moved a small stool over close to Roberto and sat down. "Howie, you have been a good friend of mine over the years. I want you to be one of the first to know something. If we win today's game, I'm going to quit baseball." But a couple of hours later, as Roberto ran in from right field after the final out, he changed his mind. When he rushed over to embrace Vera, she was crying. "Roberto," she said, "don't quit baseball now. Please don't quit now, it's your life."

The Pittsburgh locker room was a shambles. Players, coaches, newsmen, and gate-crashers were stepping all over each other, tripping on wires, embracing, yelling, laughing, soaking each other with champagne. Steve Blass, his arm around his dad—a plumber from Connecticut—was beside himself with joy and relief. All during the game he had popped in and out of the clubhouse, unable to sit still, opening up one Coke after another, taking a sip and throwing it away. "I can't believe it! I can't believe it!" he yelled. Moments before, President Nixon had called both managers. Did Blass receive a phone call, too? asked one newsman. "I sure did! It was from the first selectman of Falls Village, Connecticut, and he congratulated me!" The mikes were now thrust toward Roberto, who stood nearby. "First," he said, "I would like to say something in Spanish to my mother and father in Puerto Rico." Looking into the camera, he said, "On this, the proudest moment of my life, I ask for your blessing." Few, if any, Americans understood the meaning of that remark, but in Puerto Rico and throughout Latin America they knew. Everyone wanted to shake his hand. Jerry Hoffberger, the Orioles' millionaire board chairman, came over. "Mister Clemente, you guys are great, and you are the best of the ballclub." Pirate reserve catcher Charlie Sands edged himself in and blurted: "I want to shake the hand of the greatest ballplayer in the whole damn world."

As the Pirates continued their joyous pandemonium, Roberto drifted back to his locker and sat on the wooden stool, a smile on his face. Minutes before, he had seen Jackie Hernández and Willie Stargell rush into the clubhouse from the field with their arms around each other, crying. He later said, "To me, that I could bring together a black Latin and a black American was my joy."

Observing Roberto from across the room, trainer Tony Bartirome said to a reporter, "Look at him, look at the remarkable physical specimen he is. Not one piece of skin out of place. It's fantastic to see him and realize how great he does when he's got pain. He hurt the rotor muscle in his right shoulder this year when he threw a ball too hard after playing it off the wall. I've been treating it all season."

"Why aren't you celebrating, Roberto?" a newsman asked him. Clemente smiled, saying, "Oh, that's okay for the younger fellows." He had his own way of showing emotion, as Steve Blass recalls so vividly:

"Talk about emotional moments. I was pretty worked up about the playing the World Series, and Robby had such a great Series—it was his showcase. It was so obvious, his feeling of pride, and he was just as happy as hell because everybody in the world had a chance to see what we'd been watching for all these years. After the last game, he was surrounded by reporters over by his locker, and I had some around me, so we didn't really have a chance to see each other. Then we had two buses going to the airport—he was on one with Vera, and I was on the other with my wife, Karen. At the airport,

Karen and I got on the plane, walked back to the second section and sat down. We saw up front that Clemente and Vera were coming down the aisle, shaking hands with everybody. All of a sudden he looked up and saw me. He came close and simply said, 'Blass, let me embrace you.' "

"The Uncontaminated Man"

Efrén R. Bernier's voice is barely audible above the hum of the air conditioner in his office. A short, very soft-spoken man in his early fifties, Sr. Bernier is a distinguished lawyer and now presides over the Colegio de Abogados, Puerto Rico's bar association. And, like countless other men in a surprising variety of fields, he is a baseball buff.

I was president of the Amateur League in 1955 and had met Roberto from time to time, but it wasn't until the past five years that I came to know him intimately. I love baseball—I read anything about it that I can get my hands on—and I considered Roberto to be the finest player of all time. Whenever I went to a lawyers' convention in the United States, I took advantage and spent a few days watching him play. The first year, in 1968, I attended a seminar in San Francisco, and then saw him play series in San Diego and Los Angeles. One day, I greeted him. We dined together, and we spoke quite a bit. I recall that he got his 2,500th hit during the Los Angeles series. I told him, "Roberto, I promise you I'll be with you when you hit number 3,000." He was a bit skeptical and said, "I don't know if I'll last that long, because I don't feel very well." I told him, "No, you're going to make it, and I'll be there." And I was.

The next year I went to the United States with my whole family—my wife, four children, my mother, and a nephew. The convention was in Portland. But we drove cross-country from New York and we saw him play a five-game series in Chicago. During that season, I also stopped for a few weeks in Pittsburgh and saw him play an entire homestand. We were together almost every day. If my admiration for him as a player was great, it was even greater for him as a human being.

We became quite friendly, and he even began to ask my advice, informally, on legal matters. The next year, a man Roberto loved very much died in an auto accident and left a large family. Their family lawyer had to leave the case because he was appointed to a government job. He asked me to take over the case. The family was offered $30,000 to settle, which was about the maximum ever paid before in Puerto Rico. Roberto had been financing the family for quite some time, with considerable amounts of money, and if they won the case they could pay him back; if not, he said forget it. I explained to Roberto that $30,000 wasn't really equal to the economic loss of the person, and in the course of the conversation he displayed such a degree of logic that he even gave me a few pointers that I used in arguing the case! Finally, we settled for $348,000, although the Supreme Court later lowered it to $95,000.

Roberto and I discussed every imaginable topic; we visited each other's houses often. Once we even spoke of starting a business that wasn't really a business. He was highly skilled in ceramic work and in making lamps. His whole house is decorated with things he himself made. Roberto saw ceramics as a way for fathers, mothers, and children to work together, as a family nucleus, in their own homes, to chat, and in the meantime produce salable merchandise. The business would be to supply them with the raw materials. There was almost no profit involved. It was practically a public service.

Once, in Pittsburgh, we went to a store to buy some ceramics materials. The owner, a fellow about twenty-eight years old, refused to take Roberto's money. This happened in many places. It was a tremendous problem for Roberto to eat out in Pittsburgh. Sometimes he'd seek an out-of-the-way place, and when he went up to the register the cashier would say, "It's already paid for." Well, the fellow in the ceramics shop wouldn't take his money, either. Roberto insisted, saying that he expected to be his client for quite some time, and he wouldn't feel right if he didn't pay. Finally, the fellow told him, "Look, Clemente, you won't remember this, but when I was a kid—ten or eleven years old—I was sitting in the right-field stands at Forbes Field while you were out there. The batter hit a foul into the stands and when I went for it an older man grabbed the ball away from me. I sat there, crying. The next inning you came over and said, 'Here's a ball for the one they took away from you.' That ball slept beneath my pillow every day of my life, until I married. Now I keep it in a place of honor in my home. That's why I can't charge you."

In a certain sense, Roberto was a man from another century. Although his family was very poor and had little schooling, it was a very "cultured" family in the sense of values. They had a scale of priorities, and he was that way, too. In Pittsburgh, he was always visiting hospitals, talking with children. "The great one! The great one!" That's what they called him. And to Roberto, kids were the greatest thing in the world. To him, a child represented the "uncontaminated man," the man who still conserved his innocence. He didn't smoke, and he rarely drank—maybe one or two to be sociable—but in the presence of a child, never.

Once, the Pepsi-Cola Company offered him about $30,000 for a brief commercial that would be used only in Pittsburgh, in Puerto Rico, and in New York City, places where lots of Latinos lived. Roberto refused because it was limited to those specific places. He felt that he represented all Latino players, and the idea of a commercial that in a sense hid him from the rest of the country was denigrating to not only himself but to all Latinos.

The Sports City in Puerto Rico was his big dream. The time came when his social concern overshadowed almost everything else. Baseball was no longer his *modus vivendi*, because he didn't need the money. I'd tell him, "You can't retire now. You can't do this to the people of Puerto Rico. It's not only you now, many people are counting on you." Roberto's career had vast repercussions, among Latino players and among his people. This is why he played always as if it were the World Series, why he ran into walls, played when he was sick, with pain, his legs swollen. With proper stimulus, he had about four good years ahead of him, and perhaps a few more with this new rule of the designated batter, who only comes up to hit. In terms of base hits, he could have reached third place, only behind Ty Cobb and Stan Musial. I have all the statistics. If you count Winter League baseball, he would have reached 5,000 hits. Except for home runs and stolen bases, he would have been among the top five in singles, doubles, triples, extra-base hits, total bases, runs batted in, runs scored, assists, times at bat, games played. In a couple more seasons, he would have had 10,000 times at bat, and only two other men in that category—Cobb and Musial—would have had higher batting averages. He was a true iron horse.

But his greatness on the field was not merely due to his physical ability. He had an extraordinary drive to excel. Once, I went early with Roberto to the park in Pittsburgh so he could practice something I never thought could be done. It was drizzling, and he wanted to see how best to grip a wet ball and throw it with accuracy. He developed a different grip for wet days! Another time, I told him I would love to see the old Forbes Field, which was being dismantled. "Let's spend the morning there," he said. We strolled around there in the outfield, in this old empty stadium, and he told me how he first became so popular with the Pittsburgh fans. There were a number of steady fans who always took the same seats in right field, near him. He got to know them. One day an older woman didn't show up and he went over to the fence. "Where is she?" he asked. She had died, they told him. He knew them all. That same morning he showed me the tricky right-field wall at Forbes Field, which was like a hexagon. A wrong bounce and a simple hit became a double or triple. For hours he had players hit the ball against the wall, and he even learned that the ball spinned differently if it was a right-handed or left-handed batter. It was a question of the law of physics!

Because of his back problems, Roberto was examined by many specialists. He asked them questions and read a lot about it. It became almost an obsession, and soon he himself could perform wonders! He treated people on the big green pool table downstairs in his trophy room. A little boy would come over, his neck bent. "What's up?" "I've been this way for years. Had an accident and that's the way it is." "Here's where it hurts, right?" "*Aaaaah!*" According to his father, the kid had been to plenty of doctors. Roberto massaged him, moved his neck around, suddenly we hear like a creaking sound, and the kid was fine!

I used to warn Roberto not to do such things. He had no license, and someone might sue him. "I don't give a damn, let them sue! I'm just trying to help."

There have been a lot of stories about Roberto's problems with the U.S. press, not with all of them, of course. In my personal opinion, most sportswriters are frustrated players. They might have a tendency to try and show that they were too intelligent to be athletes, that baseball is simply a matter of physical dexterity. They ask such foolish questions! The idea, of course, is to get a foolish reply!

I wasn't in the locker room during the 1971 World Series, but a close friend of mine was there and has told me this anecdote. He repeated it to me in Roberto's presence, and he never denied it. It was just before the seventh game of the Series with Baltimore and everyone assumed that, no matter what happened, the Most Valuable Player Award would go to Roberto. At the pregame press conference, they were asking him all sorts of questions. Almost every baseball writer in the country was there. One of them asked, "Is this World Series the greatest moment in your career?" Roberto looked at him very seriously, thought for a moment and said, "The greatest moment in my career is *now*, this precise instant, when I'm going to answer your question. This is the *first* time I've ever been able to have all of you together in one room, and I want to tell all of you that *you're a bunch of good-for-nothing bums!* Now that I've got it off my chest, you'll see a different Roberto Clemente. I won't complain about anything any more."

Of course, not a word of this got published!

11

"I finally have peace of mind. Now everyone knows the way Roberto Clemente plays. I believe I'm the best player in baseball today."

Few of the people gathered at Mamma Leone's Restaurant in New York that late October afternoon would have dared dispute Roberto's claim. No one could recall when a player had last dominated a World Series so completely. Against Baltimore he had compiled a fantastic .414 batting average, with twelve hits—including two home runs, two doubles, and a triple— and he had played defense with flawless brilliance. Vera and Roberto had come to Manhattan a few days after the Series for the luncheon where he would be officially declared the winner of a car for being the outstanding player of the 1971 Series.

Now, at last, he had peace of mind, after 60 million people all over America and points beyond had seen him at his best. Roberto Clemente was now a household word. A few months later, when he met with Pirate general manager Joe Brown and signed a one-year contract for about $150,000 to play the 1972 season, he would say, "I don't have to play this game for money. I have $600,000 put away from what I have earned in baseball and have a $100,000 home that is paid for completely. I was ready to quit after the World Series, but my wife didn't want me to do it and that is the only reason I'll be back next season." There was also the matter of that 3,000th hit. Only ten had achieved that lofty figure, and Roberto stood just 118 hits away. But this was well within reach. With the financial security of his family assured, with his place as a superstar also assured, one would expect him to settle back and enjoy life. But the restless Roberto was never one to settle back. Someone once described him as a man who expected "absolute perfection from life." This was a tall order in an imperfect world. During that luncheon at Mamma Leone's—as he had in years previous and would in the few months that remained of his life—he spoke out on "touchy" issues that baseball's establishment preferred not to discuss.

He came out in strong support of black star Curt Flood's attempt to challenge the hoary reserve clause in the courts. Since the beginning of organized baseball, the reserve clause in players' contracts has kept them in a status of high-priced chattels who are the exclusive property of the clubs and can be traded or sold whenever the whim strikes the owners. The clause has been challenged, without success, several times over the years. Flood had been ostracized for his court battle—which, if victorious, could radically change the game's management-player relationship, and Roberto was one of the few prominent stars in baseball to support his militant stand.

Roberto also leveled charges at club owners for being unable or unwilling to produce a black field manager; he also criticized the press for not amply airing this vital issue. "If a black player wants to become a manager, the owners tell him he has to go to the minors to get experience," he said, "but a white player does not. And sometimes the white player has not even made it to the major leagues. I think that is a double standard." Several blacks—Ernie Banks and Frank Robinson among them—were qualified "right now" to manage in the big leagues, he insisted.

Roberto acknowledged that progress had been made in opening up sports to members of racial minorities. The proof was in Pittsburgh's twenty-five-man roster that year, which included twelve blacks, five of whom were Latinos, and they had become champions of the world. "My greatest satisfaction," Roberto said, "comes from helping to erase the old opinion about Latin Americans and blacks. People never questioned our ability, but they considered us inferior to their station of life. Simply because many of us were poor we were thought to be low-class. Even our integrity was questioned. I don't blame the fans for that. I blame the writers. They made it look like we were entirely different from the white players."

Despite the progress, Roberto continued to insist that his people did not enjoy full equality. The difficulty that blacks and Latinos encounter in securing commercial endorsements was a permanent wound to his pride. "You have to be American," he once said, his voice dripping with irony, "or you can't be my 'sweetheart next door.' If they don't like my face, they can send me to get plastic surgery."

Roberto's brilliant career and the success of Latino stars such as Juan Marichal, the Alou brothers, Orlando Cepeda, Tony Oliva, and others had inspired—and opened the doors for—many more Latinos. But most of these youths—inarticulate and unsure of themselves in America's affluent, alien culture—signed for meager bonuses and docilely accepted low salaries. They were the wetbacks of American sports. Few Latinos felt sure enough of themselves to speak out like Roberto or like young American blacks such as Pittsburgh pitcher Dock Ellis, who says, "The black man has passed the stage where he is happy just to be playing major league baseball. I say, keep the records, trophies, and awards, and just give me the money."

But few Latinos have passed that stage. In the spring of 1971, when a dozen young Puerto Rican and Dominican prospects were turned away from an "open" dance in Saint Petersburg, Florida, they said nothing until days later, when a club official noticed that they were "quiet and sullen." One shy Latino rookie went without food for three days, eating only oranges from a grove next to the ballpark, because he couldn't understand the restaurant menus. Many Latino newcomers are resigned to their difficulties. As a Dominican rookie said recently, "One has to sacrifice in life. I try to remember a saying I was taught growing up at home: In the waters, I am water. In the rivers, I am a river. Among stones, I am a stone."

At five in the afternoon on October 22, 1971, a huge Eastern Airlines 747 jet glided gently to a halt on the runway of the International Airport in Puerto Rico. Roberto Clemente, *el héroe*, was home at last. A small official delegation—his parents, a few close friends, and a handful of government officials—was there to greet him. But behind a straining cyclone fence at the edge of the landing field were thousands of his people. As the door of the plane opened and Roberto, Vera, and the children emerged in the golden late afternoon sunshine, the noisy crowd burst past a barricade of policemen and engulfed them. After a brief ceremony, the Clementes were whisked away in official cars, but they were followed down the highway by a caravan of automobiles, gaily honking their horns.

Months later, Roberto would sigh, "What a rough winter!" The demand for his presence was far beyond what any mortal could satisfy. The governor, the park administration, civic clubs, and journalists all wanted to see him. Shaking his head and smiling, he said that, for a month and a half after the Series, "my wife and I couldn't sleep. Our house was like a museum—people flocking down the street, ringing our bell day and night, walking through our rooms, even tourists!" But Roberto was the kind of man who couldn't say no. One night, after taping an interview at a San Juan television station, he spent more than an hour with a group of station employees, showing them how he hit to different fields by changing the position of his legs. Everything was happening at once. In late January, he flew to New York to accept the Babe Ruth Award as the outstanding performer in the World Series. At the award dinner in the Americana Hotel, Casey Stengel called him "the greatest rightfielder I've seen in my fifty years of baseball." The next week, he was off to Rochester for another award, then to Erie, Pennsylvania, and next on to Pittsburgh, where he, Willie Stargell, and Danny Murtaugh would be honored as the town's outstanding citizens. Catholic University in Puerto Rico gave him an honorary doctoral degree in education, because his deeds had given "international status to the good name of the island." Pirate owner John W. Galbreath even named a racehorse in his honor, and the thoroughbred Roberto won the 1972 English Derby. The pace was maddening. Vera and he tried to get away to South America for a vacation but were called back because his father took sick. They tried to escape to their small house in the mountains, where they hoped to spend much of their leisure time, and got there exactly three times all winter. At a time when most ballplayers gain weight on the "banquet circuit," Roberto lost ten pounds.

Despite his busy schedule, Roberto somehow found time to promote his concept of the Sports City. It was almost as if he were racing against time. The Sports City, he said, had now become "the biggest ambition in my life."

"One of the biggest problems we have today," he said, "is that the father doesn't have time for the kids and they lose control over the children." Explaining that he hoped to finance the project with a combination of federal and insular funds, he complained, "They spend millions for dope control in Puerto Rico, but they attack the problem after it is there. Why don't they attack it before it starts? It would help to get kids interested in sports, and give them somewhere to learn." He dreamed of building a large complex where children from all social classes could stay for weeks at a time. "I want to have three baseball fields, a swimming pool, basketball, tennis, a lake where fathers and sons can get together, all kinds of recreational sports. It's not enough to go to a summer camp and have one or two instructors for a little time and then you go home and forget everything. You go to a sports city and have people like Mays and Mantle and Williams, and kids would never forget it. If I was President of the United States, I would build a sports city and take in kids of all ways of life. What we want to do is exchange kids with every city in the United States and show all the kids how to live and play with other kids."

"He felt that sports was one of the best ways to imbue in youth the values of good citizenship," his friend Efrén R. Bernier says, "where they could play hard, win or lose, and learn that games were a collective enterprise, and that one had to respect some outside authority—the law. He felt that with sports the child learned in a natural way, at an important stage of his life, that one must sacrifice a bit for the common good. This became his life, and the rest was almost secondary."

Roberto told his old friend Bob Leith, "People keep saying that I should leave work on the Sports City until after I retire from baseball, when I will have the time to work on it. I won't do it, because now I'm a big star, but when I retire no one will listen to me. It won't get done." Tirelessly, he went to the governor's mansion in San Juan to solicit support. He had paid an architect to map out a plan of the sports complex. He told Manny Suárez, a reporter for the *San Juan Star*, "I don't think there is a place in the world that has the athletic talent Puerto Rico does. We are a small island, and yet we have fathered three prizefight champions, a Chi Chi Rodriguez in golf, a Carlitos Pasarell in tennis, and enough major league ballplayers to field two teams. But maybe we have thousands of other youths out in the *barrios* who have the ability but, because they do not have the places to play in an organized way and because they do not have the coaching, will never get the chance. The Sports City could be the place to get them all started."

"I know where it is all built for you," said Suárez, who managed a Little League team that played at the nearby San Juan Naval Base in Miramar. Immediately, Roberto wanted to see it. He and Suárez climbed into Bob Leith's big Cadillac and off they went. Suárez recalls, "When he saw the swimming pool, the big gymnasium, the small theater, ball parks, and barracks buildings that could be used for dormitories, he could not hide his enthusiasm. 'This has everything we need. Why didn't they tell me about it?' "

Roberto was told that the naval base would soon be turned over to Puerto Rico by the federal government. Although no plans had been announced for the use of the valuable property—located in the center of the San Juan metropolitan area—Suárez commented, "You can bet your life that a playground for a bunch of ragamuffins was not one of their considerations."

"But we don't need the entire base," Roberto said. "All the sports facilities are in one small area. We could use this part and the government would still have enough land to do what they want with the remainder." Roberto was determined to push ahead on the project, but time ran out. Soon, he would have to report back to the Pirates for the 1972 season.

No sooner did he reach training camp than the writers began to hound him about the 3,000th hit. He usually replied, "It means nothing. I am not playing this season because I have a chance at a 3,000th hit. I am playing because I feel good and can go another good year, and as long as I can play good, the team has a chance to win."

Why should he confide in writers, he must have asked himself, after so many of them had twisted his words. With them, he showed—to use the old Spanish expression—his *cara de palo, his* "wooden face," a mask that shielded his true feelings. But he was not *cara de palo* with men like Manny Sanguillen. Later that season—feeling fatigued, underweight, yearning to rest—he said, "Sangy, I've *got* to get those 3,000 hits. I might get sick or die, and no other Latin will do it."

Roberto looked like a million as he strolled about the grounds of Pirate City in Bradenton that spring. One writer recalls him "in his long-collar-tab shirts and brilliant slacks . . . as vivid a major leaguer as there is, with features that might be carved out in ebony . . . signing autographs with dignity and a few gracious words for clusters of fluttering retired ladies."

"He tried twice as hard as anyone to help me," recalls Bill Virdon, his former teammate who became Pirate manager in 1972 when Murtaugh retired. "He was a true professional and he knew he had to get in shape. If I asked a bunch of guys to do something, that's the way it was. Whenever you get cooperation like that, you don't have problems with the rest of the players. He felt that baseball had done a great deal for him, and in his remaining days he wanted to pay back as much as he possibly could. But he didn't have to worry about that. He'd given baseball a lot more than he ever took from it."

The Pirates, who were favored to repeat as champions of the National League's Eastern Division, got off to a fast start in 1972. So strong was their offense that Al Oliver remarked, "You just can't make the line-up unless you're hitting .300." Roberto did his share, but he was constantly hampered by physical problems: a painful Achilles tendon, symptoms of rheumatism, the flu. At one point he dropped ten pounds from his sleek 180-pound frame, the size-32 pants of his own uniform were too big, and he had to borrow a pair from his 164-pound teammate, Rennie Stennett. He carefully rationed his strength, and manager Virdon, who knew him well, allowed him to sit out the second half of doubleheaders or afternoon games when the Pirates had played the night before. He played well, when he played, and the Pirates had powerful reserves to spell him. They were winning, and Roberto was enjoying himself. "It is a pleasure to play on this ball club, because we're winning, and every game is like a holiday." Even when he rested on the bench, says former teammate Jose Pagán, "the other team not only knew he was there, they saw Roberto waving to the rightfielder to show him where to stand. Nobody knew better how to play the batters."

This was a new, self-assured Clemente. Earlier in Roberto's career, says Monte Irvin, "I'd always kind of kid him good-naturedly, tell him he never *laughed* enough. 'A handsome guy like you, why'ntcha laugh more? Why'ntcha *smile?*' He always seemed so *serious*. Even though he made a great catch, or hit a home run, he never really let himself go." But in the summer of 1972, when Irvin attended a luncheon for Roberto in New York, he noticed a change. "He was so happy, because he was finally getting some recognition for his contributions to the game. It was never money he was after. He wanted recognition."

"He was one of the most dignified human beings I ever met, but he could also be very funny," says Pirates official photographer Les Banos, who was one of Roberto's favorite dinner companions during the team's road trips the last couple of years. In 1972, he recalls, "we went to have breakfast in San Francisco. There was an elderly black woman in the restaurant who keeps looking at Clemente. Finally she comes over and says, 'Mister Blue, can I have your autograph?' 'I'm sorry,' he says, 'but I'm not Vida Blue.' 'Oh!' she says and walks away. Roberto looks at me, shrugs his shoulders and says with a smile, 'See? That's fame and fortune for you.' The time I'll never forget is when we went to a Chinese restaurant in Philadelphia. There were three of us—Roberto Clemente from Puerto Rico, Eddie Acosta of Panama, and me, a Hungarian. A real old Chinese waiter comes over. Roberto says to him, 'We want sweet and sour pork, duck almond, fried rice, won ton soup—but we don't want individual servings. We want it all in big dishes so we can serve ourselves.' The old Chinese waiter looks at me, a real puzzled look on his face. So there we are, a Panamanian, a Hungarian, a Puerto Rican, and a Chinaman. Roberto is laughing. He stands up and says real loud: 'For heaven's sake, doesn't anyone speak English in this joint?' "

On June 20, Roberto was rolling along with a solid .325 batting average when he hit a two-run homer against the Los Angeles Dodgers. The 15,430 fans at Three Rivers Stadium rose and gave him a tremendous standing ovation. It had been more than just a home run. With that blow, he had broken the club all-time record of 1,273 runs batted in, held by Pie Traynor, the old Hall of Famer who had died a few months previously. As the fans continued to applaud, Roberto stayed in the dugout. Afterward in the clubhouse, a reporter asked why he hadn't come out to tip his hat and acknowledge their cheers. Seated near his locker, his head bowed, he said, "The man whose record I broke was a great ballplayer, a great fellow. And he just died here a few months ago. That's why I didn't tip my cap. You know what I mean," he said quietly, looking up at the reporters.

As the reporters scribbled his comments into their notebooks, he added, "I wasn't even aware of the record until they flashed it on the scoreboard. You know what means more to me? It gives me more satisfaction that I am still able to go out and play at my age. I thank God . . . For me, playing this game is all that counts. In all my years of baseball, I have never held out when it came to contract time. Maybe I'm crazy, I could probably be making a lot more money, but I will never let money come between me and this game."

June faded into July, and the Pirates moved inexorably toward the division title. Their batting lineup was being hailed as a new "Murderers' Row." Roberto missed several games because of his ailments, but with a team batting average that soared as high as .291, others picked up the slack. It was a far cry from the Pirates of years ago, when Roberto was like a lone woodchopper in a huge forest. When they needed him most, he was there. In late July, after the Pirates lost five games in a row, it was Roberto's single that drove in the tying run and gave a chance to Stargell, who hit a double to clinch the decision. Another time, in Chicago, he won a game with a home run off Ferguson Jenkins.

Roberto tumbled another all-time Pittsburgh club record on September 2, when his double and three-run homer helped to sink San Francisco and preserve the Pirates' eleven-game lead over Chicago. The double was his 2,971st hit and broke the previous Pirate record for career hits, held by the great Honus Wagner, one of the original members of the Hall of Fame, who retired in 1917. The champagne flowed again in the Pirate clubhouse on September 22 as they beat the Mets and assured another Eastern Division title. Now, the hottest question in Pittsburgh—until the Pirates met the Reds in the playoff for the National League pennant—was Roberto's 3,000th hit. The pressure grew, as the number of days left in the season diminished. On September 28, Roberto got a single—hit number 2,999—against the great Philadelphia pitcher Steve Carlton. He asked to be removed from the lineup so that he could try for the 3,000th hit at home in Pittsburgh the next night.

That Friday evening, 24,000 fans turned out at Three Rivers Stadium, despite rainy weather. Roberto would face Tom Seaver, the ace of the New York Mets. "I'm tired," he said before the game. "I need a rest to get ready for the playoffs. If I don't get that hit this weekend, I'll just wait until next season."

His first time up he swung hard at one of Seaver's fastballs but touched only a piece of it. The ball bounced over Seaver's head toward second, where Ken Boswell managed to get a glove on it. Clemente stood safely on first base. More than 24,000 pairs of eyes shifted to the scoreboard. The seconds seemed like minutes. The public address system boomed, "Error, second baseman. Error, Boswell." But the big "H" for "Hit" blinked momentarily on the scoreboard, and it was suddenly like New Year's Eve at Three Rivers Stadium. The umpire recovered the ball and gave it to Roberto, who flipped it over to first base coach Don Leppert for safekeeping. Suddenly the big "E" for "Error" lit up on the scoreboard, and the crowd, its emotions defrauded, waited to see what Roberto would do in his next three times at bat. Seaver held him hitless. Only in the ninth did he come close, lining a shot down the right-field line, but Rusty Staub, playing him perfectly, caught it.

In the clubhouse, the reporters were on him like a swarm of bees, and Roberto, reacting to the tremendous pressure, popped off angrily. "The scorers have been screwing me all my life and this shows it."

"How many hits do you think you lost in eighteen years?" one newsman asked.

"How many hits? You mean how many batting titles! I should have won two more," he said.

"One year we played in Montreal and I hit a ball between third and short. The shortstop threw the ball on one hop to first. I beat the throw, but they call it an error. You can't tell me whose is the error, because the shortstop threw it and the first baseman caught it. That one time at bat cost me a batting title. I lost another to Pete Rose in my final time at bat. But before, in San Diego, I got 4-for-5, and I hit a ball over second base where the shortstop tried to get the ball but never touched it. Three weeks later a writer comes to me and says, 'I'm sorry, but they took one hit away from you. They turned that hit into an error.' How can they take a hit away three weeks after the game?"

Finally, calmer, he shrugged and said, "I'll be out there swinging again tomorrow."

The official scorer for that game had been Luke Quay, a Pittsburgh-area sports editor and a friend of Roberto's. It was learned months later that Roberto took the "almost 3,000" souvenir ball and sent it to Quay, first writing upon it, "It was a *hit*, no, it was an *error*. No, it was superman Luke Quay! To my friend Luke with Best Wishes—Roberto Clemente."

The next evening, the Mets sent a young fireballer by the name of Jonathan Trumpbour Matlack (Jon Matlack to his fans) up against Clemente and Company. Roberto had spent almost the whole night before answering phone calls from friends in New York and Puerto Rico. "Then," he said, "my wife had to be at the airport at six o'clock to meet some friends, so we didn't even bother to go to bed. When I arrived at the ballpark, I had no sleep at all."

"There was tremendous pressure that night," recalls Felo Ramirez, whose Spanish-language broadcast was being heard by countless thousands of fans in Puerto Rico and the rest of Latin America. "For the past few days, everybody in the clubhouse kept talking about the 3,000th hit, except for Roberto; he had great self-control. To relieve the pressure, his old friend and teammate José Pagán said to him, '*Damn*, Roberto, do me a favor. Lend me your bat and *I'll* hit number 3,000 for you!' That caused a great deal of hilarity."

In the first inning, with 13,117 Pirate fans cheering him on, Roberto struck out. He came up again to lead off the fourth inning. Willie Stargell took a bat from the rack, handed it to him, and said, "Go get it." Roberto walked slowly to the plate, wiping the bat handle with a rag. He looked out at the field and rolled his head around and around to relieve the chronic pressure on his neck. Finally he dug in, deep in the batter's box. He crouched, cocked his bat high, stuck his chin out over the left shoulder in that aggressive way of his, and his eyes widened, waiting for the pitch. Eighteen years ago, 2,432 big league games ago, 9,453 trips to the plate ago, a tense rookie stood at bat in Pittsburgh seeking his first major league hit against Johnny Podres of the Brooklyn Dodgers.

Matlack threw and Roberto let it go by. Strike, said the umpire. In came the next pitch and Roberto whacked a terrific line drive that bounced against the wall in left-center field. It was hit number 3,000. A double. Clean. Irrevocable. It was a historic moment, and the fans knew it.

As the cheers reverberated throughout Three Rivers Stadium, Roberto stood at second base, one foot upon the bag, and raised his batting helmet to acknowledge the fans. Then, hands upon his hips, he rolled his head around and around to relieve the pressure in his neck. Umpire Doug Harvey came over, gave the historic ball to Roberto, and shook his hand. As Willie Stargell stood in the batter's box and Matlack waited on the mound, the applause continued for a full minute. The double was the start of a three-run Pirate rally, which proved enough to defeat the Mets. Roberto played for one more inning, as the fans continued to cheer, and then returned to the dugout. Willie Mays trotted over from the Mets' side and shook his hand while the photographers popped away. They had come a long way since they met in San Juan some eighteen years before. The two of them and Hank Aaron were the only players active in baseball with 3,000 career hits, and Roberto had just become the eleventh man in the entire history of the game to join that exclusive club.

"To get 3,000 hits means you've got to play a lot," he had said to a writer in Philadelphia a few days before. "To me it means more. I know how I am and what I've been through. I don't want to get 3,000 hits to pound my chest and holler, 'Hey, I got it.' What it means is that I didn't fail with the ability I had. I've seen lots of players come and leave. Some failed because they don't have the ability. And some failed because they don't have the desire."

The post-season playoff against the Reds was a sad, but not crushing, finale. Both teams had nearly identical records during the year. They split the first four playoff decisions, and it was not until the chaotic final inning of the final game that a wild pitch allowed Cincinnati to win the pennant. With two such superbly matched clubs, glittering with talent, the element of chance loomed large. As the champagne flowed in the Cincinnati clubhouse this time, the Pirates sat silently near their lockers, just fifty yards away. But manager Bill Virdon could say, with conviction, "It was a good game

. . . I took the time to tell each player individually that we'd had a hell of a year." And for an "old man," as Clemente now jokingly referred to himself, it hadn't been a bad year at all. Playing in 102 games, he had finished with a strong .312 batting average and—for the first time in his long career—had achieved a perfect 1,000 fielding record, handling 199 putouts without an error.

Roberto had no other visible horizons to conquer in baseball, but he planned to return for the 1973 season. However, his head also buzzed with retirement plans. There was the great dream of the Sports City, and he plunged ahead, seeing more and more people, trying to convince them, trying to raise funds. He also planned to open a free chiropractic clinic in Puerto Rico. He thought of going into the heavy equipment business, to rent earth-moving machinery to small towns on the island that could not afford their own. He thought of acting as personal representative for young Latino players to ensure that they would receive adequate salaries. The Puerto Rico Telephone Company had signed him up to give a series of baseball clinics for more than ten thousand youngsters in various towns of the island. He had accepted an invitation to manage an amateur Puerto Rican team in a Worldwide Amateur Tournament that would begin in Nicaragua on November 15. During the tournament he would fly back to San Juan to act as best man at 'he wedding of his niece, Carmen Luisa. There were offers to give clinics and make appearances in Colombia, Cuba, and other nations.

With all that, "he had a phenomenal memory," says Pirate announcer Bob Prince. "In October he asked me would I come to a banquet in Puerto Rico in honor of my twenty-fifth anniversary as a broadcaster. He also knew that I'm interested in helping retarded children—I helped to found a school for them in Pittsburgh. And wouldn't you know that he brought four or five retarded youngsters to the banquet, so that he could do something for them, and also let me know that he remembered. Then, before many hundreds of people at the banquet, he related the story from way back in 1958 about my defending Orlando Cepeda on the air. He explained it both in Spanish and in English. And he recalled the time in 1960 when he won the World Series and said, 'There was a newspaperman who campaigned against my winning the award for the most valuable player in that series. I was very hurt over that. I didn't mind that my teammate Dick Groat won it, but I was very hurt that one man should campaign *against* my winning it. So I promised my mother and father I would prove to them that I was the best player in the world.' The next year, 1961, he won his first National League batting championship and they gave him the silver bat award. He gave it to his parents, who later returned it to him, and he put it in his trophy room at home. When he continued to speak at the banquet, he said, 'I've been trying to think of the *one thing* I could give to one of the best friends I have in the world, the thing that means most to me, and I found out what it is.' With that, he began to cry and gave me the silver bat from 1961. I accepted it, and I was crying, too. When I took it from him, I said, 'I make this promise to you. When I die, this bat will be returned to your children, because it belongs to them.' "

"His Hands Reflected His Spirit"

"He called me 'Luisito,' and I felt like a brother to him," says Luis Rodriguez Mayoral, an airline accountant who also represents the Pittsburgh Pirates in Puerto Rico. In 1970, he originated the idea of holding special "days" for Latin American players in different major league cities.

I met Roberto before that, in 1967, when I was just twenty-one years old. I knew Howie Haak, the Pirate scout, and one time when he was staying at the Caribe Hilton in San Juan he said, "Let's go to Roberto's house." I was very happy; he was my idol and I'd never met him. When we got to the house, around 6 P.M., it was getting dark and they were out on the balcony, where you could see the whole city. Roberto was wearing gray Bermuda shorts and had no shirt on—I think he was doing some work in the yard. I was shy and just stood over in a corner. But he noticed that and came over to chat with me. We must have talked for about twenty minutes, and I felt so good, speaking with a man who was my idol. We seemed to hit it off well, and after that I saw him often. I recall September 1970, when he came to San Juan for some treatments because his back was ailing. We met in the airport, and I told him all about my new idea for special days to honor Latin players in the big leagues. I knew this was a cause very dear to him, and he answered with a smile. That was enough for me to know how he felt.

As I came to know Roberto, I saw what a great difference there was between the real man and what the American press said of him. They simply didn't understand him. I guess it's a question of different cultures. They made fun of his injuries, and to a Latin that is the biggest insult, because a Latin—especially a man like Roberto—wants respect more than anything. It's part of our culture. Without respect, a man is nothing.

We spent many hours together, and we rarely talked about baseball. Sometimes we would just sit and philosophize about life. Sometimes, though, the stories he told me—I'm inclined to think he was joking. You never knew. He said that when he was very small he could take a six-inch nail in his hands and bend it. Then he would give you a mysterious smile, and you never knew! Another time, he said, it was a very windy day at Candlestick Park in San Francisco, and he hit a terrific shot to right-center field that appeared to be a sure home run. But the wind held it up and Willie Mays caught it. He says he got so mad that he threw his batting helmet up in the air, and the wind blew it right out of the park! "Ask Orlando Cepeda, he was there," he used to say, with that little smile of his.

One moment of great satisfaction to me was on January 29, 1972, when the Rawlings firm awarded him his eleventh Golden Glove for superior defensive play. They asked me to present it to him personally at a dinner in the Puerto Rico Sheraton. He won twelve of those gloves, but the eleventh was the last one he received while alive. One of his favorite prizes was the Dodge Charger he won for being the outstanding player in the 1971 World Series. Roberto had a fever for driving, he was like a kid in that respect. One day, I'm at my office in the airport doing some accounting work when I see a big shadow loom over the paper I'm writing on. It was Roberto, wearing a beautiful brown suit with a mustard-colored shirt. "Let's have lunch, Luisito," he says. But we never got to eat. We drove all around in that Dodge, and he kept speeding and weaving in and out of traffic. "Roberto, you're *loco!*" I yelled at him. But he sat at that wheel with such confidence. He looked over at me and smiled, saying "Relax, I'm the best driver in the world." He did everything with such zest. Later that year, at spring training in Bradenton, I flew up there and arrived very early in the morning. I was very tired. I had breakfast with him, Jackie Hernández, and Manny Sanguillen. Then he told me to take a nap in his room. After practice later that morning, he came into the room and said, "Luis, I'm going to prepare you a punch—the kind that keeps me strong."

Well, he took two bottles of grape juice, and then, one by one, he dropped about eight eggs in there. It almost made me laugh to see the dedication he had in preparing that punch! It was good. Not *that* good, but I drank it anyway.

His hands were large and beautiful, and I believe that, more than anything else, his hands reflected his spirit. On the field, he gripped the bat with the strength of a tiger. But when he saw a little child and patted its head, his hands were extremely gentle. He had great talent with his hands. He made ceramic objects. He had never studied music, but he could play an electric organ quite well. He cured people with his hands. Late one night, he told me, an old lady knocked at his door. He opened and asked, "What's the matter, *señora?*" She said to him, "God has sent me!" She was all bent over. He took her into the house and treated her. He told me later, very happily, "*Muchacho*, I gave her such a 'pop' of the back and 'crack' of the neck that she walked away fine!"

He had such a passion for getting that 3,000th hit. When he finally did, he felt very shy about it. The locker room was shut tight, and lots of press people were crowded near the door. I yelled, "Rober-TO!" He knew that call and told Hully, the equipment manager, to let me in. Earlier that day I spoke with his mother on the phone, and she told me, "Give an embrace and a kiss to my son." He was sitting on his wooden stool near his locker in his underpants and sweatshirt. I walked over and hugged him and gave him a kiss on the side of his neck. He looked up at me and laughed, and I said, "That's from your mother and me." Then he looked down at floor and said, "*Chico*, I felt so uncomfortable when all those people applauded me."

I had brought with me a very special prize from Puerto Rico for his 3,000th hit, and the next day I gave it to him in a small ceremony at Three Rivers Stadium. It was a trophy that included a clod of earth from the place where he was born, Barrio San Antón in Carolina. He was very touched and said, "How great, and yet how small is the world. More than twenty years ago, I played upon this grass, so far away, and now here I am in Pittsburgh, playing on artificial turf." That 3,000th hit meant so much to him. He told me, "Now, at last, they know me for the player that I am." He didn't use the words "best" or "greatest," but simply "the player that I am."

12

oward R. Hughes, the recluse billionaire, woke with a start early in the morning of December 23, 1972. For nearly five months he had been cloistered in the lavish seventh-floor suite of the Managua Intercontinental Hotel. But now the curtains quivered strangely, porcelain on shelves and tables rattled. Hughes dressed quickly, alerted his staff, and hurried down a darkened back stairway to a rented car. Soon afterward his personal Learjet took off from the trembling earth of Nicaragua and deposited him safely in London.

The people of Managua were less fortunate. By nightfall, the earthquake had devastated their city, killing 6,000 injuring 20,000 more, and leaving about 3,000 homeless. Relief efforts sprung up throughout the hemisphere. A friend of Nicaraguan leader General Anastasio Somoza said later, "Hughes still hasn't sent a damn thing."

The night of December 23, Roberto Clemente went with Vera to the San Jeronimo Hilton in San Juan, where he would receive another award for his crowded trophy room. After the ceremony, in the hotel lobby, he met a local television producer, Luis Vigoreaux, who suggested that they form a committee to direct local relief efforts for the "sister country" of Nicaragua. Not long before, Vigoreaux explained, he had befriended several Nicaraguans at a convention of broadcasters in Mexico City. Roberto, too, had personal reasons for sharing the sorrow of the earthquake victims. That November he had managed Puerto Rico's entry in the Seventh Annual World Series of Amateur Baseball, held in Nicaragua, and made numerous friends. Osvaldo L. Gil, president of Puerto Rico's

Amateur Baseball Federation, had accompanied Roberto and the team on the trip. He vividly recalls one incident: "Julio Parrales, a poor orphan about fourteen years old, had lost both legs in an accident. When we learned that he needed only $750 to buy a pair of artificial legs, the Puerto Rico team raised $100 to start the collection. With about $200 more needed, it was suggested that an article be prepared for the newspapers to publicize the case. I said no, our team didn't want any credit for our donation. Roberto overheard me and came over to congratulate me for 'not allowing them to exploit a humanitarian act.' Then asked me to allow him to 'quietly put up the rest of the money.' Just Roberto and I went to see the child, to tell him that he would get his artificial legs, and the conversation between Clemente and that boy is simply beyond my poor powers of description. We returned from Managua on December 6, and about ten days later Roberto gave a little *fiesta* at his home for the Puerto Rican team. During the *fiesta*, he asked me when we would start practice again. I told him that my term as league president expired and that I planned to return to my private business. 'You can't leave yet; we have to win a world title first, and we can do it in two years,' he said. He spoke with tremendous enthusiasm and said he was sure the new government that took over in Puerto Rico on January 2 would give stronger backing to sports. He told me, 'We have to make the government understand that our athletes abroad are like national ambassadors. They can't go without being properly dressed and trained, otherwise they give a bad name to the island.' "

About that time, in mid-December, Edwin J. Morgan, a Pittsburgh photographer, visited Puerto Rico with his wife for a brief vacation, and also to take a few color photos of Roberto for his paper. As he walked up to the house he greeted Vera: "Haven't seen you since Cincinnati."

Shaking her head, recalling the playoff defeat in October, she smiled and said, "Forget Cincinnati." Morgan gave a quizzical look at a cage on the front lawn of the house. "Oh, that's Roberto's," she said. Moments later, Roberto pulled up, followed by several carloads of ballplayers. "How you get here, Ed?" Roberto shouted, clasping his hand and smiling. After they chatted for a while, Morgan says, "Roberto went into his garage and emerged with a monkey on a leash and put it into the cage. This brought squeals of glee from his three children, who were running around wearing Pirate hats. A little later, as we watched Roberto pulling away in his car, I shouted that I would see him at spring training."

It was more than a week before Christmas, but in Puerto Rico *las navidades* is a season, not a single day. The Christmas spirit begins to effervesce early in December and bubbles on through to January 6, Three Kings Day. Puerto Rican hospitality glows brightest during the Christmas season; it is a time for visiting and eating and drinking heartily. *Villancicos* (carols) are sung, and friends organize *parrandas*, groups of roving merrymakers who go from house to house with *asaltos* (attacks or surprise visits) until all hours of the morning, waking their friends with boisterous singing and noisemaking and demanding drinks and snacks. Night after night, Roberto's friends had "assaulted" the spacious house atop the hill in Rio Piedras, bringing music and cheer, and Roberto had sat down at the big electric organ in his living room, playing as they sang. It was a time when the Puerto Rican family swelled large, as cousins and uncles and aunts, nieces and nephews, godparents and *compadres* sped up and down the highways, from town to town, *barrio* to *barrio*, renewing the familial ties that might have slackened during the year. It was a time for all the old traditional delicacies: roast pig, pigeon peas, rice pudding, spicy blood sausage known as *morcilla*, and Puerto Rico's answer to eggnog, *coquito*, which is prepared with coconut milk and rum, preferably the "white lightning" variety that is manufactured in some remote country still.

This was the gay atmosphere in which Roberto was immersed, and from which he tore himself away, the night of December 23, when he agreed to join with Luis Vigoreaux in forming a Managua relief drive. As they chatted in the hotel lobby, they were joined by Ruth Fernández, an immensely popular local singer—"the soul of Puerto Rico," she was called—who that November had won a seat in the island Senate. On December 24, known as *nochebuena* in the Hispanic world, Roberto and Luis met at Ruth's house to map out the details of the relief drive. That afternoon, in the studios of WAPA-TV, they taped a spot urging the public to donate cash, medicine, clothing, and food to the Nicaragua earthquake victims. The collection point would be the parking lot of Hiram Bithorn Stadium, a modern ball park in the center of metropolitan San Juan.

On Christmas Day and the day after, Roberto's gifts lay unopened as he worked tirelessly at the stadium, while cars and trucks
poured in with donations. His friend Luis Rodriguez Mayoral went
to the stadium on Christmas and recalls, "He was working hard,
packing clothes and food into a big carton. He was bent over and
didn't see me at first. I walked by and gave him a pat on the behind,
the way ballplayers do. He sort of jumped, looked around, and when
he saw me he laughed." Alejandro and Aida Sórraga, Roberto's
friends from San Francisco, had moved back to the island and also
went to see him on Christmas. "We spent almost the whole day
with him at the stadium," Aida recalls. "He forgot all about eating.
About two in the afternoon, I asked him if he'd eaten, and he said
he'd had a small piece of *morcilla*. I asked him to come to the house
for lunch; we lived nearby, but he said 'no, just bring me a little
coffee.' I went home and we were out of milk, but we finally found
some and I made him a thermos of coffee and brought it to him.
Neither Roberto nor Ruth Fernández had eaten all that day. That
night we left, saying we'd see him as soon as the Nicaragua thing
was over with."

By now, thousands of people in Puerto Rico were answering
Roberto's broadcasts for help. Several civic and professional groups
joined in. A group of Puerto Rican doctors volunteered to fly to
Managua to help the understaffed medical teams there. The Rotary
and Exchange clubs pledged $50,000 in cash and had already gath-
ered two tons of beans and many boxes of antibiotics for shipment.
"This is wonderful, people are really responding to our appeal,"
Roberto said, as more and more *sanjuaneros* flocked to the ballpark
with cartons of gifts. Roberto had installed a radio-telephone near
his home and kept in touch with the Managua airport to coordinate
air shipments of materials from Puerto Rico. As in every other en-
deavor, he plunged into the relief drive with every ounce of his energy. On December 27, the collection center moved across the street
to the huge parking lot of the Plaza las Americas shopping center,
since there would be a game at the ball park that night. That same
day, Roberto flew to Aguadilla on the west coat to give a baseball
clinic for youngsters at Colón Stadium, and also to collect donations
for Managua. In previous weeks, while under contract to the local
telephone company, he had offered clinics to thousands of young-

sters at ball fields in various island towns. The date in Aguadilla was last on the agenda. Fernando González, a young Puerto Rican infielder who plays for the Pirates, was there that day.

"I knew of him from the time I was a *chamaquito*, a little boy," says Fernando. "I was always the mascot of the Arecibo Winter League team, and when he came to play in Arecibo I watched his every move. We got to know each other when I spent the spring of 1972 at the Pirate camp in Bradenton. Manny Sanguillen would joke with him, '*Mira*, González is here and he says you never taught him a *thing!* He says that you and Stargell are a couple of bums!' But Roberto always invited me and the other Latins out to eat and told us all kinds of stories. I was sent back to the minors before the season ended, so I didn't see him again until December 27, when he gave the clinic in Aguadilla, not far from my home. I spoke to him for quite some time that day. Joe Brown, the general manager, was coming to see me soon about my first big league contract, and I wanted his advice. He told me to go to his house next week, right after New Year's. He was very busy. In early January, he planned to go to Cuba. When he was in Nicaragua with the Puerto Rican amateur team, he met some players from the Cuban delegation and their government invited him to go there. Then we got to talking about when he might retire, and he said that whenever people asked he would say 'this year and one more.' He'd say the same thing every year. He said he never felt that tired, because whenever he felt bad he would lie down in bed and think back to when he was a boy, and how he worked with his father, carrying big cans of water to the cane-cutters. He would say, 'Just think of all those people, waking up so early in the morning, cutting cane in the hot sun.' And then he'd ask himself, 'How can I feel tired if all I have to do is play baseball?' When he thought of that, it gave him more spirit. He always said, 'The mind controls the body.'

"That day in Aguadilla he spent the whole afternoon under the sun giving a clinic for the kids. People kept coming up to give him money for Nicaragua, and he insisted that they write out checks so that there'd be no chance of the money being mishandled. At one point, he was giving batting pointers, and there was a kid—about eighteen years old—pitching to him. The people in the stands kept yelling, 'Roberto, bet you can't hit a homer!' Finally, on the last pitch, he smacked the ball right out of the stadium. He gave the kid the bat as a souvenir, and somebody else got the ball. Afterward, they erected a small monument to mark the spot where the ball fell. I think that was the last time Roberto swung a bat, and he hit a home run."

Later that day, Roberto dashed back for a press conference in San Juan. He and Luis Vigoreaux announced that one large airline had offered to fly 80,000 pounds of cargo to Nicaragua for $20,000, but Roberto found another company that would make three trips in a small plane, carrying 114,000 pounds for $11,500. They also revealed that the cargo vessel *San Expedito* would sail for Nicaragua Saturday night laden with donations, and would make the trip free, thanks to its owner, Demistocles Ramirez de Arellano. When Roberto told a reporter that he "might" accompany the first air shipment to Managua on Thursday, December 28, Vigoreaux took him aside, saying, "I don't think you should go. You don't know what shape these cargo planes are in. You're too valuable to Puerto Rico." Roberto remained in San Juan, working long hours on the relief program. On Friday, December 29, he saw Manny Sanguillen, who was playing in the Puerto Rican winter league, and couldn't resist joking for a few moments with his likable teammate. In parting, he put his arm around Manny and said, "I bought a monkey the other day and I call him Sangy for you. *Adiós, amigo.*" It was the last time Manny saw him. That night, Roberto made a television appeal for volunteers to come to the docks Saturday and help load the *San Expedito*. By then, three flights had already been made to Managua, with three or four Puerto Rican volunteers accompanying each flight. At the television station, Roberto told Vigoreaux that he had rented another plane, for $4,000, to make a final trip on Sunday, December 31. "We must do it, Luis," he said, explaining that he had received an urgent request from Managua for sugar, tracheotomy tubes, anesthetics, a water pump, and an X-ray machine. All these items were secured and packed for the flight.

Later that Friday night, Roberto Marín, Mrs. Marín, and a few friends "raided" the Clemente household. "At Christmas time," says Marín, "we Puerto Ricans have what we call *asaltos*, where we raid a friend's house and eat, drink, and have a good time. Since they had so many friends, I called his wife, Vera, my *comadre*, and warned her not to go out that night. It was a very gay evening. At the height of the party, there must have been twenty people in the house. Roberto played the organ in the living room with one finger, but he was quite good at it. We had roast pig and rice and beans—Roberto loved rice and beans, he would even have it for breakfast, with fried chicken! The night went on and on, until there were only five of us left, Roberto and Vera, my wife and I, and a singer, Polito Galíndez, who was singing lovely Christmas carols as we looked out from the balcony, watching all the lights in the city below. Finally, about six in the morning, we said goodbye."

On Saturday, as crews of volunteers loaded the San Expedito at the pier, Roberto tried to persuade Vigoreaux to accompany him on the Sunday flight. "But my son was getting married Sunday in Ponce, on the south coast," says Vigoreaux. "I tried to dissuade him from going, too, but he said, 'I have to go, Luis. We have eleven people from Puerto Rico there. I don't know how they are. Also, I have to arrange for the Red Cross to take charge of the goods on the *San Expedito* when it arrives.' "

Roberto heard disturbing news that day from Narciso Rabell, executive director of the Engineers, Architects, and Surveyors Association, who had led a delegation to Managua three days before and just returned. Rabell told him that the Venezuelan and Mexican delegations in Nicaragua were directing their own relief efforts very smoothly, but the supplies from Puerto Rico and the United States were being distributed by the Nicaraguan national guard, and their operation was "neither the most efficient nor effective." The supplies from the *San Expedito* were assigned to the Red Cross in the town of Masayas; it had not been hit by the quake, but its normal population of 30,000 was swollen by 100,000 refugees from Managua, and the situation there was desperate. Rabell said he had confidence in the Red Cross but was concerned about the overland transportation from the port to Masayas. Roberto assured him that he would go to Nicaragua to personally guarantee the safe arrival of the materials.

Late Saturday, as Roberto pitched in with the rest of the volunteers in loading cargo onto the *San Expedito*, he spotted TV cameraman Mike Benítez and invited him to fly to Nicaragua on Sunday to cover the arrival of the donations. "I've got a seat for you, Mike.

See you at the airport, sport." But when Mike drove home, he thought it over and decided not to spend New Year's Eve away from his family. "I'll excuse myself with Roberto when he gets back," he thought to himself.

Roberto was awake at his home Sunday morning before sunrise. He had barely slept in the past few days. Ruth Fernández pleaded with him, "Don't go, Roberto. It's the thirty-first. Stay here with the children, with Vera. Go tomorrow." But he insisted. "I sent eleven people there. All of them have families in Puerto Rico. The least I can do is be with them tonight." Vera, too, asked him to postpone the trip. "But he told me, 'Babies are dying over there, they need these supplies.' Roberto had been to Managua with the Puerto Rican team in November and the people there were very kind to us. There was also a little boy; Roberto had raised money to buy artificial legs for him. He wanted to see if he was still alive. He wasn't even sure if the hospital was still standing. Finally, he asked me what I thought, and I told him he must do what he thought best. He said to me, 'What the heck, I'll go. Just be sure to save me some roast pork for when I get back.' "

About four that Sunday morning, Roberto got a call from San Juan airport. There was some trouble with the plane, and a pilot and copilot had not yet been hired. The rest of the day, Roberto drove back and forth to the airport, checking on the status of the flight.

The four-engine DC-7 cargo plane was nearly twenty years old. The previous owner had flown it back and forth on cargo trips between San Francisco and Australia, and the plane had suffered two minor accidents. It lay unused in Miami for about four months until it was purchased by the Interstate Air Service Corporation, whose president was Arturo Rivera. The plane was brought to San Juan in early December, and, as it was being moved from its hangar to another section of the airport, the hydraulic system failed. The plane went over an abutment and plowed into a ditch next to the runway. Two damaged propellers had to be replaced.

A crew was finally found. Jerry Hill, a retired Air Force captain who had planned to spend New Year's in Miami with his wife and three sons, responded when he heard a pilot was needed. When no copilot appeared, Mr. Rivera, the owner, offered his services. The flight engineer was Francisco Javier Matías, a mechanic for a local airline who was free that day. He had four children, and his wife Margarita was eight months pregnant (a seven-pound boy would be born on January 30). Another passenger was Angel Lozano, a friend of Clemente's, who owned a trucking company.

A few hours before going to the airport, Vera took the children to her mother's house in Carolina, since she knew she might return late. "As I left them there," she says, "Robertito asked me, '*Mami*, is the earthquake finished? Is *papi* all right?' I reassured him and left. Later, my mother says that when she was fixing Robertito's bed, he told her, 'Grandma, grandma, *papi* is going to Nicaragua, and he won't be back. That plane is going to crash, I know it. Call *mami* and tell her not to let *papi* leave.' But he is just a young child, and my mother decided not to call me."

At 3:30 Sunday afternoon, Roberto and Vera were driven to the airport by a close friend, Cristobal "Caguitas" Colón. House guests of the Clementes were arriving from Allentown, Pennsylvania, early that evening. And after Vera saw Roberto off she planned to pick them up at the arrival gate.

The plane's flight plan called for it to leave San Juan at 4 P.M. "But," says Vera, "they were still having trouble with the plane. At about 5 o'clock, it seemed ready to leave and I kissed Roberto goodbye. He asked me not to wait there any longer, so that I could pick up our friends at the other end of the airport. It was the only time I remember not waiting to see Roberto's plane actually take off. I began to leave as he climbed the stairway into the plane. The sad look on his face frightened me. It wasn't like him."

A few minutes later, the plane taxied down the runway, but again there was a delay and the mechanic made more adjustments. Impatient, Roberto said, "One more delay and I won't go tonight. I'll wait until tomorrow." His friend Cagüitas Colón tried again to persuade him not to leave. But Roberto answered, "*Si se va a morir, se muere.*"—*the* idiomatic equivalent is: "When your number is up, it's up." Arturo Rivera, the owner of the plane, said reassuringly, "Look, *señores*, if I knew the plane were in bad shape I wouldn't go, because I love myself above anyone else."

About 5:30 P.M., Nevin Rauch and his family—the Clementes' friends from Allentown—had arrived. It took them nearly an hour to pick up their luggage at the crowded airport. Not knowing that

Roberto was nearby, they drove to Vera's mother's house for a brief visit and then continued to the Clemente house to ring in the New Year.

"I remember I got home at twenty minutes to eight," says Vera. "When I raised the garage door, the phone was ringing. But when I picked up the receiver, the other party hung up. The thought struck me, 'Could this be Roberto calling? No, it can't be. He's half-way to Managua by now.' "

Shortly after 9 P.M. on December 31, as millions of people gathered to celebrate the coming of 1973, the DC-7 cargo plane with five passengers taxied slowly down the runway, ready at last to take off for Managua.

The plane was in the air at 9:22 P.M. An airport control tower official saw it take off and bank to the left as prescribed by the flight plan. Another airport employee recalls that its number one engine was "vibrating excessively" before takeoff. Still another recalls seeing "fires on the left wing as it lifted off." Moments later, pilot Hill tried desperately to swing back to the landing field. The last words on the tape recording in the control tower are "coming back around . . ." Suddenly, the plane disappeared from the radar screen.

José Antonio Paris, who lives near the beach at Punta Maldonado, a strip of land that juts into the Atlantic about a mile east of the airport, saw the plane flying low as it veered back toward the field. "I was afraid it would hit one of the palm trees," he says. José Ayala, another area resident, was in bed when he heard the plane zoom above his house. "Suddenly the motors appeared to sputter and go dead, and my wife said to me, 'That plane is going to crash.' " Gregorio Rivera was awakened by his son, who heard a loud impact. They ran outside and saw the plane floating atop the water, about a mile out to sea. "I went to tell my other son to call the police. When I came back, moments later, the plane was gone."

Several of Roberto's Pirate teammates were playing in the Puerto Rican league that winter. They had gathered for a New Year's party in Bob Johnson's apartment on the twenty-seventh floor of a building that overlooks the Atlantic. "We heard about a plane crash," says Richie Zisk, "and we saw the search crews looking for bodies and debris. We watched the searchlights as one year went out and the new one came in." The usually jovial Manny Sanguillen was quiet and withdrawn. "What's the matter?" his wife asked. They left the party soon afterward. Roberto's niece, Rafaela Rivera, was with a group partying from house to house when a friend told her the radio was saying that Roberto's plane had crashed. She ran to a phone and called Vera.

"It's not possible," Vera kept repeating.

"It must have been about ten or twenty minutes after midnight when someone called Vera to say the plane had crashed in Nicaragua," says Nevin Rauch, the visitor from Allentown. "Vera was so nervous she couldn't speak any more, so my daughter Carol, who speaks Spanish, took the phone. We thought it might be a prank. We sped out to the airport, and they told us the accident happened here, not in Nicaragua. The Coast Guard had lit up the sky with flares, and police cars shone their headlights into the ocean. We stayed there a few hours, but it was raining and Roberto's father was with us. We decided to take him home before he got very sick." By then, the big Clemente house on the hill was rapidly filling with friends and relatives, who stood around in numb, tearful silence.

About 4 A.M. the phone rang at an apartment in Pittsburgh, where Steve Blass, Dave Giusti, their wives, and some friends had ushered in the New Year. It was Pirate trainer Tony Bartirome, who had heard the news on the radio. "After that," says Blass, "we couldn't sleep. We just kept pacing in and out of our rooms, past each other." Another call wakened general manager Joe L. Brown. Soon Blass and Giusti were at his house, sipping coffee, staring vacantly at the walls. Al Oliver and his wife had just returned from Willie Stargell's New Year's Eve party in another part of Pittsburgh. The phone rang at 5 A.M. It was Stargell. He could barely speak. After Oliver hung up, he walked into his living room, turned on the radio, and sat, trembling, in his reclining chair. "I think that was the first time my wife has ever seen me cry," he says.

New Year's Day, 1973. It was cloudy and drizzling ("even the sky seems to be in mourning," observed one Puerto Rican journalist) as the Coast Guard and several private boats contined the search for the missing plane in the choppy seas off Punta Maldonado. The curving shore is ringed by gray coral reef, below which is a seemingly endless labyrinth of caverns. The swells were as high as twelve feet. By now, the whole world knew. Cars jammed the narrow Boca de Cangrejos road that leads to the beach, as thousands of motorists inched their way toward the site of the tragedy. Men, women, children stood on the shore—some with the sea washing up to their ankles—looking out, listening to small portable radios.

Relatives and friends had kept an all-night vigil at the Clemente household. People crowded around to console Vera, who sat in a big chair in her bedroom, saying over and over, "God, give me strength." The room was crowded and stuffy, and someone opened the aluminum blinds to let in some cool air. "I wanted to go with him," said Vera, "but he didn't let me." A few miles away, in Carolina, more cars crowded the street near the home of Roberto's parents. People stood in the front driveway, some of them crying. In the bedroom, *don* Melchor lay awake, staring, hands crossed upon his chest. Next to him in another bed lay *doña* Luisa, wearing a black dress. She was under sedation and slept soundly. Near her bed lay a bible, the page open to the Twenty-third Psalm. All night she had read, seeking strength: "The Lord is my shepherd, I shall not want. . ."

Planes brought more mourners from the United States. Phil Dorsey, Roberto's "brother" from Pittsburgh, came to the house, tears in his eyes, and from then on was fiercely and lovingly protective of Vera and the children. Strangers wandered into the quiet, crowded house. A man started to preach the Gospel in the living room and suddenly began to shudder, saying he had been possessed by a spirit. Dorsey and another man guided him out the front door. The phone kept ringing. That night, a spiritualist from New York called and swore that he had "seen" Roberto still alive, his leg broken, lying near a big rock by the shore in Old San Juan, just below the La Perla slum settlement. Desperately seizing any strand of hope, a group of friends—Sanguillen, Pagán, Stennett, Rodriguez Mayoral—drove ten miles to the spot; as the rain fell and the waves crashed against the black rocks, they blinked their flashlights in the gloom, searching for Roberto. From one until four in the morning they searched, and then returned sadly to the Clemente home. Later, Sanguillen, a fervently religious man, would shake his head and say, "The spiritualists were working against God's will, because only

He knows all things, and to show that He is all-powerful, He didn't reveal Roberto."

The next day, there was to be a festive celebration to mark the inaugural of a new governor, thirty-six-year-old Rafael Hernández Colón. Municipal bands, concert orchestras, parades, equestrian shows, a ballet performance, fireworks at the Condado Lagoon. All but the swearing-in ceremony and a few private gatherings were canceled. The capitol building stands on a cliff facing north, out over the Atlantic, and as the ceremony began on the marble steps helicopters and Coast Guard cutters searched the waters ten miles to the east for the wreckage of the plane. The crowd stood, heads bowed, for a minute's silence in Roberto's honor, as only the rumble of the Atlantic surf was audible. "Our people have lost one of their glories. All our hearts are saddened," said the new governor in his first speech.

On Wednesday, the shattered body of the pilot, Jerry Hill, floated to the surface and was recovered. This inspired hopes that more bodies would be found, but the plane's wreckage lay nearly a mile off the coast in choppy water that was more than one hundred feet deep. The next day, the entire Pittsburgh Pirate team flew to San Juan to attend a special mass in Roberto's home town. Through the sunny plaza of Carolina they filed into the old church: all of his teammates and their wives, baseball commissioner Bowie Kuhn, Pirate president Dan Galbreath, manager Bill Virdon, former managers Harry Walker and Danny Murtaugh. Archbishop Luis Aponte Martinez was assisted in the solemn mass by the Reverend Salvador Planas, who at the same pastel-colored altar, some eight years before, had pronounced Roberto and Vera man and wife. In Pittsburgh's old Trinity Cathedral, more than 1,300 people attended an ecumenical service. Many wept. In the Hispanic *barrios* all over America—New York, Newark, Paterson, Chicago, Philadelphia—people joined in silent marches through the streets and solemn masses to mourn the loss of their hero. Many of the mourners were Americans, fans who had admired Roberto and whose hearts were touched by the humanitarian gesture on New Year's Eve that led him to his death.

One friend was not in church. Every day since Roberto's disappearance, Manny Sanguillen drove to the beach, stripped to a pair of swim trunks, and searched about in the murky waters.

"He's all over the place," said a police officer at the beach. "He goes out in the Coast Guard's lifeboat and holds the oxygen tank. He's tired, but he's always there."

"It was dark," says Sanguillen, recalling his futile attempts to dive for Roberto's body. "I don't see anything. The ocean got rough for a while, so I come up. Every day I jump out of the boat, and go looking. I see when they discover the body of the pilot. It was completely destroyed. This was when I gave up on finding Roberto. I went down in the water for the last time five days after the crash, when they said they saw a body. It was only a green fish. I also saw this big shark, I saw lots of sharks. This one was really big—it didn't scare me, but it made me sad, very sad."

"Roberto's body didn't appear," says Ruth Fernández, "because God wanted us to remember him as he was: that handsome *negro*, so strong, so beautiful within and without."

Each day during the first week, Vera and a few relatives sat in a roped-off area of the beach, keeping vigil as the fruitless search went on. Hour after hour, Vera peered through binoculars, scanning the choppy surface of the sea. Bit by bit, remnants of the crash were found: vials of medicine, hunks of wreckage that washed ashore or floated westward with the tide toward San Juan. Navy divers found the plane's cockpit, split in two, and pieces of propeller, rubber tubing, and an oxygen mask. On Saturday—Three Kings Day, the festive climax of the holiday season—the divers spotted the tail and fuselage of the DC-7 about 400 yards offshore. The only personal effects salvaged from the sea were a pair of eyeglasses, believed to be the pilot's, and a small black suitcase, apparently Roberto's, that contained a single brown sock. Finally, after a week more, when the divers had descended to depths of 120 feet, the search was called off.

"I was unable to meet with you earlier for emotional reasons," Vera said softly at her first press conference on January 12. She sat in her living room, her three sons beside her. "But I have been anxious to express to the people of Puerto Rico, Latin America, and the United States my gratitude for their concern and support at a time when it was so greatly needed . . . Now that Roberto is not here, I shall try to fill the void that he has left, working with the Managua relief committee so that an orphanage can be built for the many children who lost their parents during the earthquake. We have also formed another committee to work on the Sports City, to insure that Roberto's dream is realized."

A final, solemn *adiós* was bid to Roberto Clemente that Sunday, January 14, with an ecumenical service on the baseball diamond at Hiram Bithorn Stadium. Manny Sanguillen, holding little Enrique in his arms, led Roberto's two older sons onto the field for the ceremony. Thousands of people sat quietly in the stands and later raised their voices in song. Among the hymns was Roberto's favorite: "*Sólo Dios Hace el Hombre Feliz*," "Only God Makes a Man Happy." Afterward, the Clementes were taken to the beach. A police helicopter flew over the crash site and dropped five floral wreaths into the ocean, one by one, for Jerry Hill, Francisco Matías, Rafael Lozano, Arturo Rivera, and Roberto Clemente.

"For me, he's still alive," Vera told a visitor to the house weeks later. "All his clothes are in the same place. I just think he left on one of his trips and is coming back." The big electric organ in the living room was unplugged. Outside was a lone police guard assigned to round-the-clock custody of the Clemente home. His old sedan was parked at the curb, a black handkerchief fluttering at half-mast from the antenna. Vera had kept busy answering thousands of cards, letters, and telegrams. Downstairs in the trophy room, hundreds of silver and gold awards glittered in their glass cabinets. The closets upstairs were filled with more, and a big carton of trophies, for Roberto's 3,000th hit, lay unopened.

As all hope of finding Roberto's body vanished, his memory loomed even larger. The city of San Juan named its new coliseum, adjacent to the ballpark, in his honor. (The ballpark was named after Hiram Bithorn, a former big-league pitcher from Puerto Rico who was killed in an altercation with a policeman while traveling in Mexico on New Year's Day, 1952. He was thirty-five.)

Funds poured in from everywhere to build the Sports City, Roberto's long cherished dream. "If he were alive, nobody would give him a cent for it," says his old friend Arturo Garcia. "God took him, and now comes the Sports City. One suffers, and then gets what he wants. Now the government gives a million dollars. Even President Nixon writes out a check. The team gives, the city of Pittsburgh gives, and Puerto Rico has gone overboard with generosity. That's because he's not alive."

Column after column in sports pages all over the country urged that Roberto Clemente be elected to baseball's Hall of Fame, waiving the rule that a candidate must be retired from the game for five years before he is eligible. In 1939, New York Yankee first baseman Lou Gehrig was stricken with a rare terminal disease while still in his prime. The Baseball Writers Association of America voted Gehrig in by acclamation. But the five-year rule did not exist at the time. In early February, Jack Lang, secretary-treasurer of the Baseball Writers Association, drove to a post office near his Long Island home and deposited ballots in the mail for a special poll of the members. Three-fourths of those polled would have to vote "yes" to make Roberto's entry valid. On March 20, eleven weeks after his death, Roberto Clemente became the first Latin American to enter the Hall of Fame. Of the 424 votes cast, an overwhelming 93 per cent were in his favor. There were two abstentions and 29 "no" votes, with most of these explaining in separate notes that they opposed only the waiving of the five-year rule. Only six other players had received such a landslide vote. Thus, on August 6, 1973, a plaque bearing Roberto's likeness and briefly recounting his deeds would be placed in the Hall of Fame at Cooperstown, New York. That same day a handful of other stars would be enshrined at Cooperstown, among them Monte Irvin, Roberto's childhood hero.

The day that the official results were announced at a banquet in Saint Petersburg, Florida, Vera presented a special Roberto Clemente Award for good citizenship to Detroit Tiger star Al Kaline (it would be an annual award henceforth). After that ceremony, Vera told a reporter that her eldest son Robertito had asked her to relay a special message to Pirate general manager Joe Brown. "I asked him, 'What is it?' He said, 'Tell him not to give away right field. Tell

him it's my position.' I said, 'Oh, you mean when you grow up.' And
he said, 'No, I'll play it right now for my father.' "

The sports pages were filled with reminiscences of Roberto
that day. Phil Musick, the Pittsburgh writer, lamented, "Now it's
too late to tell him there were things he did on a ball field that made
me wish I was Shakespeare."

"Never again," said Rafael Pont Flores, the Puerto Rican
sportswriter, "never again will I see him perform miracles before
my eyes; those hits, those running catches, and those throws. Poetry in motion. Never again."

But the days passed. Up north in the spring of 1973, the green
buds burst through the earth. In Puerto Rico, the tall, silver-topped
canestalks glistened in the sun, and a new generation of strong,
sinewy young men issued forth from the island to "do battle"—not
with the cane as in years past, but in the stadiums of America's
cities. The Saint Louis Cardinals played an exhibition game against
the Yankees in Saint Petersburg and made baseball history. The three
Cruz brothers of Arroyo, Puerto Rico—Cirilo, Hector, and José—
took charge of the Cardinal outfield for nine innings and batted one,
two, three in the lineup. "They're good ballplayers," said manager
Red Schoendienst. "They have six brothers back home, and if they
come to town I'll play them, too!" On the Yankee club was twenty-
two-year-old Otto Vélez from Ponce, Puerto Rico. His shyness and
halting English recall a young man who left Carolina some eighteen
years before. A reporter asked Vélez if he had an idol, someone he
would like to emulate. "Clemente," he said quietly, looking down at
the ground. "I knew him. I talked to him a couple of times."

Epilogue

It is cold the morning of April 5, 1973, at Three Rivers Stadium in Pittsburgh; a few snowflakes float down upon the soggy Tartan Turf. The Pirates, wearing warm-up jackets, flip baseballs back and forth, catching them gingerly to avoid the sting. A cylindrical flame-throwing machine blows its hot breath at the pitcher's mound to soften the frozen earth.

It had been different a few days before in Florida, as they baked in the sun, upon the scarred green bench outside the clubhouse, tying the laces of their spikes, as white gulls swooped and keened above a nearby marshland. There are three baseball diamonds back to back at Pirate City, and as the tourists and retirees stood behind the metal backstops and watched, they limbered up. First, on the outfield grass, with calisthenics. "C'mon, let's go, reach down and *touch* those toes!" Thirty men, hatless, their tan leather gloves resting on the grass nearby. Arms swinging side to side, then hands behind the head, then on their backs, groaning, stretching, sweating off the winter lard, limbering up the stiff muscles. Then infield practice. The sounds of ball and bat, ball and glove, ball and earth—toc! splat! thwump!—as they perform their intricate ballet. Blass, pitching batting practice from the mound behind a metal protective screen, a wire basket full of baseballs at arm's reach; Hebner, with a slim fungoe bat, behind the cage on the third base side, whacking high flies to the outfielders; a coach, Dave Ricketts, over on the first base side, slapping grounders to the infielders, who throw to the first baseman standing behind another protective screen. Two, three, four baseballs in the air at the same time, like an incredible juggling act. Bill Mazeroski, his cheek bulging with a huge chaw of tobacco, throws to the hitters now. A pitch backs Jackie Hernández away from the plate, and Maz says, grinning, "I never liked Cubans anyhow." Then, looking at the empty basket and raising his hand, he says, "Wait! Let me get some more *pelotas*." Later, inside the clubhouse, sweaty men, walking around half-clad, their hips and legs marked with old scars and new raspberries. Shouts, curses, laughter echo off the concrete walls, bats clatter on the hard floor, a radio blares rock music. On the cork bulletin board, schedules, reminders, and a poem about Roberto Clemente written by a fan. Fifty yards away, at the Pirate City motel, room number 231—Roberto's room—is locked. On the door is a small metal plaque: "I want to be remembered as a ballplayer who gave all he had to give—Roberto Clemente, 1934–1972."

Back in Pittsburgh, at Three Rivers Stadium, the Pirates look smaller. Smaller and more remote. In the easy informality of Florida, one could mingle with them. Here, concrete barriers, wire fences, and men in uniform will separate them from the thousands of fans. Here, beginning tomorrow, every throw, every swing of the bat will count.

A plane from San Juan late that night brings Vera, her three children, *doña* Luisa, and Senator Ruth Fernández. They are driven downtown to the Pittsburgh Hilton, where the lobby is filled with many Puerto Ricans—from San Juan, New York, Philadelphia—who have come for the special memorial ceremony that will honor Roberto before the opening game. Upstairs, Robertito, Luis, and Enrique romp around in pajamas, laughing and throwing a big yellow balloon, while "Uncle Phil" Dorsey, ever serious, tries to herd them into their bedroom. In an adjacent room of the suite, Vera talks with a reporter. *Doña* Luisa, all alone, sits upon a sofa, looking slightly lost. In another suite, two floors above, Luis Rodríguez Mayoral briefs Ruth Fernández on her role in tomorrow's pregame ceremony, when she will represent the government of Puerto Rico. Senator Fernández, a black woman in early middle age, exudes dignity and strength. But now she is distraught. She was to sing the island's anthem, "*La Borinqueña*," but there is no Puerto Rican flag. "Roberto Clemente was so proud of his Puerto Rican heritage," she says indignantly. "It would be a sacrilege to sing the anthem without a flag." It is well past midnight, but a hurried call is made to a Pirate official. Not only is there no flag, she is told, but Three Rivers Stadium has just one flagpole, for the Stars and Stripes, and there is no place to fly the island's colors. "Find me a flag," she says, rising from her chair and stretching her arms out. "If I must, I'll hold it in my *arms* as I sing!" More calls are made—to New York, to Washington. Finally, someone remembers that a firm near Philadelphia manufactures Puerto Rican flags, and messages go out to fly one to Pittsburgh the next morning. "This is impossible!" says Senator Fernández. "How can there not be a single Puerto Rican flag in all of Pittsburgh?"

The next afternoon, opening day of the 1973 season, a record crowd of 51,695 fans begins to fill Three Rivers Stadium. It is a warm, sunny day. Thousands of people walk from the parking lot through the small Roberto Clemente Memorial Park—formerly North Shore Park—and file past the bronze monument to stocky Honus Wagner, frozen in the follow-through of a mighty swing that must have launched the ball for miles. Inside, the traditional Dixieland combo plays behind home plate as the Pirates warm up, wearing circular patches with the number 21 on their left sleeves. A television crew prepares to tape the pregame ceremony and show it in Puerto Rico the next day. Several returned Vietnam POW's— pale, thin, looking too small for their beribboned uniforms—are also guests of honor. In a simple ceremony at home plate, Roberto's uniform—Number 21—is delivered to Vera and *doña* Luisa. Now it will be retired, together with Pie Traynor's Number 20 and Honus Wagner's Number 33. As the ceremony proceeds, Roberto's old friend Cagüitas Colón sits in the Pirate dugout, wearing a white suit and black shirt. His eyes are red and moist, and his shoulders tremble.

The crowd rises, and the players, removing their caps, stand at attention along the foul lines, facing the flagpole in center field. Standing on the field, Ruth Fernández, accompanied by the stadium organist, begins to sing the lilting melody of *"La Borinqueña."* The special courier from Philadelphia never arrived, and only the American flag flutters from its pole in the outfield. But suddenly, miraculously, in the grandstand a few Puerto Rican flags appear, together with black cloths of mourning. Roberto's compatriots from San Juan and the *barrios* of America, have come prepared.

The game commences, and Bob Gibson, the star pitcher of the Cardinals, is throwing what the pressbox scribes like to call "aspirin tablets." For five innings he holds the Pirates scoreless, as Saint Louis builds a 5–0 lead. It feels strange to see Manny Sanguillen out in right field, Roberto's fiefdom for the past eighteen summers. But Manny plays well and draws cheers for one long, hard throw to third base. Nevertheless, the mood is subdued in the radio booth above home plate where Teddy Garcia broadcasts the game back to Puerto Rico in his staccato style. Several Puerto Ricans are in the booth. Senator Fernández sits next to Teddy on a metal folding chair. "Gee," someone says, "how nice it would be if the Pirates could win this one for Roberto. Vera and the kids and *doña* Luisa are here. Who knows when they'll come back?" Pittsburgh chips away for single runs in the sixth and seventh innings, and in the bottom of the eighth the Pirates shell Gibson from the mound. When Richie Hebner bloops a double to put the Pirates just one run behind, Senator Fernández closes her eyes and crosses her fingers. With two outs and two men on base, Gene Clines takes the pitcher's turn at bat and wallops a triple that sends Pittsburgh ahead 7 to 5. The stadium and the radio booth go wild. Opening her eyes, smiling, Senator Fernández says, "You know, it may sound incredible, but just a moment ago I felt his presence."

In the top of the ninth, manager Bill Virdon chooses Ramon Hernández, a native of Roberto's hometown of Carolina, to pitch the final three outs against Saint Louis. With his sweeping curves, the Puerto Rican left-hander quickly sets down the first two batsmen. The last man, Lou Brock, hits a high fly ball, very high, to—of all places—right field. Manny Sanguillen stands there, gazing skyward, waiting, waiting. The ball settles in his glove, and he lopes toward the dugout as the cheering crowd slowly vanishes through the exits.

Statistics

Roberto Clemente's Record

Year—Club	League	Pos.	G.	AB.	R.	H.	2B.	3B.	HR.	RBI.	B.A.	PO.	A.	E.	F.A.
1954—Montreal†	Int.	OF-3B	87	148	27	38	5	3	2	12	.257	81	1	1	.988
1955—Pittsburgh	Nat.	OF	124	474	48	121	23	11	5	47	.255	253	18	6	.978
1956—Pittsburgh	Nat.	*OF-2-3B	147	543	66	169	30	7	7	60	.311	275	20	*15	.952
1957—Pittsburgh	Nat.	OF	111	451	42	114	17	7	4	30	.253	272	9	6	.979
1958—Pittsburgh	Nat.	OF	140	519	69	150	24	10	6	50	.289	312	*22	6	.982
1959—Pittsburgh‡	Nat.	OF	105	432	60	128	17	7	4	50	.296	229	10	*13	.948
1960—Pittsburgh	Nat.	OF	144	570	89	179	22	6	16	94	.314	246	*19	8	.971
1961—Pittsburgh	Nat.	OF	146	572	100	201	30	10	23	89	*.351	256	*27	9	.969
1962—Pittsburgh	Nat.	OF	144	538	95	168	28	9	10	74	.312	269	19	8	.973
1963—Pittsburgh	Nat.	OF	152	600	77	192	23	8	17	76	.320	239	11	11	.958
1964—Pittsburgh	Nat.	OF	155	622	95	*211	40	7	12	87	*.339	289	13	10	.968
1965—Pittsburgh	Nat.	OF	152	589	91	194	21	14	10	65	*.329	288	16	10	.968
1966—Pittsburgh	Nat.	OF	154	638	105	202	31	11	29	119	.317	318	*17	12	.965
1967—Pittsburgh	Nat.	OF	147	585	103	*209	26	10	23	110	*.357	273	*17	9	.970
1968—Pittsburgh	Nat.	OF	132	502	74	146	18	12	18	57	.291	297	9	5	.984
1969—Pittsburgh	Nat.	OF	138	507	87	175	20	*12	19	91	.345	226	14	5	.980
1970—Pittsburgh	Nat.	OF	108	412	65	145	22	10	14	60	.352	189	12	7	.966
1971—Pittsburgh	Nat.	OF	132	522	82	178	29	8	13	86	.341	267	11	2	.993
1972—Pittsburgh	Nat.	OF	102	378	68	118	19	7	10	60	.312	199	5	0	1.000
Major League Totals			2433	9454	1416	3000	440	178	240	1305	.317	4697	269	142	.972

† Drafted by Pittsburgh Pirates from Montreal (Brooklyn Dodgers' organization), November 22, 1954.
‡ On disabled list May 25 through July 3.
* Led league.

Roberto Clemente's Record (Continued)

WORLD SERIES RECORD

Year	Club	League	Pos.	G.	AB.	R.	H.	2B.	3B.	HR.	RBI.	B.A.	PO.	A.	E.	F.A.
1960—Pittsburgh	Nat.	OF	7	29	1	9	0	0	0	3	.310	19	0	0	1.000
1971—Pittsburgh	Nat.	OF	7	29	3	12	2	1	2	4	.414	15	0	0	1.000
World Series Totals			14	58	4	21	2	1	2	7	.362	34	0	0	1.000

CHAMPIONSHIP SERIES RECORD

Year	Club	League	Pos.	G.	AB.	R.	H.	2B.	3B.	HR.	RBI.	B.A.	PO.	A.	E.	F.A.
1970—Pittsburgh	Nat.	OF	3	14	1	3	0	0	0	1	.214	7	0	0	1.000
1971—Pittsburgh	Nat.	OF	4	18	2	6	0	0	0	4	.333	12	0	0	1.000
1972—Pittsburgh	Nat.	OF	5	17	1	4	1	0	1	7	.235	10	0	0	1.000
Championship Series Totals			12	49	4	13	1	0	1	12	.264	29	0	0	1.000

ALL-STAR GAME RECORD

Year	League	Pos.	AB.	R.	H.	2B.	3B.	HR.	RBI.	B.A.	PO.	A.	E.	F.A.
1960—National (both games)		OF	1	0	0	0	0	0	0	.000	2	0	0	1.000
1961—National (both games)		OF	6	1	2	0	1	0	2	.333	2	0	0	1.000
1962—National (both games)		OF	5	0	3	1	0	0	0	.600	4	0	0	1.000
1963—National		OF	0	0	0	0	0	0	0	.000	0	0	0	.000
1964—National		OF	3	1	1	0	0	0	0	.333	1	0	0	1.000
1965—National		OF	2	0	0	0	0	0	0	.000	0	0	0	.000
1966—National		OF	4	0	2	1	0	0	0	.500	2	0	0	1.000
1967—National		OF	6	0	1	0	0	0	0	.167	6	0	0	1.000
1969—National		OF	1	0	0	0	0	0	0	.000	0	0	0	.000
1970—National		OF	1	0	0	0	0	0	1	.000	2	0	0	1.000
1971—National		OF	2	1	1	0	0	0	1	.500	1	0	0	1.000
All-Star Game Totals			31	3	10	2	1	0	4	.323	20	0	0	1.000

Other Career Highlights

All-Time Pittsburgh Pirate Leader in		All-Time Standing in National League	All-Time Standing in Major Leagues
Games played	2,433	10th	19th
Times at bat	9,454	7th	15th
Hits	3,000	7th	11th
Singles	2,154	6th	16th
Total bases	4,492	8th	12th
Runs batted in	1,305	11th	31st
All-Time Third-ranking Pittsburgh Pirate in			
Doubles	440	11th	39th
Triples	166	11th	28th
Runs scored	1,416	11th	49th
Home runs	240	20th	39th

Clemente's Hitting Record in Puerto Rico Winter League *

Season	Team	AB.	R.	H.	2B.	3B.	HR.	RBI.	B.A.
1952–53	Santurce	77	5	18	3	1	0	5	.234
1953–54	Santurce	219	22	63	13	2	2	27	.288
1954–55	Santurce	273	65	94	9	4	6	38	.344
1955–56	Santurce	278	45	85	11	3	7	30	.306
1956–57	Santurce -Caguas	225	36	89	17	3	2	29	.396
1957–58	Caguas	32	0	8	2	0	0	1	.250
1958–59	Caguas				(didn't play)				
1959–60	Caguas	215	38	71	9	6	4	42	.330
1960–61	San Juan	109	12	31	5	1	1	14	.284
1961–62	San Juan	66	9	18	3	0	0	8	.273
1962–63	San Juan				(didn't play)				
1963–64	San Juan	177	27	61	11	2	4	39	.345
1964–65	San Juan	39	6	15	3	2	2	7	.385
1965–66	San Juan	2	0	0	0	0	0	0	.000
1966–67	San Juan				(didn't play)				
1967–68	San Juan	68	15	26	4	0	4	15	.382
1968–69	San Juan				(didn't play)				
1969–70	San Juan	135	20	40	9	1	3	14	.296
1970–71	San Juan	4	1	1	1	0	0	0	.250
Totals		1,919	301	620	100	25	35	269	.323

On San Juan club roster in 1971–72 and 1972–73 but didn't play.

* Compiled by Panchicu Toste of *El Nuevo Día* newspaper, San Juan, Puerto Rico.

MEMORABLE MOMENTS

Clemente's First Major League Game

April 17, 1955

BROOKLYN (N.L.)　　　　　　　　PITTSBURGH (N.L.)

	ab	r	h	po	a
Gilliam, 2b	3	1	0	3	5
Reese, ss	5	1	2	1	2
Snider, cf	4	1	2	3	0
Hodges, 1b	4	1	2	13	0
Amoros, lf	4	1	1	0	0
Robinson, 3b	4	1	2	1	6
Furillo, rf	4	0	1	5	0
Campanella, c	5	3	3	2	1
Podres, p	5	1	2	0	0
Totals	38	10	15	27	14

	ab	r	h	po	a
E. Smith, cf	4	0	0	5	0
E. Freese, 2b	3	0	0	4	0
Roberts, 2b	2	0	0	0	2
Clemente, rf	4	1	1	2	0
Thomas, lf	4	1	1	3	0
Gordon, 3b	4	0	0	1	0
Ward, 1b	4	1	1	7	1
Shepard, c	3	0	2	2	3
Groat, ss	4	0	1	1	2
Thies, p	0	0	0	0	0
King, p	0	0	0	1	1
aR. Smith	0	0	0	0	0
Bowman, p	0	0	0	0	0
bG. Freese	1	0	0	0	0
Law, p	0	0	0	0	1
cCole	1	0	0	0	0
Totals	34	3	6	27	10

a Walked for King in fifth; b Flied out for Bowman in sixth; c Grounded out for Law in ninth.

Brooklyn	0 1 1	4 0 0	3 0 1 — 10
Pittsburgh	2 0 0	0 0 1	0 0 0 — 3

Errors—Reese, E. Freese, Amoros.
Runs batted in—Thomas, Robinson, Hodges, Snider 2, Shepard, Campanella 3, Podres. Two-base hits—Hodges, Furillo, Reese 2, Campanella 2, Podres, Ward. Three-base hit—Thomas. Home runs—Snider, Campanella. Stolen base—Shepard. Sacrifice—Gilliam. Sacrifice flies—Robinson, Hodges. Double plays—Robinson, Gilliam and Hodges; Law, Shepard and Ward. Left on bases—Brooklyn 8, Pittsburgh 8. Struck out—by Podres 3. Bases on balls—off Podres 3, Thies 3. Hits—off Thies 3 in 3⅔ innings, King 2 in 2⅓, Law 7 in 3, Bowman 1 in 1. Runs and earned runs—off Podres, 3 and 2, Thies, 5 and 2, King, 1 and 0, Bowman, 0 and 0, Law, 4 and 4. Hit by pitcher—by Thies (Amoros), Podres (E. Smith). Passed ball—Shepard. Winning pitcher—Podres (1-0). Losing pitcher—Thies (0-1). Umpires—Englen, Pinelli, Beggess and Gordon. Time—2:27.

Clemente Breaks Record with Three Triples

September 8, 1958

CINCINNATI (N.L.)

	ab	r	h	rbi
Temple, 2b	4	0	0	0
Lynch, rf	4	0	1	0
Bell, lf	3	0	1	0
eWhisenant, lf	1	0	0	0
Robinson, cf	3	0	0	0
Burgess, c	4	0	0	0
Crowe, 1b	4	1	0	0
Grammas, 3b	4	0	2	0
McMillan, ss	1	0	0	0
aNewcombe	1	0	0	0
bHenrich	0	0	0	0
Hoak, 3b	0	0	0	0
Acker, p	1	0	0	0
cThurman	0	0	0	0
dDropo	1	0	0	0
Schmidt, p	0	0	0	0
Total	31	1	4	0

PITTSBURGH (N.L.)

	ab	r	h	rbi
Virdon, cf	4	1	1	0
Clemente, rf	4	1	3	1
Stuart, 1b	4	0	1	1
Skinner, lf	4	0	1	0
Thomas, 3b	3	0	0	0
Mazeroski, 2b	3	0	0	0
Groat, ss	3	0	0	0
Hall, c	3	1	1	0
Raydon, p	2	1	1	0
Gross, p	1	0	0	0
Total	31	4	8	3

a Safe on fielder's choice for McMillan in 7th; b Ran for Newcombe in 7th; c Announced as pinch-hitter for Acker in 7th; d Grounded into a double play for Thurman in 7th; e Flied out for Bell in 8th.

Cincinnati	000 000 100 1
Pittsburgh	000 030 01x 4

E—Crowe, Stuart 2. A—Cincinnati 10, Pittsburgh 14. DP—Mazeroski, Groat and Stuart 2. LOB—Cincinnati 6, Pittsburgh 3.
2B—Lynch, Skinner, Hall, Virdon. 3B—Clemente 3.
Umpires—Boggess, Dixon, Gorman, Burkhart. Time—2:23. Attendance—11,577.

1961 All-Star Game

Candlestick Park, San Francisco

Tuesday, July 11, 1961

AMERICAN LEAGUE　　　　　　　　NATIONAL LEAGUE

	ab	r	h	rbi		ab	r	h	rbi
Temple, 2b	3	0	0	0	Wills, ss	5	0	1	0
fGentile, 1b	2	0	0	0	Mathews, 3b	2	0	0	0
Cash, 1b	4	0	1	0	Purkey, p	0	0	0	0
gFox, 2b	0	2	0	0	bMusial	1	0	0	0
Mantle, cf	3	0	0	0	McCormick, p	0	0	0	0
Kaline, cf	2	1	1	1	eAltman	1	1	1	1
Maris, rf	4	0	1	0	Face, p	0	0	0	0
Colavito, lf	4	0	0	1	Koufax, p	0	0	0	0
Kubek, ss	4	0	0	0	Miller, p	0	0	0	0
Romano, c	3	0	0	0	iAaron	1	1	1	0
hBerra, c	1	0	0	0	Mays, cf	5	2	2	1
Howard, c	0	0	0	0	Cepeda, lf	3	0	0	0
B. Robinson, 3b	2	0	0	0	F. Robinson, lf	1	0	1	0
Bunning, p	0	0	0	0	Clemente, rf	4	1	2	2
dBrandt	1	0	0	0	White, 1b	3	0	1	1
Fornieles, p	0	0	0	0	Bolling, 2b	3	0	0	0
Wilhelm, p	1	0	0	0	Zimmer, 2b	1	0	0	0
Ford, p	1	0	0	0	Burgess, c	4	0	1	0
Lary, p	0	0	0	0	Spahn, p	0	0	0	0
Donovan, p	0	0	0	0	aStuart	1	0	1	0
cKillebrew, 3b	2	1	1	1	Boyer, 3b	2	0	0	0
Howser, 3b	1	0	0	0	Totals	37	5	11	5
Totals	38	4	4	3					

a Doubled for Spahn in 3d; b Flied out for Purkey in 5th; c Hit home run for Donovan in 6th; d Struck out for Bunning in 8th; e Hit home run for McCormick in 8th; f Struck out for Temple in 9th; g Ran for Cash in 9th; h Safe on error for Romano in 9th; i Singled for Miller in 10th.

American	000	001	002 1　4
National	010	100	010 2　5

E—Cepeda, Kubek, Boyer 2, Burgess, Zimmer, Gentile. 2B—Stuart, Cash, Mays. 3B—Clemente. HR—Killebrew, Altman. SB—Robinson. Umpires—Landes, Umont, Crawford, Runge, Vargo, Drummond. T—2:53. A—44,115.

2,000th Career Base Hit

September 2, 1966

CHICAGO (N.L.)	ab	r	h	rbi	PITTSBURGH (N.L.)	ab	r	h	rbi
Kessinger, ss	4	0	0	0	Alou, cf	4	1	2	0
Beckert, 2b	4	1	1	0	Alley, ss	4	0	2	0
Williams, rf	4	0	1	0	Clemente, rf	4	1	1	3
Santo, 3b	3	1	2	0	Stargell, lf	4	1	0	0
Banks, 1b	3	0	0	0	Clendenon, 1b	3	0	0	0
Boccabella, lf	4	0	1	2	Mazeroski, 2b	4	0	1	1
Hundley, c	4	0	1	0	Bailey, 3b	3	2	1	0
Browne, cf	3	0	0	0	Pagliaroni, c	4	1	2	1
Thomas, ph	1	0	0	0	Veale, p	3	1	1	0
Jenkins, p	2	0	0	0	Cardwell, p	1	0	1	2
Phillips, p	0	1	0	0	Totals	34	7	11	7
Simmons, p	0	0	0	0					
Altman, ph	1	0	0	0					
Totals	33	3	6	2					

```
Chicago      000  002  100  3
Pittsburgh   000  131  02x  7
```

E—Veale, Jenkins, Cardwell, Clendenon. DP—Pittsburgh 1. LOB—Chicago 7, Pittsburgh 9. 2B—Hundley, Beckert, Cardwell. 3B—Bailey. HR—Clemente. SB—Alou, Alley. S—Alou, Alley.

HBP—By Jenkins (Stargell). WP—Veale, Cardwell. T—2:31. A—13,677.

Ten Hits in Two Consecutive Games—A Baseball Record

August 22, 1970

PITTSBURGH (N.L.)   LOS ANGELES (N.L.)

	ab	r	h	rbi		ab	r	h	rbi
Patek, ss	7	0	0	0	Wills, ss	7	0	1	0
Alou, cf	7	0	0	0	Mota, lf	7	0	1	0
Clemente, rf	7	1	5	1	Davis, cf	5	0	1	0
Oliver, lf	4	0	1	0	Parker, 1b	4	0	0	0
Jeter, lf	3	0	1	0	Sizemore, 2b	5	1	1	0
Robertson, 1b	7	0	0	0	Sudakis, c	5	0	2	0
Sanguillen, c	4	0	0	0	Russell, rf	5	0	1	0
Stargell, ph	0	0	0	0	Grab'kewitz, 3b	5	0	0	1
Ellis, pr	0	0	0	0	Haller, c	1	0	0	0
May, c	1	0	1	1	Sutton, p	3	0	0	0
Pagan, 3b	5	0	1	0	Brewer, p	1	0	0	0
Alley, 3b	2	0	0	0	Lefebvre, ph	1	0	0	0
Mazeroski, 2b	5	1	1	0	Mikkelson, p	0	0	0	0
Moose, p	4	0	1	0	Gabrielson, ph	1	0	0	0
Giusti, p	0	0	0	0	Totals	51	1	7	1
Clines, ph	1	0	0	0					
Lamb, p	0	0	0	0					
Cash, ph	0	0	0	0					
Totals	57	2	11	2					

```
Pittsburgh    001 000 000 000 000 1  2
Los Angeles   010 000 000 000 000 0  1
```

E—Mazeroski, Sudakis. DP—Pittsburgh 2, Los Angeles 1. 2B—Davis, Pagan. SB—Wills, Sutton, Jeter, Cash, Clemente. S—Parker, Davis, Mazeroski. HBP—by Lamb (Russell), Mikkelson (Cash). PB—Sanguillen, May. T—4:21. A—38,829.

August 23, 1970

PITTSBURGH (N.L.)   LOS ANGELES (N.L.)

	ab	r	h	rbi		ab	r	h	rbi
Patek, ss	6	2	3	1	Wills, ss	3	0	0	0
Alou, cf	6	1	3	0	Hough, p	0	0	0	0
Clemente, rf	6	4	5	3	Gabrielson, ph	1	0	0	0
Clines, rf	0	0	0	0	Mota, lf	1	0	1	0
Oliver, lf	6	1	1	3	Crawford, lf	3	0	0	0
Robertson, 1b	4	0	1	0	Davis, cf	3	0	1	0
Sanguillen, c	6	1	3	3	Parker, 1b	3	0	0	0
Pagan, 3b	6	0	1	0	Sudakis, c	3	0	1	0
Mazeroski, 2b	6	1	4	0	Sizemore, 2b	3	0	0	0
Blass, p	4	1	2	0	Lefebvre, 3b	3	0	0	0
Totals	50	11	23	10	Russell, rf	2	0	1	0
					Foster, p	1	0	0	0
					Norman, p	0	0	0	0
					Joshua, ph	1	0	0	0
					Grabar'z, ss	1	0	0	0
					Totals	28	0	4	0

```
Pittsburgh    210 311 210  11
Los Angeles   000 000 000   0
```

E—Norman. DP—Pittsburgh 2. LOB—Pittsburgh 15, Los Angeles 2. 2B—Patek, Clemente, Sanguillen, Mazeroski, Russell. HR—Oliver, Clemente. T—2:21. A—20,678.

1971 WORLD SERIES

Game One

Saturday, October 9—At Baltimore

PITTSBURGH (N.L.)	ab	r	h	o	a	e
Cash, 2b	4	0	1	1	3	0
Clines, cf	4	0	0	1	0	0
Clemente, rf	4	0	2	2	0	0
Stargell, lf	3	0	0	2	0	0
Robertson, 1b	3	1	0	8	1	0
Sanguillen, c	4	1	0	6	0	0
Pagan, 3b	4	0	0	2	0	0
Hernandez, ss	2	1	0	0	4	0
bOliver	1	0	0	0	0	0
Ellis, p	1	0	0	1	0	0
Moose, p	1	0	0	0	1	0
aMazeroski	1	0	0	0	0	0
Miller, p	0	0	0	1	1	0
Totals	32	3	3	24	10	0

BALTIMORE (A.L.)	ab	r	h	o	a	e
Buford, lf	4	2	2	4	0	0
Blair, cf	0	0	0	0	0	0
Rettenmund, cf-lf	4	1	1	4	0	0
Powell, 1b	3	0	0	6	0	0
F. Robinson, 1b	4	1	2	3	0	0
Hendricks, c	4	0	1	9	0	1
B. Robinson, 3b	4	0	1	0	3	0
Johnson, 2b	4	0	1	1	1	0
Belanger, ss	4	1	2	0	2	2
McNally, p	3	0	0	0	1	0
Totals	34	5	10	27	7	3

```
Pittsburgh    0 3 0  0 0 0  0 0 0   3
Baltimore     0 1 3  0 1 0  0 0 x   5
```

aFlied out for Moose in seventh. bStruck out for Hernandez in ninth. Runs batted in —Hernandez, Cash, F. Robinson, Rettenmund 3, Buford. Two-base hit—Clemente. Three-base hit—Rettenmund. Home runs—F. Robinson, Rettenmund, Buford. Sacrifice hit—Hernandez. Left on bases—Pittsburgh 5. Baltimore 6. Earned runs—Pittsburgh 0, Baltimore 5. Bases on balls—Off McNally 2, off Ellis 1. Struck out—By McNally 9, by Ellis 1, by Moose 4, by Miller 1. Pitching records—Off McNally 3 runs and 3 hits in 9 innings; off Ellis 4 runs and 4 hits in 2⅓ innings; off Moose 1 run and 3 hits in 3⅔ innings; off Miller 0 runs and 3 hits in 2 innings. Wild pitches—McNally, Moose. Losing pitcher—Ellis. Umpires—Chylak (A.L.), Sudol (N.L.), Rice (A.L.), Vargo (N.L.), Odom (A.L.), Kibler (N.L.). Time—2:06. Attendance—53,229.

Game Two

Monday, October 11—At Baltimore

PITTSBURGH (N.L.)

	ab	r	h	o	a	e
Cash, 2b	5	0	0	2	6	0
Hebner, 3b	3	1	1	0	0	0
Clemente, rf	5	0	2	2	0	0
Stargell, lf	3	0	1	2	1	0
Giusti, p	0	0	0	0	0	0
Oliver, cf	5	0	1	1	0	1
Robertson, 1b	3	0	0	8	1	0
Sanguillen, c	5	0	1	4	0	0
Hernandez, ss	2	1	1	2	1	0
dMay	1	0	0	0	0	0
R. Johnson, p	2	0	0	2	0	0
Kison, p	0	0	0	0	0	0
Moose, p	0	0	0	0	0	0
Veale, p	0	0	0	0	1	0
aSands	1	0	0	0	0	0
Miller, p	0	0	0	0	0	0
cDavalillo, lf	1	1	1	1	0	0
Totals	36	3	8	24	10	1

BALTIMORE (A.L.)

	ab	r	h	o	a	e
Buford, lf	5	0	0	2	0	0
Rettenmund, cf-rf	5	1	2	3	0	0
Powell, 1b	5	1	1	4	3	0
F. Robinson, rf	4	2	3	1	0	0
bBlair, pr-cf	1	1	1	1	0	0
Hendricks, c	3	2	2	10	0	0
B. Robinson, 3b	3	2	3	0	1	0
D. Johnson, 2b	5	1	2	1	3	0
Belanger, ss	3	1	0	2	1	1
Palmer, p	2	0	0	2	0	0
Hall, p	0	0	0	1	0	0
Totals	36	11	14	27	8	1

Pittsburgh	0 0 0	0 0 0	0 3 0	3
Baltimore	0 1 0	3 6 1	0 0 x	11

aStruck out for Veale in sixth. bRan and scored for F. Robinson in sixth. cSingled and scored for Miller in eighth. dGrounded out for Hernandez in ninth. Runs batted in —B. Robinson 3, D. Johnson 2, Palmer 2, Hendricks, Buford, Rettenmund, Hebner 3. Two-base hit—Clemente. Home run—Hebner. Double plays—Cash and Hernandez; Stargell and Sanguillen. Left on bases—Pittsburgh 14, Baltimore 9. Earned runs— Baltimore 11, Pittsburgh 3. Bases on balls—Off Palmer 8, off R. Johnson 2, off Kison 2, off Veale 2, off Giusti 1. Struck out—By Palmer 10, by R. Johnson 1, by Miller 1. Pitching records—Off Palmer 3 runs and 7 hits in 8 innings; off Hall 0 runs and 1 hit in 1 inning; off R. Johnson 4 runs and 4 hits in 3⅓ innings; off Kison 0 runs and 0 hits in 0 innings (pitched to two batters in fourth); off Moose 5 runs and 5 hits in 1 inning; off Veale 1 run and 1 hit in ⅔ inning; off Miller 1 run and 3 hits in 2 innings; off Giusti 0 runs and 1 hit in 1 inning. Winning pitcher—Palmer. Losing pitcher —R. Johnson. Save—Hall. Umpires—Sudol (N.L.), Rice (A.L.), Vargo (N.L.), Odom (A.L.), Kibler (N.L.), Chylak (A.L.). Time—2:55. Attendance—53,239.

Game Three

Tuesday, October 12—At Pittsburgh

BALTIMORE (A.L.)							PITTSBURGH (N.L.)					
	ab	r	h	o	a	e		ab	r	h	o	a	e
Buford, lf	4	0	0	3	0	0	Cash, 2b	4	1	1	2	2	0
Rettenmund, cf	4	0	0	3	0	0	Oliver, cf	4	0	0	2	0	0
Powell, 1b	4	0	0	7	0	1	Clemente, rf	4	1	1	3	0	0
F. Robinson, rf	4	1	2	2	0	0	Stargell, lf	1	1	0	2	0	0
Hendricks, c	3	0	0	4	1	0	Robertson, 1b	4	1	1	8	1	0
B. Robinson, 3b	3	0	1	1	5	1	Sanguillen, c	4	1	2	8	0	0
Johnson, 2b	3	0	0	3	2	0	Pagan, 3b	4	0	2	0	0	0
Belanger, ss	3	0	0	1	2	0	Alley, ss	2	0	0	1	2	0
Cuellar, p	1	0	0	0	0	1	Hernandez, ss	1	0	0	0	1	0
Dukes, p	0	0	0	0	0	0	Blass, p	4	0	0	1	2	0
aShopay, ph	1	0	0	0	0	0	Totals	32	5	7	27	8	0
Watt, p	0	0	0	0	0	0							
Totals	30	1	3	24	10	3							

```
Baltimore      0 0 0   0 0 0   1 0 0    1
Pittsburgh     1 0 0   0 0 1   3 0 x    5
```

aGrounded out for Dukes in eighth. Runs batted in—Clemente, Pagan, Robertson 3, F. Robinson. Two-base hits—Cash, Pagan, Sanguillen. Home runs—F. Robinson, Robertson. Double play—B. Robinson and Johnson. Left on bases—Baltimore 4, Pittsburgh 9. Earned runs—Baltimore 1, Pittsburgh 4. Bases on balls—Off Cuellar 6, off Blass 2. Struck out—By Cuellar 4, by Watt 1, by Blass 8. Pitching records—Off Cuellar 5 runs and 7 hits in 6 innings (pitched to three batters in seventh); off Dukes 0 runs and 0 hits in 1 inning; off Watt 0 runs and 0 hits in 1 inning; off Blass 1 run and 3 hits in 9 innings. Losing pitcher—Cuellar. Umpires—Rice (A.L.), Vargo (N.L.), Odom (A.L.), Kibler (N.L.), Chylak (A.L.), Sudol (N.L.). Time—2:20. Attendance—50,403.

Game Four

Wednesday, October 13—At Pittsburgh

BALTIMORE (A.L.)	ab	r	h	o	a	e
Blair, cf	4	1	2	2	1	1
Belanger, ss	4	1	1	3	4	0
Rettenmund, lf	4	1	1	1	0	0
F. Robinson, rf	2	0	0	2	0	0
B. Robinson, 3b	3	0	0	1	1	0
Powell, 1b	3	0	0	6	0	0
Johnson, 2b	3	0	0	3	2	0
Etchebarren, c	2	0	0	6	0	0
Dobson, p	2	0	0	0	3	0
Jackson, p	0	0	0	0	0	0
aShopay, ph	1	0	0	0	0	0
Watt, p	0	0	0	0	0	0
Richert, p	0	0	0	0	0	0
Totals	28	3	4	24	11	1

PITTSBURGH (N.L.)	ab	r	h	o	a	e
Cash, 2b	4	1	1	3	3	0
Hebner, 3b	5	1	1	1	1	0
Clemente, rf	4	0	3	0	0	0
Stargell, lf	5	1	2	1	0	0
Oliver, cf	4	0	2	6	0	0
Robertson, 1b	4	1	1	11	0	0
Sanguillen, c	4	0	2	4	0	0
Hernandez, ss	3	0	1	1	2	0
bDavalillo, ph	1	0	0	0	0	0
Giusti, p	0	0	0	0	0	0
Walker, p	0	0	0	0	0	0
Kison, p	2	0	0	0	1	0
cMay, ph	1	0	1	0	0	0
dAlley, pr-ss	0	0	0	0	2	0
Totals	37	4	14	27	9	0

Baltimore	3 0 0	0 0 0	0 0 0	3
Pittsburgh	2 0 1	0 0 0	1 0 x	4

aGrounded into fielder's choice for Jackson in seventh. bReached first on Blair's error for Hernandez in seventh. cSingled for Kison in seventh. dRan for May in seventh. Runs batted in—B. Robinson, Powell, Stargell, Oliver 2, May. Two-base hits—Stargell, Oliver, Blair. Stolen bases—Sanguillen, Hernandez. Sacrifice flies—B. Robinson, Powell. Double plays—Hernandez, Cash and Robertson; Belanger, Johnson and Powell. Left on bases—Baltimore 4, Pittsburgh 13. Earned runs—Baltimore 3, Pittsburgh 4. Bases on balls—Off Dobson 3, off Jackson 1, off Walker 1. Struck out—By Dobson 4, by Watt 1, by Richert 1, by Kison 3, by Giusti 1. Pitching records—Off Dobson 3 runs and 3 hits in 5⅓ innings; off Jackson 0 runs and 0 hits in ⅔ inning; off Watt 1 run and 4 hits in 1⅓ innings; off Richert 0 runs and 0 hits in ⅔ inning; off Walker 3 runs and 3 hits in ⅔ inning; off Kison 0 runs and 1 hit in 6⅓ innings; off Giusti 0 runs and 0 hits in 2 innings. Passed ball—Sanguillen. Hit by pitcher—By Kison 3 (Johnson, F. Robinson, Etchebarren). Winning pitcher—Kison. Losing pitcher—Watt. Save—Giusti. Umpires—Vargo (N.L.), Odom (A.L.), Kibler (N.L.), Chylak (A.L.), Sudol (N.L.), Rice (A.L.). Time—2:48. Attendance—51,378.

Game Five

Thursday, October 14—At Pittsburgh

BALTIMORE (A.L.)	ab	r	h	o	a	e
Buford, lf	3	0	0	1	0	0
Blair, cf	4	0	0	3	1	0
Powell, 1b	3	0	1	8	0	0
F. Robinson, rf	3	0	0	1	0	0
Hendricks, c	2	0	0	4	3	0
B. Robinson, 3b	3	0	1	2	2	1
Johnson, 2b	3	0	0	3	1	0
Belanger, ss	3	0	0	2	3	0
McNally, p	1	0	0	0	1	0
Leonhard, p	0	0	0	0	0	0
aShopay, ph	1	0	0	0	0	0
Dukes, p	0	0	0	0	0	0
bRettenmund, ph	1	0	0	0	0	0
Totals	27	0	2	24	11	1

PITTSBURGH (N.L.)	ab	r	h	o	a	e
Cash, 2b	4	0	0	5	2	0
Clines, cf	3	2	1	3	0	0
Clemente, rf	4	0	1	4	0	0
Stargell, lf	4	0	1	2	0	0
Robertson, 1b	3	1	1	9	0	0
Sanguillen, c	4	1	1	2	0	0
Pagan, 3b	4	0	1	0	6	0
Hernandez, ss	3	0	2	2	1	0
Briles, p	2	0	1	0	1	0
Totals	31	4	9	27	10	0

```
Baltimore     000  000  000  0
Pittsburgh    021  010  00x  4
```

aFlied out for Leonhard in sixth. bGrounded out for Dukes in ninth. Runs batted in —Robertson, Briles, Clemente. Three-base hit—Clines. Home run—Robertson. Sacrifice hits—Briles 2. Stolen bases—Clines, Sanguillen. Double plays—Hernandez, Cash and Robertson; Pagan, Cash and Robertson. Left on bases—Baltimore 2, Pittsburgh 9. Earned runs—Pittsburgh 3. Bases on balls—Off McNally 2, Leonhard 1, Briles 2. Struck out—By McNally 3, Dukes 1, Briles 2. Pitching records—Off McNally 4 runs and 7 hits in 4 innings (pitched to two batters in fifth); off Leonhard 0 runs and 0 hits in 1 inning; off Dukes 0 runs and 2 hits in 3 innings; off Briles 0 runs and 2 hits in 9 innings. Wild pitch—McNally. Hit by pitcher—By Dukes (Hernandez). Losing pitcher—McNally. Umpires—Odom (A.L.), Kibler (N.L.), Chylak (A.L.), Sudol (N.L.), Rice (A.L.), Vargo (N.L.). Time—2:16. Attendance—51,377.

Game Six

Saturday, October 16—At Baltimore

PITTSBURGH (N.L.)

	ab	r	h	o	a	e
Cash, 2b	5	0	1	3	4	0
Hebner, 3b	4	0	0	0	2	1
Clemente, rf	4	1	2	2	0	0
Stargell, lf	4	0	0	2	0	0
Oliver, cf	5	1	1	2	0	0
Miller, p	0	0	0	0	0	0
Robertson, 1b	4	0	2	9	0	0
Sanguillen, c	4	0	3	8	0	0
Hernandez, ss	4	0	0	2	2	0
Moose, p	1	0	0	0	2	0
R. Johnson, p	1	0	0	0	0	0
Giusti, p	0	0	0	0	0	0
bDavalillo, ph-cf	1	0	0	1	0	0
Totals	37	2	9	*29	10	1

BALTIMORE (A.L.)

	ab	r	h	o	a	e
Buford, lf	4	1	3	3	1	0
D. Johnson, 2b	5	0	1	5	1	0
Powell, 1b	5	0	1	9	1	0
F. Robinson, rf	4	1	0	0	0	0
Rettenmund, cf	5	0	1	4	0	0
B. Robinson, 3b	4	0	1	1	0	0
Hendricks, c	4	0	0	6	0	0
Belanger, ss	1	1	1	2	5	0
Palmer, p	2	0	0	0	1	0
aShopay, ph	1	0	0	0	0	0
Dobson, p	0	0	0	0	0	0
McNally, p	0	0	0	0	0	0
Totals	35	3	8	30	9	0

Pittsburgh	0 1 1	0 0 0	0 0 0	0	2
Baltimore	0 0 0	0 0 1	1 0 0	1	3

aFlied out for Palmer in ninth. bLined out for Giusti in tenth. *Two out when winning run scored. Runs batted in—Robertson, Clemente, Buford, D. Johnson, B. Robinson. Two-base hits—Oliver, Buford. Three-base hit—Clemente. Home runs—Clemente, Buford. Sacrifice hits—Moose, Palmer. Sacrifice fly—B. Robinson. Stolen bases—Belanger, Cash. Double play—Hebner, Cash and Robertson. Left on bases—Pittsburgh 9, Baltimore 10. Earned runs—Pittsburgh 2, Baltimore 3. Bases on balls—Off Moose 2, off R. Johnson 1, off Giusti 1, off Miller 1, off Palmer 1, off Dobson 1, off McNally 1. Struck out—By Moose 3, by R. Johnson 2, by Giusti 3, by Palmer 5, by Dobson 1. Pitching records—Off Moose 1 run and 4 hits in 5 innings (pitched to three batters in sixth); off R. Johnson 1 run and 1 hit in 1⅔ innings; off Giusti 0 runs and 2 hits in 2⅓ innings; off Miller 1 run and 1 hit in ⅔ inning; off Palmer 2 runs and 8 hits in 9 innings; off Dobson 0 runs and 1 hit in ⅔ inning; off McNally 0 runs and 0 hits in ⅓ inning. Umpires—Kibler (N.L.), Chylak (A.L.), Sudol (N.L.), Rice (A.L.), Vargo (N.L.), Odom (A.L.). Time—2:59. Attendance—44,174.

Game Seven

Sunday, October 17—At Baltimore

PITTSBURGH (N.L.)   BALTIMORE (A.L.)

	ab	r	h	o	a	e		ab	r	h	o	a	e
Cash, 2b	4	0	0	4	3	0	Buford, lf	3	0	1	0	0	0
Clines, cf	4	0	0	2	0	0	Johnson, 2b	4	0	0	2	2	0
Clemente, rf	4	1	1	2	0	0	Powell, 1b	4	0	0	12	0	0
Robertson, 1b	4	0	1	11	1	1	F. Robinson, rf	4	0	0	3	0	0
Sanguillen, c	4	0	2	5	0	0	Rettenmund, cf	4	0	0	2	0	0
Stargell, lf	4	1	1	0	0	0	B. Robinson, 3b	2	0	0	1	5	0
Pagan, 3b	3	0	1	0	2	0	Hendricks, c	3	1	2	7	0	0
Hernandez, ss	3	0	0	2	5	0	Belanger, ss	3	0	1	0	3	0
Blass, p	3	0	0	1	2	0	Cuellar, p	2	0	0	0	3	0
Totals	33	2	6	27	13	1	aShopay, ph	0	0	0	0	0	0
							Dobson, p	0	0	0	0	0	0
							McNally, p	0	0	0	0	0	0
							Totals	29	1	4	27	13	0

Pittsburgh   0 0 0   1 0 0   0 1 0   2
Baltimore   0 0 0   0 0 0   0 1 0   1

aSacrificed for Cuellar in eighth. Runs batted in—Clemente, Pagan, Buford. Two-base hits—Hendricks, Pagan. Home run—Clemente. Sacrifice hit—Shopay. Caught stealing—Buford. Double play—Cash and Robertson. Left on bases—Pittsburgh 4, Baltimore 4. Earned runs—Pittsburgh 2, Baltimore 1. Bases on balls—Off Blass 2. Struck out—By Blass 5, by Cuellar 6, by Dobson 1. Pitching records—Off Blass 1 run and 4 hits in 9 innings; off Cuellar 2 runs and 4 hits in 8 innings; off Dobson 0 runs and 2 hits in 2/3 inning; off McNally 0 runs and 0 hits in 1/3 inning. Umpires—Chylak (A.L.), Sudol (N.L.), Rice (A.L.), Vargo (N.L.), Odom (A.L.), Kibler (N.L.). Time—2:10. Attendance—47,291.

3,000th Career Hit

September 30, 1972

NEW YORK (N.L.)	ab	r	h	rbi	PITTSBURGH (N.L.)	ab	r	h	rbi
Garrett, ss	4	0	0	0	Goggin, 2b	4	0	2	0
Boswell, 2b	4	0	1	0	Stennett, cf	4	0	0	0
Milner, lf	3	0	0	0	Clemente, rf	2	1	1	0
Staub, rf	3	0	0	0	bMazeroski	1	0	0	0
Rauch, p	0	0	0	0	Davalillo, rf	1	0	0	0
dMarshall	1	0	0	0	Zisk, lf	1	2	0	0
Kranepool, 1b	3	0	1	0	Sanguillen, c	3	1	1	1
Fregosi, ss	0	3	0	0	Pagan, 3b	3	0	0	0
Schneck, cf	3	0	0	0	J. Hernandez, ss	3	0	1	2
Dyer, c	1	0	0	0	Ellis, p	2	0	0	0
aNolan, c	2	0	0	0	cClines	1	0	0	0
Matlack, p	2	0	0	0	Johnson, p	0	0	0	0
Hahn, rf	0	0	0	0	Totals	28	5	6	3
Totals	29	0	2	0					

aFanned for Dyer in 5th; bPopped out for Clemente in 5th; cFlied out for Ellis in 6th; dFlied out for Rauch in 9th.

```
New York     0 0 0  0 0 0  0 0 0  0
Pittsburgh   0 0 0  3 0 2  0 0 x  5
```

ER—Pittsburgh 3. LOB—Pittsburgh 4, New York 5. 2B—Clemente. 3B—J. Hernandez. DP—New York 3. E—Garrett. PB—Dyer, Nolan. Winning pitcher—Ellis (15-7). Losing pitcher—Matlack (14-10). T—2:10. Umpires—Kibler, Pulli, Harvey, Crawford. A—13,117.